Praise for Lit

Best Book of the Year

New York Times Book Review (Top Ten)

Michiko Kakutani (Top Ten)

The New Yorker (Reviewer Favorite)

Entertainment Weekly (Top Ten) · Time (Top Ten)

Washington Post · San Francisco Chronicle

Chicago Tribune · Christian Science Monitor · Slate

St. Louis Post-Dispatch · Cleveland Plain Dealer · Seattle Times

A National Book Critics Circle Award Finalist

"[Karr] seems to have been born with the inability to write a dishonest—or boring—sentence."   —Lev Grossman, Time

"In a gravelly, ground-glass-under-your-heel voice that can take you from laughter to awe in a few sentences, Karr has written the best book about being a woman in America I have read in years."
—Susan Cheever, New York Times Book Review

"Searing. . . . [Karr] has written a book that lassoes you, hog-ties your emotions, and won't let you go. . . . Karr writes with such intensity and poetry. . . . This struggle to reconcile her past and present, her family and her future, is the steel-wired ribbon that not only runs through this affecting book, but that also connects it to Ms. Karr's two earlier memoirs—the bright, elastic thread on which she so deftly strings the colored beads of her tumultuous life."   —Michiko Kakutani, New York Times

"Howlingly funny. . . . The overall impression is of a sorrowful narrative poem as humble and funny as it is beautiful. Karr is an 'inveterate check grabber,' she tells us, out of 'the poor girl's need to prove solvency.' Perhaps a similar need drives her generosity on the page. Certainly her readers, once again, are the lucky beneficiaries."
—Mary Pols, *Time*

"Mary Karr restores memoir form's dignity with *Lit*."
—*Vanity Fair*

"[Karr] writes with a singular combination of poetic grace and Texan verve, which allows her to present the experiences as fresh, but she also brings a potent, self-condemning honesty and a palpable sense of responsibility and regret to the narrative. . . . Will ring as true in American-lit classrooms as in church support groups—an absolute gem that secures Karr's place as one of the best memoirists of her generation." —*Kirkus Reviews* (starred review)

"A master class on the art of the memoir. Mordantly funny, free of both self-pity and sentimentality, Karr describes her attempts to untether herself from troubled family in rural Texas, her development as a poet and writer, and her struggles to navigate marriage and young motherhood even as she descends into alcoholism."
—*New York Times Book Review*

"[Karr] is a gifted storyteller who can make horrific events seem grotesquely funny without minimizing the pain and fear they caused. . . . Believers and nonbelievers have long been drawn to confessions, like Saint Augustine's, that read like dispatches from the knock-down, drag-out encounter between God and the stubborn sinner. *Lit* . . . is one of those."
—Francine Prose, *The New York Review of Books*

"You do not have to be a rehabilitated drunk or go to church, or have had a terrible childhood, or get so swept up in a book you forget to let the dog out to pee to find yourself in this book—you have only to be human. *Lit* is a testament to the healing power of love that beats at the heart of every good story."
—Melanie Gideon, *San Francisco Chronicle*

"A redemptive, painfully funny story."
—Bob Minzesheimer, *USA Today*

"A brutally honest, sparkling story."
—*Glamour*

"Karr movingly depicts her halting journey into AA, making it clear her grit and spirit remain intact."
—Michelle Green, *People* (3½ out of 4 stars)

"This is a story not just of alcoholism but of coming to terms with families past and present, with a needy self, with a spiritual longing Karr didn't even know she possessed. It sounds as if she was hellish to be around for much of the time she describes here, but she is certainly good company now."
—Valerie Sayers, *Washington Post*

"*Lit* shows that a first-rate writer doesn't need to repeat herself or trump up false epiphanies in order to craft a fascinating autobiography. The book glows with Karr's descriptions—coming to terms with her alcoholism, her early lean years as a poet and teacher, her chaotic love life—but there's nothing sentimental or self-congratulatory about her prose."
—Ken Tucker, *Entertainment Weekly*

"Karr tells the story with the same down-to-earth writing—some of it funny—that she brought to her first two memoirs. . . . Her willingness to show herself in this light and the humility with which she writes about recovery and faith are testaments to the honesty of both her writing and her life."

—Nancy Connors, *Cleveland Plain Dealer*

"With grace, saltiness, and profanity galore, Karr . . . reestablishes herself as one of our finest memoirists and storytellers."

—*San Francisco Chronicle*

"Karr's too smart and accomplished a writer to not acknowledge her genre's limitations. But while it's fashionable for memoirists to fess up that memoir is a fuzzy thing, Karr sincerely and passionately believes in the truth. . . . If what we expect from Mary Karr is to deliver transcendence . . . she delivers."

—Elizabeth Foy Larsen, *Minneapolis Star Tribune*

"*Lit* matches its predecessors in candor and outstrips them in insight."   —*Commonweal*

"Karr has managed to raise the bar higher still on the genre of memoir."   —Steve Ross, *Huffington Post*

"[*Lit*] completes a landmark trio of literary confessionals from best-seller Mary Karr . . . and complements the story of her mother's destructive drinking that the Texas-born Karr has previously captured so colorfully and painfully. . . . A body-and-soul-baring memoir."

—*Elle*

"What distinguishes Karr's book from most others . . . is her mordant humor and exceptional writing. Throughout, her descriptions are startling and poetic. . . . This is a truly harrowing story, but so poetically written that unlike many memoirs, the material seems riveting rather than repugnant. And not once does the author paint herself as the heroine of her own life. (There isn't a single false note in *Lit*.) Her hard-won contentment is inspiring and, above all, miraculous."

—Carmela Ciuraru, *Christian Science Monitor*

"Confessional, raw, urgent, vividly funny, and blazing. . . . [Karr] may, in fact, be the only writer on Earth who can make hitting rock bottom as an out-of-control alcoholic humorous, compelling, profound, and uplifting, all at the same time. . . . Karr continues to deliver the goods. . . . Magnificent."   —Tricia Snell, *Oregonian*

"*Lit* contains more than a whiff of the standard recovery narrative as Karr gropes her way toward her new faith. The saving grace, so to speak, is that she, better than anyone, can reinvigorate a tired tale. . . . The yarn-spinning skill she inherited from her father and the love of words bequeathed by her mom . . . remain in full display."   —Ellen Emry Heltzel, *Seattle Times*

"As powerful as *Liars' Club*, as restless as *Cherry*, and as exquisitely written as any of Karr's award-winning collections of poetry."

—David Sheets, *St. Louis Post-Dispatch*

"[Karr] continues to delight with her signature dark humor and pitch-perfect metaphors. . . . Karr's prose moves at a quick and seductive clip, delivering large doses of wit and painful insights. . . . There are plenty of memoirs about being drunk, but this one has Karr's voice—both sure-footed and breezy—behind it. . . . Even when Karr is writing about church, *Lit* has flashes of brilliance to keep you under its intoxicating spell."

—Beth Greenfield, *Time Out New York*

"Riveting. . . . As unsparing and unsentimental as her first two memoirs and, like the others, by turns hilarious and gut-wrenching. She again brings to the task her acerbic wit and poet's eye for lyrical detail. . . . Karr's entire body of work attests to this simple truth: that the past, until you reckon with it, will remain in hot pursuit. In other words, what you don't bring into the light will destroy you. *Lit* brings this process full circle. That pleasingly monosyllabic title encapsulates this writer's entire journey thus far—one that is about drinking and the illuminating revelations of sobriety, about the redemptive power of literature and how the act of writing can save a soul." —Katherine Wyrick, *BookPage*

"[Karr's] poetic sensibility infuses every sentence of her story with an alliterative and symbolic energy, conjuring echoes of poet Gerard Manley Hopkins and, occasionally, Sylvia Plath. . . . [Her] wry wit and deft prose do not render her slow conversion to Catholicism in a sentimental or proselytizing manner."

—*Publishers Weekly*

"Her tale is riveting, her style clear-eyed and frank. That Karr survived the emotional and physical journey she regales her readers with to become the evenhanded, self-disciplined writer she is today is arguably nothing short of a miracle, and readers of her previous two books won't be disappointed." —*Library Journal*

LIT

Also by Mary Karr

Poetry

Sinners Welcome

Viper Rum

Devil's Tour

Abacus

Nonfiction

Cherry

The Liars' Club

The Art of Memoir

LIT

A Memoir

Mary Karr

This is a work of nonfiction. The events and experiences detailed herein are all true and have been faithfully rendered as the author has remembered them, to the best of her ability. Some names, identities, and circumstances have been changed in order to protect the privacy and/or anonymity of the various individuals involved. Others have vetted the manuscript and confirmed its rendering of events.

A hardcover edition of this book was published in 2009 by HarperCollins Publishers.

An extension of this copyright page appears on pages 437–438.

HarperCollins books may be purchased for educational, business, or sales promotional use. For information please e-mail the Special Sales Department at SPsales@harpercollins.com.

FIRST HARPER PERENNIAL EDITION PUBLISHED 2010.

FIRST HARPER PERENNIAL OLIVE EDITION PUBLISHED 2015.

The Library of Congress has catalogued the hardcover edition as follows:

Karr, Mary.
    Lit : a memoir / Mary Karr.—1st ed.
        p.   cm.
    ISBN: 978-0-06-059698-9 (hardcover)
    1. Karr, Mary—Mental health.   2. Poets, American—20th century—Biography.   3. Recovering alcoholics—United States—Biography.   4. Mental illness—United States—Case studies.   5. Alcoholism—United States—Case studies.   6. Karr, Mary—Childhood and youth.   7. Karr, Mary—Family.   8. Problem families—Texas.   9. Texas—Biography. I. Title.
    PS3561.A6929Z4683   2009
    811'.54—dc22
    [B]   2009024810

ISBN 978-0-06-242109-8 (Olive Edition)

15   16   17   18   19   DIX/RRD   10   9   8   7   6   5   4   3   2   1

For Chuck and Lynne Pascale
and for Dev:
Thanks for the light.

Passage home? Never.

—*THE ODYSSEY*, BOOK 5, HOMER
(TRANS. ROBERT FAGLES)

Contents

IV Being Who You Are Is Not a Disorder

LIT

Prologue: Open Letter to My Son

Side A: Now

Any way I tell this story is a lie, so I ask you to disconnect the device in your head that repeats at intervals how ancient and addled I am. It's true that—at fifty to your twenty—my brain is dimmer. Your engine of recall is way superior, as you've often pointed out.

How many times have you stopped me throwing sofa cushions over my shoulder in search of my glasses by telling me they're tipped atop my own knobby head? The cake we had on that birthday had twelve candles on it, not ten; and it wasn't London but Venice where I'd blindly bought and boiled and served to our guests a pasta I mistakenly believed was formed into the boot of Italy.

And should I balk at your recall, you may bring out the video camera you've had strapped to your face since you were big enough to push the red Record button. You'll zoom in on the 1998 bowl of pasta to reveal—not the Italian boot—but tiny replicas of penis and testicles. Cock and balls. That's why the guys who sold it to me laughed so maniacally, why the au pair blanched to the color of table linen.

Through that fishbowl lens, you've been looking for the truth most of your life. Recently, that wide eye has come to settle on me, and I've felt like Odysseus, albeit with less guile and fewer escape routes, the lens itself embodying the one-eyed cyclops. You're not the monster; my face reflected back in the lens is. Or replay is. Or I am.

Still, I want to show that single eye the whole tale as I know it, scary as that strikes me from this juncture.

However long I've been granted sobriety, however many hours I logged in therapists' offices and the confessional, I've still managed to hurt you, and not just with the divorce when you were five, with its attendant shouting matches and slammed doors.

Just as my mother vanished from my young life into a madhouse, so did I vanish when you were a toddler. Having spent much of my life trying to plumb her psychic mysteries, I now find myself occupying her chair as plumbee. Believe me. It's a discomfiting sensation.

Last week specifically: a gas leak in your apartment drove you to my place, where I was packing for a trip. So I let go my cat sitter and left you prowling old video footage like a scholar deciphering ancient manuscripts. How much plea-sure your concentration gave me. From the raw detritus of the past, you're shaping your own story, which will, in your own particular telling of it, shape you into a man.

Days later, when my taxi pulled up, you came down to help haul bags. At six-two, you're athletic like your father, with his same courtly manner—an offhanded chivalry that calls little attention to itself. While manhandling my mammoth suitcase through two security doors, you managed to hold each one open for me with your foot. The next instant I registered—peeking from the top of your saggy jeans—the orange boxers spattered with cartoon fish from Dr. Seuss's *One Fish, Two Fish* that I read you as a kid.

Inside, loading books into your messenger bag, you mentioned watching for the first time a video of Mother and me, filmed years ago by your camera (borrowed) in the cracker-box house of my kidhood. Mother was recounting her psychotic episode—the seminal event that burned off whatever innocence a kid in backwater Texas has coming.

You know the story in broad outline and have steered clear of my writing about it—a healthy fence blocking my public life from your private one. But the old video stirred something in you.

It was kind of crazy, you said.

You were wrapping up wires for one of your cameras.

I thought you meant Mother's story of taking a carving knife to kill my sister and me when we were little. How she hallucinated she'd butchered us and called the doctor, who called the law, who took her away for a spell.

Not that, you said. Your blue eyes fixed me where I stood.

This curiosity about my family past has a new gravity to it, countered by your T-shirt, which reads DON'T GIVE ME DRUGS.

You told me all that, you said. The way Grandma told it was strange, like it happened to somebody else. Crazy. She said, *You were just so precious, I thought I'd kill you before they all got to hurt you.*

Then your girlfriend called from the next room, and the instant was over.

I'd all but forgotten the tape. So after you'd gone, I played it—maybe for the first time all the way through.

It's a summer afternoon in a yellow kitchen we've yet to remodel. A few tiles still bear bullet holes from Mother's pistol-wagging arguments with my daddy and two subsequent romances. The florid robe she's wearing would suit a Wiccan priestess. Ditto her short, ashwhite hair, and her pale as marble skin, which still looks dewy.

She reads some gnostic texts about goddesses and gods and the Christ within each of us. She pauses every now and then to say, Isn't that wild? or to relight her long cigarillo.

Next to her is a giant plastic sunflower my nephew gave her for Mother's Day. She flips a switch on it, and it blinks to life, singing, *You are my sunshine, my only sunshine*—a song my daddy used to sing to me on the way to fishing.

Don't you love that? she says. It's silly, but I love it.

I ask what she was thinking on the night in question, and she says, I just couldn't imagine bringing two girls up in a world where they do such awful things to women. So I decided to kill you both, to spare you.

How long had you been drinking?

Oh I wasn't drunk, Mother says. Maybe I'd had a few drinks.

This completely counters her earlier version, in which she'd claimed to have been shitfaced. But I don't press it. She shrugs at me, adding, *Sheesh*.

I'd never think to go over this footage myself but for you, Dev. You're showing my life to me through a new window—not just the video, either. Your birth altered my whole posture on the planet, not to mention my role vis-à-vis Mother.

For I partly see her through your vantage. You never knew the knife-wielding goddess of death. She's your gray-haired grandmother, the one I was always trying to protect you from, even though she was sober when you knew her. Her rages had dissipated, but her child-rearing judgment never improved.

You still think it's funny that she let you screen—at age eight—the über-violent *Pulp Fiction* because she found your interest in nonlinear film methods *artistic*. But I'd stood before her sputtering, What about the *sodomy*, Mother?

From the corner of the room, you asked what exactly sodomy was.

Mother said, When the man hurt the other man.

You asked her if it was the guy with the bondage ball in his mouth.

Jesus, Mother, I said. You see!

Well, he was interested in the movie when his cousin talked about it, Mother said.

It's a testament to your desire to avoid further conflict that you waited till we were on the plane to tell me she'd also shown you—at the outset of our visit—a pearl-handled revolver in her pocket-book. Her rationale? She didn't want you coming across it in her purse.

I'd never go through Grandma Charlie's purse, you said.

Still, you considered the pistol incident something I'd want to know, while you reassured me you were disinclined to play with a loaded weapon.

Mostly, Mother couldn't hurt you. But I both could and did.

The time I'm mostly thinking of, you were barely four, which—I would argue—is less like being a miniature person than like a dog or cat who can talk. Your father and I were coming to pieces, and not long after, you came to see me in the hospital.

You remember the embossed smiley faces on my green

slippers. You remember the red-haired woman so psychotic she once landed in four-point restraints just about the time you got there with your Ninja Turtle lunch box, and you could hear her howls.

We had a picnic one summer afternoon when you visited, and the hospital grounds so evoked the playing fields where your father distinguished himself that you told your teachers at daycare that I was at a slumber party at Harvard.

We both remember, albeit in varying tones of gray and black and shit brown, the misery I mired us in.

That's the story I want to tell: how I started getting drunk. How being drunk got increasingly hard, and being not drunk felt impossible. In Odyssean terms, I'd wanted to be a hero, but wound up—as Mother did—a monster.

But because of you, I couldn't die and couldn't monster myself, either. So you were the agent of my rescue—not a good job for somebody barely three feet tall.

Blameless, the Greek translators call it. That's what Odysseus wished for his son, Telemachus: to live guilt free. As a teenager myself, reading how Odysseus boffed witches and fought monsters, I inked the word *blameless* on the bottom of my tennis shoe. And my favorite part was always when he came home after decades and no one knew him.

As you get older, you look at me more objectively—or try to. As I become strange to you in some ways, you've become more familiar to yourself. Maybe you could loan me some of the shine in your young head to clear up my leftover dark spaces. Just as you're blameless for the scorched parts of your childhood, I'm equally exonerated for my own mother's nightmare. Maybe I can show you how I came to peace, how she and Daddy wound up as blameless in my story as you are.

Before you left the other night, you added—in the form of

afterthought—what was, to me, the most dramatic news I'd heard that night: after the tape of your grandmother, you'd read nearly fifty pages of my own memories.

You added, I'm gonna use that and some footage of Grandma for my documentary class.

I watched you disappear down the stairs and wanted to call you back but thought better of it. Your girlfriend was with you, and you were so loaded down with bags and equipment. And something about those orange boxers with their cartoon fish—they draw from me such a throat-clenching nostalgia for a younger version of you—an image at odds with the man you are.

You're disembarking now, I can see it. Maybe by telling you my story, you can better tell yours, which is the only way to get home, by which I mean to get free of us.

Side B: Then

At the end of my drinking, the kingdom I longed for, slaved for, and at the end of each day lunged at was a rickety slab of unreal estate about four foot square—a back stair landing off my colonial outside Cambridge, Mass. I'd sit hunched against the door guzzling whiskey and smoking Marlboros while wires from a tinny walkman piped blues into my head. Though hours there were frequently spent howling inwardly about the melting ice floe of my marriage, this spate of hours was the highlight of my day.

I was empress of that small kingdom and ruled it in all weathers. Sleet, subzero winds, razor-slicing rain. I'd just slide a gloved hand over my tumbler, back hunched against the door. I defended my time there like a bull with a lowered head, for that was the only space in the world I had control of.

However I thought things were in that spot, so they were. No other place offered as much. My sole link to reality was the hard plastic baby monitor. Should a cough or cry start, its signal light stabbed into my wide pupil like an ice pick.

That's a good starting point, the red pinpoint eye. If I squint inward at it and untether my head from the present, time stops. I close my eyes. From that center dot, I can dive into the red past again, reenter it. Blink, the old porch blooms around me, like a stage set sliding into place, every gray industrial board. Holding the monitor is my smooth thirty years' hand. The cuticles are chewed raw, but there's nary vein nor sun blotch. On the yellow fisherman's coat over my pajamas, rain goes *pat pat pat*.

Not one thing on the planet operates as I would have it, and only here can I plot my counterattacks.

Problem one: The fevers my year-old son gets every few weeks can spike to 105°, which means waking the husband, a frantic trip to Children's Hospital, a sleepless night in the waiting room. No reason for this, nothing wrong with his immune system or growth. They'll give him the cherry-flavored goop that makes him shit his brains out, and the cough will ease, but his stomach will cramp, and on the nights he ingests that medicine, he'll draw his stumpy legs to his chest in agony and ball up tight, then arch his back and scream, and though no one suggests this is my fault, my inability to stop it is my chief failure in the world.

Problem two: If he's sick, I'll have to cancel classes so maybe the real professors who just hired me on a friend's recommendation—despite my being too muttonheaded to sport a very relevant diploma—will fail to renew me next semester. I've published one slim volume of verse and some essays, but so has every other semiliterate writer in Cambridge. It's like owning a herd of cattle in my home state of Texas, publishing a book is.

Problem three: Our landlords, the Loud Family. This time, they're after Dev's blue blow-up wading pool. They left a message: If there's a yellow circle in the lawn, our security deposit must cover the cost of sodding. Sod off, I said to the answering machine, shooting it the finger, both barrels, underhanded, like pistolas from a holster. Double-dog damn them. Mr. Loud plans to spend all spring and summer painting the house. All today he stood on a ladder scraping—meticulously by hand—lead paint. Meanwhile, his old-time transistor blares the so-called easy-listening channel—zippity doo-dah for nine hours—and he's only cleared a four-foot square, and I have to tape shut Dev's room so no lead gets in. Mr. Loud's bringing a boom box tomorrow, and all his *Peter, Paul & Mary* tapes. Do I remember *Puff the Magic Dragon,* he wants to know. Do I? On my fun scale, it ranks with the Nuremberg Trials. Virtually every hour, Mr. Loud trudges loudly in to pee—age maybe seventy, one plaid thermos, yet the guy pees like Niagara Falls. By dusk, he's washing his brushes in my sink, while in my mind, I'm notching an arrow in my bow and aiming it at his ass.

Problem four—minor but ongoing: I'm just a smidge further in the bag tonight than I'd planned on, which keeps happening. The yard hasn't started to spin like a roulette wheel yet. I'm upright, but even the slightest list can set it off. Posture's what I need, balance, like walking with a book on my head, which I always sucked at. Unless I keep that bubble exactly in the middle, the whirlies will start. Tip my head even one inch to the left, the oak tree pitches right. Unless I focus extra-hard at something close, I'll tumble off the face of the planet, trailing puke as I fly. What helps is staring at the index finger. Just foreground it and let the rest fuzz up. I sit upright against the kitchen door, staring at my own finger like it's the Delphic oracle.

And there I sit, poised as if on a flagpole, feeling with my free hand for my drink, when the wisp of an idea trails through my head. It doesn't last, but it's audible: you're the bad mom in the afterschool special, the example other moms—little parentheses drawn down around their glossy mouths—go to the principal about.

Oh, horseshit, I think. Mother fell down and pissed her pants, Daddy got in fistfights and drank himself to death. (Who but a drunk, I wonder looking back, could sit on the porch alone and get in an argument?) I turned out half okay; well, a quarter—at least a tenth okay.

As a new mother, I used to cup my son's downy head with wild tenderness and marvel at his heavy slump in my arms, and for the few moments his china-blue eyes fixed on mine before they closed, it was as if the sky had been boiled down and rendered into that small gaze. Those first months, I fed him from myself. And doing so felt like the first true and good act I'd managed in my whole slipshod life.

Then I started drinking every day and stopped breast-feeding, and tonight, while holding the bottle to his working mouth, I averted my eyes for fear he'd see the gutshot animal I'm morphing into, which mirrors the mother I fled to keep from becoming, the one who shoved me off—*Don't hug me, you're making me hot* her tagline.

Problem five, the husband: Should he come home early after work and grad school, should he round the corner and peer in with an expectant grin, I'll shoo him away. Sex of the calf-roping variety still takes place, but otherwise, I'd felt so alone with my son that first year when night after sleepless night I'd gotten up while the husband slept like a hog in his wallow with a white-noise machine to mask the loud misery I gave off—now we connect at no point.

Now nights, I sit downstairs on the porch and stare into the black hole of the garage, which, in my childhood cosmology, was where my oil-worker daddy sat in the truck and drank himself to death. After he staggered into the house to pass out—first bumping against the sides of the hall like a train conductor—I'd go out to the garage and stand with my back to the wall, waiting for the headlights of my mother's vehicle to come swerving up the dead-end street we lived on. Through sheer force of will, I'd draw her drunk ass home alive. Daddy was steady and stayed. Mother was an artist and left. Those two opposing colossi tore a rip in my chest I can't seem to stitch shut.

The garage faces me like an empty pit, and I sit on the house's threshold facing it till the edges of the square hole go blurry. If I were a real poet, I'd be composing a sonnet about the fairy mist in yon oak. Instead, I stare at my finger with dwindling success, for behind it, the view is getting wavery, and in an attempt to adjust, to regain my bearings, I tip my face up slightly into summer rain, which move makes the world take an unprecedented lurch. My head pitches back like a Pez dispenser. The postage-stamp backyard whips from view.

I am leaning the top of my head against the door when I spot for the zillionth time—Problem Six?—the burnt-out lightbulb I fail every day to change, the cartoon idea I every night fail to get.

PART I

Escape from the Tropic of Squalor

I was miserable, of course, for I was seventeen,
and so I swung into action and wrote a poem,

and it was miserable, for that's how I thought
poetry worked: you digested experience and shat

literature.

—WILLIAM MATTHEWS, "MINGUS AT THE SHOWPLACE"

They all followed a circuitous route, which very
often took them to foreign countries, but led only
to disintegration and death, and meanwhile their
parents, their brothers and sisters and other rel-
atives, drank themselves to death at home. . . .
They existed in a ceaseless delirium of accusation
and blame, which amounted to a deadly disease.

—THOMAS BERNHARD, *GATHERING EVIDENCE*

1

Lost in the Golden State

Here lies one whose name was writ in water
—GRAVESTONE OF JOHN KEATS

Age seventeen, stringy-haired and halter-topped, weighing in the high double digits and unhindered by a high school diploma, I showed up at the Pacific Ocean, ready to seek my fortune with a truck full of extremely stoned surfers. My family, I thought them to be, for such was my quest—a family I could stand alongside pondering the sea. We stood as the blue water surged toward us in six-foot coils.

No way am I going in that, I said, being a sissy at heart. My hair was whipping around.

Easy and Quinn were unhooking their boards from the truck that had choked and sputtered through twelve hundred uncertain miles.

Wasn't that the big idea? Doonie snapped back, rifling

through the back for towels and a wet suit. He was my best friend and maybe the biggest outlaw, point man on our missions. He tended to land the most spectacular girls. The ocean roar was majestic enough that I quoted Robert Frost:

The shattered water made a misty din.
Great waves looked over others coming in
And thought of doing something to the shore
Water had never done to land before . . .

Pretty, Doonie said.

Quinn spat in the sand and said, She's always like Miss Brainiac, or something, or like she's fine.

He zipped up his outsize wet suit with force. The crotch of it hung down so low that for him to walk, he had to cowboy swagger.

My hair was three days without soap, and my baggy cutoffs were held up with a belt of braided twine a pal of ours made in prison.

That's me, I said. Miss California.

Quinn himself was no Adonis. We called him Quinn the Eskimo, since he'd just moved to Leechfield from the Alaskan oil fields where his daddy had worked. Blond as Jean Harlow, pimply, he was also skinny enough to crash a junior high dance. His sole source of pride was the obvious lie that his old man had invented the water bed, then tragically had his patent pinched by some California engineer. From the time we'd hit the state line, he'd been going into phone booths to skim directories for the guy's name.

Doonie tucked his board under his arm, saying, Y'all little bitches stand here and fight it out. I'm gonna carve those waves up like your mama's Christmas turkey.

Then they were running down the immaculate white sand with their boards—Doonie and Dave, Quinn and Easy and the quiet Forsythe.

But by Orange County standards, the surf sucked. I overheard the California guys bitching about it as breaking in water too shallow: *Not worth wasting the wax on, dude.* They stood in small bands along the beach, tanned and bleached and orthodontured. And Lord, were they fetching, those boys. I spotted no stitches on anybody, no keloid scars from boiling water. They'd suffered no car wrecks in which an ancient axle had snapped. Nobody was missing any obvious teeth, either.

In the ocean, long waves came with open-fanged mouths, drooling where the spray blew back only to bite down on my pals, who'd thrown themselves onto their homemade boards and were digging in.

From the beach, it was a bitch to witness—not just the ass-whipping the sea was delivering but the massive cheer of my friends taking it, the small and concentrated energy of repeatedly hurling themselves at impenetrable force.

Mocking their inadequacy against those waves, one guy walking past said to his small-boned girlfriend, *This is why they send the white trash to Vietnam.*

At some point, a guy as wasp-waisted as a Ken doll, with stomach muscles you could have bounced a quarter off, strolled over to where I sat. The sun shone through his long dark hair, making a halo around him. Maybe he'd seen our license plates, for he said to me, You Texan?

I allowed as how I was.

You interested in some acid? Ken said.

When I told him I didn't have any money, he smirked, saying, They make chicks pay for drugs in Texas?

Which seemed to have no right answer to it, like the

school bully in *A Portrait of the Artist* who asks Stephen
Dedalus, *Do you kiss your mother?* Any answer seems cause
for a butt-whipping.

I shrugged. What do y'all do here?

He unfolded a small square of surf magazine to reveal an
orange tab of LSD.

I knew right off I didn't want it, but this boy was teen-
idol darling. So I set the tab atop my tongue and faked swal-
lowing, hoping for a weak dose.

He also invited me to a graduation party a few weeks
down the line in Laguna. Soon as he'd scrawled out an address and sketched a map for me, I hightailed it back to the
truck to spit the tab out and wash my mouth with water from
a sand-gritty milk jug.

At dusk, we parked in an apartment lot where a hometown dope dealer had left his pink Lincoln Continental with
its busted steering column. Easy knew somebody who lived
there, and in the way of poor hippies, they cooked us noodles and let us use their bathroom in exchange for the free pot
Doonie could lay on them. Secreted inside the freakishly fat
surfboard—in a scooped-out hollow in its foam core—he'd
ratholed a few fragrant bricks of pot and a baggie of question-
ably acquired pills. These investments—tucked away from
the law under sheets of fiberglass and squeegeed over with
resin—would free him from the factory jobs we'll all eventually take.

For the first time in days, inside a rank plastic shower
curtain flowering with mildew, water poured over me. And
it was in the shower that the acid kicked in—not full bore,
just enough to keep me holding myself very still. The suds
swirled down my torso like chrysanthemums in a Japanese
wood-block print. And my body seemed to smoke.

By the time I'd dressed, beers were being handed around. Black speakers thumped out music. The guys agreed I could sleep in the palatial luxury of the Lincoln, not that sleep was possible on that acid. Doonie helped me run an extension cord with a caged mechanic's light so I could read. But with the nearby ocean buzzing like a hornets' nest, I could only puzzle over the black letters squiggling off the edges of the white page.

At some point, a looming figure glided up to the foggy side window, and I jerked huffing in air to holler, but the scream got stuck, just added itself onto the large round scream that all my life had been assembling in my chest. It felt like a huge lump of cold clay. Someday I was gonna holler so long, glass would shatter and walls explode.

But it was just Doonie's thin shape with black frazzled hair. His knuckles whapped the glass.

I body-blocked the heavy car door open, saying, You scared the fuck out of me.

Each word materialized between my lips like a tiny pink balloon that rose with other balloons in a birdlike drove.

Doonie had his sleeping bag over his shoulder like a corpse. He said, Sorry, man. Mind if I grab the front seat?

As I stared at him, his edges grew more solid, and when I told him to go ahead, there were no more balloons blipping from my lips. He plucked an azalea off the nearby bush, saying, Can you believe how this place even smells? I didn't know the outside could smell like this.

I breathed in the living green of it, then asked if the others were asleep.

Yeah, Doonie said, except Dave keeps busting out hollering shit. He just sat up and said, *We're all gonna die!* Like he's in Nam or something.

Doonie looked around. Man, ain't it the Ritz up in here? Don't you know, those side lights used to light up like the Superdome.

I looked at the long bank of dead bulbs and felt a sinking at how dim and broken everything could get.

I told him I sometimes felt like smacking Quinn for mocking me anytime I recited poetry.

Nah, it ain't like that, Doonie said. He just associates poems with some teacher telling him he's a dumbass.

He put his callused feet up on the dashboard behind the steering wheel. I asked him what Quinn's momma was like.

Doesn't have one. I don't know.

How do you not have a mother? I said, but somehow I knew, because mine had always lived on the brink of evaporation. (Strange, we never—not one time—talked about the doped-up or drunk-assed backgrounds some of us were fleeing.)

Doonie said, Quinn's died or ran off or something. This is according to Dave, of course, so who knows. And get this, Dave also says Quinn brought a pistol to kill the waterbed king with. If he can't get his old man's money back. A no-shit gunslinger pistol like we used to shoplift from Woolco. You'd get a little plastic sheriff's badge with it. He's got some fantasy he's gonna get even for his daddy.

The word *daddy* hung in the air outlined in gold. Closing my eyes, I found it in blue on my eyelids. I could feel the roots my daddy had grown in me—actual branches in my body. His was the ethos of country folk: people who kept raked dirt yards rather than grassy lawns because growing grass was too much like field work; people who kept the icebox on the porch, plugged in with an extension cord run through a window, so folks driving by would know they had one. I could feel Daddy's roots in me, but I couldn't fit him into any version of my life I could concoct. He'd been going away for years, out into the garage at night, down into the bottle he secreted under his truck seat.

I adapted to Daddy's absence partly by smoking enough reefer to float me through a house where—increasingly—nobody's path intersected with another.

Doonie's voice jolted me back into the warm car. He said, You know what I'm gonna do?

A lot of obscene and illegal stuff, I'd wager.

He said, I'm gonna fix this Lincoln up and drive it back to Leechfield. My senior year ride. No more Mama's Torino.

Like you will, I said.

Like I won't.

My brain was starting to melt and soften again around an old image of Daddy from childhood. How he'd come home at dawn in his denim shirt, and I'd be the only one up, peering out the back drapes till he walked across the patio. Lots of times, he'd come in and lie on his stomach on the bare boards of our yet-to-be-carpeted floor, and I'd walk barefoot along his spine. I'd have to hold on to the bookcase to keep from sliding off the sloping muscles of his back, but I'd work my toes under his scapular bones, and he'd ask, You feel my wings growing under there, Pokey? And I'd allege that I did. He claimed it always helped him get to sleep in the daylight. It was maybe the only time I felt like a contributor to the household, somehow useful in our small economy.

In the Lincoln, the image faded inside me, and I heard myself say, What use am I now?

Doonie said, Something wrong?

What the hell *was* wrong? Here I was, where I'd planned to be, but it felt like . . . like nothing. Some black and rotting cavity of wrongness still stank somewhere inside me. I could smell it but not name it.

I lay in the dark a long time and had just about forgotten Doonie was there at all when he tossed the azalea blossom over the backseat and it fell in the middle of me, as if dropped from a cloud.

Within a week or so, the party the Ken doll had invited me to rolled around. It was my only day off from the T-shirt factory where I sewed on size labels with a bunch of Mexican ladies in their sixties. Before that, we'd starved, living on what we could fetch out of grocery store dumpsters plus some raids on local orange and avocado orchards.

Walking the canyon roads that day, I couldn't find the posh Laguna address, so I spent hours flip-flopping up and down, getting the occasional whiff of coconut oil and chlorine, overhearing the soft Spanish spoken by some pool cleaners.

But I rounded each corner believing rescue would show up. Passing a road called Laurel Canyon, I remembered a folksinger with a record named that and near-expected her to show up with a basket of sunflowers. Or Neil Young would amble toward me in a fringed leather jacket. Or J. D. Salinger himself, who'd become my mentor and order up poems from me like so many diner pancakes. . . .

(What hurts so bad about youth isn't the actual butt whippings the world delivers. It's the stupid hopes playacting like certainties.)

At one point a town car glided up, and my heart bounded like a doe as the window silently slid down. But it was a wrinkled lady in tennis whites, asking in bad Spanish if I was Luz from the agency.

Parched, covered in dust, with blisters the size of half

dollars on both feet, I finally stood on the coastal high-way, having adopted the most desultory hitchhiking man-ner in history. Holding up a cardboard sign that read SAN CLEMENTE—where my pals had been surfing all day—I tried to look bored, like a girl who didn't actually need a ride. I was a hitchhiker to aspire to.

Toward dusk, a black Volkswagen pulled up, its driver a tattered-looking doper with sleek raven hair and pork-chop sideburns. He jumped out and ran around to open my door, announcing that Tennessee men were bred to manners. Sam-u-el, his name was—short version Sam—a guy old enough to be sporting an incipient widow's peak flanked by bald spots.

The car smelled like something left in an ice chest too long, and the back seat had been torn out, trash piled in. He claimed his old lady was gonna fry his ass if he didn't get that mess cleaned up, but he'd driven down from Oregon and was wore out.

I said my fiancée was the same way, thus believing we'd entered into some chaste understanding. We pulled from the road's shoulder, peace-sign roach clip swinging from the rear-view.

He was a slow driver, puttering along at a tractor's pace, and in that landscape, I had no reason for fear. Along the pop-ulated beach were tanned, bemuscled men; women whose hands bore diamonds the size of gumballs. I tried to roll the window down more, but it stuck about halfway. He drove on, head-banging to the backbeat of Ozzy Osborne's *Paranoid*. On a steep hill, he downshifted and said, Mary, do you be-lieve you live by what you earn?

I said sure, stunned less by the question than by the breath he'd exhaled—real snake-shit breath.

He shouted, Some live by what their own hands take. Others feed like buzzards on the carcass's leftovers.

That's right, I said, wondering what he was getting at. Maybe he wanted me to sell Tupperware or cosmetics door-to-door. Some of the want ads I'd answered offered that.

He said, Samson after his haircut could not break his chains, and the stones of the temple rained down.

I nodded at the King James Bible cadence he'd slid into, his accent no longer evoking Grandpappy on the porch with a slab of pie, but a preacher whose fire and brimstone maybe came from a guilty conscience about underage choristers. I tried to adopt the big-eyed face of a church girl with a well-armed brother. A crumb of fear.

He drew a snuff can out from under his seat and tucked a pinch in his jaw, saying around it, You dip?

No, sir, I said.

He said, Not a pretty habit on a young woman. After an awkward silence, he added, Here's the real truth, if you can dig it. He reached into the backseat and handed over a be-draggled paperback whose inside-back ads involved books on UFOs and Nostradamus.

Looks real interesting, I said.

You believe in presences? he said.

I lied that I knew ESP and ghosts existed, though I believed in nothing, naught, *nada*. (When I got to college and found the word *nihilist*, I'd glom onto it the way a debutante does an alligator handbag.)

He shook his head. Those are just circus tricks for the weak mind.

That's when I noticed that no aspect of this hillbilly matched up with the surfboard lashed on top. Sam's sunken chest mean this only swimming included water wings. *Or—*

the ghost of reason said to me—*when he was weighing down corpses in some black sunken lagoon.*

He said, My granny back in Tennessee was born with the web of a caul over her head like a wedding veil, and I come into this world wearing that same veil. I see what others don't. I am wed to the truth and a missionary of it.

He studied me in black-eyed silence for a while. You're not a Jew, are you? I didn't peg you for a Jew.

Me? No, sir. Actually, do you know a good church around here for me and my fiancée? As if, I thought, I'd ever enter a church other than carried by handles.

He spat in a coffee can and pointed out my window, saying, Look at this cathedral we been give here.

Sun was spattering the indigo water with silver sequins. Girls who seem to have stepped from chewing gum commercials jogged in bikinis along the shoreline. It was a lobster-salad-eating crowd.

I said, They say it never rains here hardly at all.

With two fingers, he stroked the edges of his thick mustache like some diminutive Chinese emperor about to sign a death order. He said, We're not made to wallow in pleasure. Pleasure is joy's assassin. He paused to spit in the coffee can. He said, I can see past this day to the time when these same waves will be made of blood. You believe that?

Sounds like you know the Bible, I said.

That I do. I've studied on it pretty good. You don't mind, he said, brightening up—you don't mind, I gotta make a quick stop by a friend's house right this side of San Clemente.

With that statement, his manner altered. He smiled, showing the pointy incisors of a gerbil. Which change hit my adrenal system like jumper cable voltage. He was suddenly trying to be charming. For the first time, I could see how wildly high he was. I must have had heatstroke to miss it. His eyes were tar pits, his body slick with sweat. This wasn't cannabis sativa high, nor heroin nod-off high, nor John Lennon's imagine-all-the-people-living-in-one-world high. This was eyeball-boiling, grind-your-teeth-to-bloody-stubs high. In short, crystal meth high.

Sorry, I said. I gotta make my old man dinner.

Why, I thought, why didn't I just go to the midwestern college I'd weaseled my way into early admission, then chickened out of? A premed student I had a crush on went there. At the time school had seemed repellently conventional. Plus the education fund Mother and Daddy had—all our lives—reassured us we'd have turned out to be nonexistent. Mostly, though, I knew I'd fail in such a place, having once secured a D in art class—even, maybe not accidentally, given that Mother was a painter.

Sam tucked his long black hair behind his ear, the smile still rigid on his face. He said, This is a cool scene. You'll dig it. My friend used to jam with the Grateful Dead. (A claim ubiquitous among West Coast guitar players circa 1972.)

Cars zipped by. I bent over and pretended to rummage through my big fringed purse as though I were a woman who clipped recipes. Lifting my knees to block my right hand from sight, I got a tight grip on the door handle.

He said, This won't be but a minute.

We slowed down for a curve, and I scanned the empty road behind us before I hoisted the handle and hit the door.

Nothing happened. The handle was floppy loose. It could have spun in a tractionless circle like a pinwheel, no connection to the mechanism. Now I knew why he'd been Sir Galahad with the door.

He downshifted, and the car's loose hull rattled around us. His solvent breath was so strong, one match and he'd belch out dragon flames. He said, It's the truth that saves us, but some people's truth is bitter gall. You're a woman, Mary, with the curse of Eve on you.

I wondered where were the ubiquitous squad cars that had plagued my friends and me. The doughnut-munching bastards.

You wanna see my truth? Sam asked.

I firmly doubted I had a choice. I said of course I'd be honored to see his truth, wise in the arcana as he seemed to be. Then I waited for him to raise up the hatchet or samurai sword with which he would surely split my skull to the gizzard.

With some ceremony, Sam drew from under his shirt a suede pouch on a leather cord slung around his neck. Opening it, he drew out a thin object a few inches long and wrapped in red silk with tiny Chinese ideograms on it. On his lap, he unfolded it with one hand—a small brownish-black burnt-looking thing like an umbilicus. A root or charm, I thought.

That's my twin brother's finger, he said.

I looked at him, white stuff at the sides of his mouth, flecks of tobacco on his bottom lip. I felt my right hand on the floppy door handle.

Sam had been on a tarmac bagging bodies unloaded from a helicopter fresh from the carnage of the Tet Offensive. He'd peeled back one tarp and looked down into his own face. Which was his brother's, of course.

Mary, he said, pray the Lord you never see a face like that. One half was like the inside of a roast you left outside. Just blown slap off. His ear had stayed perfect, though. I wanted something of my brother's power. And I'd had a vision before I got shipped in-country. In a big cathedral, he was, wearing his dress blues. He was praying over my casket. That's what was supposed to of happened. Instead, he got his face shot off.

The wind eked in the window seals, and the car shook. What scared me most was the crying part of Sam had been cauterized already. He was a living scar.

All my life I'd met people bearing wounds far deeper than my own. I'd thought California would change me, heal me, free me from attracting all that. And now I'd flagged it down and climbed in a car with it.

We rounded the curve into Dana Point.

The car lunged up to a light. It shuddered and died. I jammed my skinny arm through the window slot, slick as a length of licorice, and yanked the door open. I didn't so much jump from the car as eject myself out on the roadside slope. The effort launched me downward, sliding. Over gravel and scrub oak, rocks scraping my shins.

I could hear Sam crank the dead VW back up to a stunted idle, its ragged engine coughing. I scrambled up the gravel incline, losing a flip-flop in the process, hollering as if somebody at the light might take notice. I raised my head and bawled for some driver to see me, hear me.

He was calling my name, looking like a guy ditched by his prom date—sweaty and short and like his feelings were hurt. The light changed. Horns. I sprinted across the yellow line before oncoming traffic to the other side of the road. Sam hollered over, Hey, you forgot your pocketbook.

I was sprinting so shards of rock got embedded in one foot. Even then I was doubting my instincts. Maybe he was harmless.

By the time the shakes hit, I was speed-walking with a single flip-flop along the road's shoulder, a kind of inner earthquake starting in my middle—a shaking that spread outward and nearly buckled me.

At a fish joint famous for not letting the beach-weary use its facilities, I rushed past counter traffic to the bathroom.

Soon as I locked the door, I hunched over the sink, washing my unstable limbs with brown paper towels and pink soap as if they belonged to some patient I was paid to tend. The shaking receded like a tide.

Sometime after that—maybe even the next day—I stopped smoking pot, stopped going to the beach. Sam had spooked from me the notion that the hippies I'd once revered were benevolent characters identifiable by roach clips and tie dye. Plus, the crash pad my friends and I had rented had gotten too raggedy for any girl to stand. The sink stayed piled with scabby dishes from when I'd cooked everybody spaghetti a month before. When you hit the light switch at night, the roaches didn't even run anymore. Yet night after night the guys lazed around puffing weed and telling dick jokes. When they headed to the beach, I'd lose myself down the valley of a book or scribble longhand on loose pages that I stashed under my sleeping bag.

College was the thing. I'd scammed my way into that small midwestern school too good for me, but then I'd put it on hold as too square. Now it looked like an escape from flagging down another satanic hobo, or it was suddenly an excuse to read nonstop. I longed for its library walled with books, a desk with gooseneck lamp, a bulletin board.

Taking my collect call, Mother agreed—her life's goal being college for perpetuity. She phoned the school's financial officer, who promised as much in work and loans as I needed. I was sweltering inside the open accordion door of a phone booth.

You've tried it your daddy's way, Mother said.

How is this Daddy's way? Daddy wants me to stay home and hone my pool game.

Yeah, but the T-shirt factory job, the whole working-class-hero pose. Who knows, maybe you'll meet some suave intellectual. . . .

I told her the phone was making my face sweat, but she'd already relaunched into her plan to auction off my unemployable ass to some husband as if I were chattel. She sketched for me an artsy, wire-rimmed guy with a wardrobe of turtlenecks, a shiny car unmarred by the blurring circle of the sanding machine. Which hunk of whimsy failed to account for the fact that I'd bolt like a startled cheetah before such a man—a beast of an unknown phylum.

On my last day, dropping an armload of ratty cutoffs and salt-crusted bikinis into the apartment complex's garbage cans, I spied a thrown-out notebook and nicked it for my disheveled pages—for some reason, all unlined typing paper. I used a pen to poke holes into every margin, which seemed to take a long time, hole by hole. It was dusk when the sheets slid bumpily together and the notebook's silver claws snapped shut. There was sweat on my upper lip.

I stepped out the sliding door into the dusty odor of eucalyptus, a light wind. Over the valley of orange tile roofs, you could catch just a gray strip of sea from there. I set out walking the hills for the last time. With my ponytailed hair and the sweater tied around my neck like a sitcom coed, I looked into any undraped picture window at the families around lamplit tables, pretending they'd celebrate my homecoming at term break.

2

The Mother of Invention

If Jesus had said to her before she was born, "There's only two places available to you. You can either be a nigger or you can be white-trash," what would she have said? "Please. Jesus, please," she would've said, "just let me wait until there's another place available."

—FLANNERY O'CONNOR, "A GOOD MAN IS HARD TO FIND"

Mother's yellow station wagon slid like a Monopoly icon along the gray road that cut between fields of Iowa corn, which was chlorophyll green and punctuated in the distance by gargantuan silver silos and gleaming, unrusted tractors glazed cinnamon red. Mother told me how the wealth of these farmers differed from the plight of the West Texas dirt farmers of her Dust Bowl youth, who doled out mortgaged seed from croker sacks.

But because I was seventeen and had bitten my cuticles

raw facing the prospect of fitting in at the private college we'd reach that night—which had accepted me through some mixture of pity and oversight—and because I was split-headed with the hangover Mother and I had incurred the night before, sucking down screwdrivers in the unaptly named Holiday Inn in Kansas City, I told Mother something like, Enough already about your shitty youth. You've told me about eight million times since we pulled out of the garage.

She asked me if we had any more of the peaches we'd bought in Arkansas.

We got peaches galore, I said.

The car was fragrant with the bushels of fruit we'd been wolfing for two days while our bowels grumbled. I picked through the soft bottom peaches for an unbruised one to hand her. I asked, Wasn't that the name of some famous stripper, Peaches Galore?

Pussy Galore, I believe, Mother said. She bit the peach with a zeal that made me cringe, as did her cavalier use of the word *pussy*, though I myself used it with alacrity.

To look at her behind the wheel, with the mess she could make of a peach, appalled me. She was so primordial. She had to wipe the juice off her chin with the back of her hand.

Out the window, legions of neat corn about to tassel announced a severe order I longed to enter into, one that would shut out the sprawling chaos of Mother.

She tapped her cup of watery ice, saying, I could use a little dollop of vodka in there. The cup was in its sandbagged holder on the bump in the car floor next to her streamlined legs in exercise sandals. And if, as Samuel Johnson said, everyone has the face they deserve at fifty, Mother must have paid some demon off, for despite her wretched habits, her face looked amazing at her half century—with her shock of salt-and-pepper hair, pale skin, and fine features.

She said, Don't look at me that way. We got up at five. It's cocktail hour by our schedule. We got any more ice?

I fixed her drink, then lowered myself on the spider's silk of my attention back into *One Hundred Years of Solitude* and the adventures of the Buendía family. The prodigal José Arcadio, once stolen by the gypsies, returned wearing copper bracelets and with his iron body covered in cryptic tattoos to devour roast suckling pigs and astonish the village whores with his appetites. The scene where he hoisted his adopted sister by her waist into his hammock and, in my translation, *quartered her like a little bird* made my face hot. I bent down the page, whose small triangle still marks the instant.

Touching that triangle of yellowed paper today is like sliding my hand into the glove of my seventeen-year-old hand. Through magic, there are the Iowa fields slipping by with all the wholesome prosperity they represent. And there is my mother, not yet born into the ziplock baggie of ash my sister sent me years ago with the frank message *Mom ½*, written in laundry pen, since no one in our family ever stood on ceremony.

It was sometime on that ride that Mother asked me what was I reading. So lucid is the memory that I feel the power of resurrection. I can hear her voice made harsh by cigarettes asking, What's in your book?

This was a hairpin turn in our life together—the pivotal instant when I'd start furnishing her with reading instead of the other way round.

Her hazel eyes glanced sideways at me from her face, pale as paper.

I said, A family.

She said, Like ours?

Even then I knew to say, What family is like ours?

Meaning: as divided as ours. We passed some Jersey

cows staring at us like they expected us to stop. I said, I wish
Daddy had come with us.

Oh, hell, Mary, she said, upending her drink, rattling the
ice in the cup's bottom. Read me some.

I tried to explain how little sense the book would make
starting from there, and how I was too engrossed to go back.
But she was bored and headachey from the drive and said,
Well, catch me up.

It was an old game for us. Tell me a story, she liked to
say, meaning charm me—my life in this Texas suckhole is
duller than a rubber knife. Amaze me. If I ever wonder what
made me a writer—if I tug the thread of that urgent need I
have to put marks on paper, it invariably leads me back to
Mother, sprawled in bed with a luminous hangover, and how
some book of rhymes I've done in crayon and stapled together
could puncture the soap bubble of her misery.

On the road that day, I did the same, only with better
material, and—no doubt skimming past the sex stuff—I let
those elegant sentences issue from my mouth like mystery
from a well rubbed magic lamp. She was rapt. She gasped.
She asked me to read parts over. By the time we pulled in to
the Minneapolis Holiday Inn, my voice was a croak.

In the room, I got puking drunk for the third night in a
row. Hair of the dog, Mother said. The first screwdriver had
smoothed me right out. However expert I was at drugs, I re-
mained an amateur imbiber, yet drink was all I had that night
to blind me to the presence growing slurry in the next bed.

Maybe any seventeen-year-old girl recoils a little at the
sight of her mother, but mine held captive in her body so
many ghost mothers to be blotted out. If my eyelids closed,
I could see the drunk platinum-blond Mother in a mohair
sweater who'd divorced Daddy for a few months and fled
with us to Colorado to buy a bar. Or the more ancient Mother

in pedal pushers might rise up to shake the last drops from the gasoline can over a pile of our toys before a thrown match made flames go *whump*, and as the dolls' faces imploded so the wires showed through, the very air molecules would shift with the smoke-blackened sky, so the world I occupied would never again be fully safe.

I had to sit up and breathe deep and make my stinging eyes wide so all the shimmery-edged versions dispersed, and she once again lay in filmy underpants and a huge T-shirt with jagged writing on it announcing HERE COMES TROUBLE.

She said, You can't go now. I'm not done with you yet. *Sob sob sob.* She had on one of the derby hats she'd bought each of us in Houston the day we left—pimp hats, they were, trailing long peacock feathers in their brims.

Later, Mother patted my back as I threw up into the toilet. I remember the smell of Jergen's lotion from her hands, and how the tenderness of her gesture repelled me even as part of me hungered for it. I passed out sending prayers up at machine-gun speed, like a soldier in a foxhole to a god not believed in, *Don't let me be her, don't let me be her.* For however she'd pulled herself together for this trip, she could blow at any second.

In the morning when I stirred, my eyes lasered on to her supine form in the next bed. She was nearly done with *Hundred Years of Solitude.* She still had her hat on, pushed back on her head to give her the wondering expression of Charlie Chaplin. My hat had a hole in it, which I didn't remember incurring. My first blackout.

When I pulled up to the green lawn of my college where dogs caught Frisbees in their chops, I decided to reinvent myself for that leafy place.

I'd probably gotten in by wheedling a reference from the

only professor back home I'd known well enough to bother. A lumbering drinking pal of Mother's from the technical university where she'd gotten her teaching degree, he sported a meager russet beard with a skunk stripe and a French accent I later learned was fake. He'd first materialized on our sofa one morning, shoeless, his coat draped across him. The conventioneer's name tag pasted to the breast pocket—apparently printed by the wife I never met—read DON'T BRING HIM HOME. HE'S GOT THE CAR!!!

I liked the sentences he could spin out in midair, with commas and clauses and subclauses woven through. I liked how he oohed at the poetry I'd been encouraged to press on him since about age eleven. It was tricky to find the right moment—after I'd faked interest in Ming porcelain but before he got too lubricated to talk right.

Having not seen him since I was in grade school, I felt pushy showing up in his office brandishing recommendation forms. But he'd said on the phone I could come, so I leaned in his open door slot to ask was he busy.

He sat behind a desk sprawled with papers, hands interleaved before him as if by a mortician. He closed the door behind me, then steered me to a chair facing his desk. I figured he'd decided against recommending me, having found the poems and essays I'd sent him in advance dim-witted. I felt oafish before him. No sooner did he sit down than he bobbed back to his feet like he'd forgotten something. He walked to my side and—with a kind of slow ceremony I did nothing to stop—lifted my T-shirt till I was staring down at my own braless chest. With his trembling and sweaty hand, he cupped first one breast, then the other, saying, *By God, they're real!*

Such was the interview that landed me in a school far beyond my meager qualifications.

For years I stayed grateful that the whole deal had been fast—a small price to pay for getting out of Leechfield. Though it was smaller than more violent assaults that had happened as a kid, which I paid for longer, it touched the same sore place—did I draw these guys somehow? But for ten years or more, when I was spent or hurt and totting up unnecessary gloom, his bearded face would float to mind, and I'd conjure a deep fry pot big enough to lower the pasty bastard into. Later, I pitied him more, for he was no doubt writhing in his own private hell. Which point is moot, since by now the worms have eaten him, and slowly.

What's a typical journey to college? I couldn't tell you. I hope my son, Dev, had one last summer. His dad was staring owlishly into the computer screen, trying to download music, while I slipped folded shirts into fiberboard drawers and ran extension cords. Before I left, Dev heard a series of moist-eyed platitudes till he said, Mom, don't Polonius me with this nagging. Still, he hugged me—his huge form ripe with shaving lotion—hugged me right in front of his backward-ballcap-wearing roomies. Dev's parting words: Love you. Don't forget to mail those CDs.

My passage involved three blue-ribbon hangovers and the genial loneliness of a South American novel and an image of Mother charging out of a liquor store in blinding sun holding a gallon of vodka aloft like a trophy.

On the morning Mother's yellow station wagon deposited me at a dorm and pulled away from the curb, I was seventeen, thin and malleable as coat hanger wire, and Mother was the silky shadow stitched to my feet that I nonetheless believed I could outrun. I didn't cry when she pulled away, for there were cute hippie boys playing guitar cross-legged on the lawn, but my throat had a cold stone lodged in it. I was thirsty.

3

Lackluster College Coed

*. . . I had a friend who thought the secret
was turning a turntable backwards.
One pill made you stronger, one pill
and you could fly. I had a friend
who crashed us through a cornfield
and all the husks could do was sing,
but that was all right, it was singing
that mattered to us, had weight,
occupied space, in motion tended
to stay in motion, in rest rest.*

*You start with a darkness to move through
but sometimes the darkness moves through you.*
        —DEAN YOUNG, "BRIGHT WINDOW"

When Mother and I had taken off for college, Daddy had

stood on the back porch under the clothesline with the white cat slung over his shoulder like a baby he was burping, and he swore he'd come visit his first vacation. He said, Come Halloween, Pokey, at the latest. Old Pete'll come walking up the road, making the rocks fly high. So stop that snubbing, you and your momma both. Make me wanna hork.

He spoke these words out of his own wet face, wiped with the back of his rawboned hand, but it was all bullshit, his promise. I knew, and he knew I knew. Between us stood the tacit contract that come vacation time, old Red would need Daddy's help nailing asbestos siding up at his camp, or our backyard fence would require mending, or so-and-so would be laid up and Daddy could use the overtime. He'd never set foot on this campus. His drinking schedule had become too inviolable. Plus, these college folks with whom I was hobnobbing wouldn't know how to speak to a man who'd graduated grade six and spent days off cleaning his squirrel gun.

In our household, I'd been assigned Daddy's sidekick. Starting as a toddler, I'd kept a place standing beside him in his truck, and for the rest of his days, his lanky arm still reflexively extended itself at stop signs, as if to stop a smaller me from pitching through the windshield. But all through my drug-misty high school years, Daddy had floated through the house with an increasingly vacant stare, leaving a wake of Camel smoke.

Over time, I followed the books Mother set down like so many bread crumbs to her side, and soon she was leaning in my doorway to hear Otis Redding or the sardonic Frank Zappa squawk. Once, she'd coiled my hair into a pinned twist that matched her own and we'd sat in an opera house half floodlit as a mournful soprano pined: *Vissi d'arte, vissi d'amore*—I lived for life, I lived for love. That was Mother's altar. Forget our scattered Sunday sorties into yoga and Christian Science. The theology Mother pored over—Buddhism mostly—was more theory than pursuit, and Lord knows why they baptized my sister, Lecia, Methodist. But I saw the shine in Mother's eyes as that opera washed over her.

Which music Daddy cared diddly for. The volumes that towered around Mother's bed were partly stacked up to block him out. For his part, a book was a squatty form of two-by-four—useful, say, for propping open a window with a broken sash.

Yet at college, I never stopped expecting to find Daddy reborn beside me, showing me how to tie a slipknot, or run a hunting blade under a rabbit's hide so the blue carcass could be disassembled and peppered and dredged in flour. And crossing the campus as leaves scratched along the sidewalks, I could sense whatever thinly stretched rubber bands on my back that once tethered me to Daddy had already snapped.

How he'd taught me to talk—*Y'all fixing to go to class?*—busted up the average midwesterner. Even his voice on the dorm phone could draw a crowd. Kids who answered tended to ape the drawl I'd started to lose, mimicking Daddy, they sounded like cornpone hillbillies from *Hee Haw*.

But I missed him enough to write a letter swearing fealty to the very self I was smothering:

> *Dear Daddy:*
>   *Thanks for the five-spot. You didn't have to do that, since I have actual jobs making money. The food service feeds me like the little oinker I am. You'd just put your head under the milk spout and guzzle. I*

know you would. Thanks to all this chow, I'm weighing
over a hundred again, so I'm less of a gimlet ass.

There's a really nice art history teacher named
Armajani (he's from Iran) who takes kids fishing on
weekends at his cabin. He claims the bass are big
as my arm. I told him in Texas we'd throw those
little fellers back. I sure wish you were here to yank
a few out of the water with me. I miss you more
than black eyed peas, more than oysters. Your baby,
Mary

Without Daddy, the wide plain of Minnesota was a vast
and empty canvas, me a flealike pin dot scurrying across.

So I sought the favor of my all male professors, becoming
the kind of puppyish suckup I'd hated in high school. Getting
to class early, I shot my hand in the air.

The white-haired psychology prof, Walt Mink, was a tall,
barrel-chested man whose foreshortened leg, damaged from
a drunk driver's head-on, gave him a slightly heaving walk
he never slowed down for. No doubt, a knack for tending the
troubled—including the occasional too-many-mushrooms
psychosis—kept him moving at that clip. Specializing in
brain physiology, he kept labs full of pigeons and rats to teach
conditioning theory in intro psych. In a sleep lab he sometimes ran, he wired kids up to a high-tech EEG.

I'd signed up for his freshman seminar, Paradigms of
Consciousness, under the delusion that *consciousness* was code
for *drugs*—the sole subject in which I had a leg up. Early on,
he spotted me pulling bobby socks on my hands after class.
Having lost the leather mittens Daddy had bought me at GI
surplus—stiff leather with Korean script on the inside tag—
I'd taken to wearing footwear.

He said, This another fashion trend I've let slide by?

Chronic mitten loser, I told him.

My department collects strays, he said. Stop by my office tonight. We'll see what we can find.

But during the day, the prospect slid back and forth in my skull like a BB. Why did he want to see me at night?

Leaving my library job, I faced sparse snow on the ground, scraped at by winds like straight razors. It was cold, you betcha. So I loped over to the science building, where the gleaming labs with black counters and curvy gas jets creeped me out.

There was a warm amber light spilling from Walt's doorway. I craned around the door, and he waved me through. In a green towel on his lap, he held a white lab rat, stretched on her side, taking sips of air while her fidgeting, thimble-sized offspring—pink as young rosebuds—were nursing. She'd given birth earlier, he said, and seemed to have some kind of infection. Can you hold her so I can maneuver this eyedropper? he said.

I sat down in a side chair, and he eased the wriggling small weightlessness onto my lap.

It was puzzling to me, his tenderness for that rat, since where I grew up, rats were target practice—nutria rats big as terriers with their bright orange enamel fangs. You went to the dump with a .22 or a pistol to pick them off. Doonie had given me a nutria rat skull one Valentine's Day.

She just had a rough time delivering today, Walt said. I was at home and kept thinking about her. Wondering how the babies were doing. . . .

He fixed the eyedropper between her teeth and eased out a half drop, dabbing off her whiskers with a tissue. Then he idly ran his thumb along her muzzle.

Watching that, I couldn't live another instant without

unloading into his care my whirling insides. My every woe came spilling out. No money to go home. No place to stay over Thanksgiving. A boy I liked, then didn't, then did. Plus the four jobs I held down were eating me alive. Walt handed me one pink flounce of tissue after another.

Worst of all, the only reason I'd come there was to write, but I'd refused to sign up for a lit class, being too ill read not to shame myself. At a freshman mixer early on, I heard kids hurling around like fastballs opinions about Russian novels it had taken me a week to figure out the characters in—I had to make a chart in back. They were talking Dostoyevsky's blah-blah and the objective correlative of the doodad. They'd studied in Paris and Switzerland. The closest I'd come to speaking French was ordering boudain sausage from the take-out window of Boudreaux's Fat Boy.

What small whiz-kid luster I'd given off in grade school had gone to mist starting my sunglassed junior year. I knew some Shakespeare plays, and I'd read a couple great books till their spines split. But I'd never had to form an opinion about any of that. I'd just blink at it like a bass.

Instead, I'd signed up for classes related to linguistic philosophy, for which I had even less talent. In Walt's own seminar, we were reading neo-Kantian Ernst Cassirer—a brick I broke my brain on.

Walt would help me with all that, he said, adding, Come in to talk if you're feeling bad.

From bawling so hard, my eyes were squinty as a boxer's, and my salty face felt drawn up as by too-tight pigtails. But the deep calm Walt gave off had stilled me inside. I stared down at the mice, each small enough to fit into a sugar spoon.

Finally, I said, I thought you were here to put stuff in our heads.

Unless we deal with what's already in there, he said, I can't accomplish that.

In the hallway, Walt reached into a cardboard box of lost clothes and fished around till he raised up a pair of gray suede gloves. Sliding my hand in one, I felt the silky warmth of rabbit fur. I'd have felt too greedy taking them myself, but he nudged me on.

I was in the hall when he called me back to him, saying, One more thing . . .

I stopped. The unheated hall was shadowy, and watching him heave toward me, I felt a sick fear bubble up. If he makes a pass at me, I thought, I'll run.

He said, Mind if I ask you something personal?

I stared past him into the lab behind him, where silver faucets—curved like swans' necks—glinted in the dim light. His blue-eyed face was dominated by a hawk's-beak nose. He said, Are you sleeping okay? Gained or lost any weight?

Actually, I'd used a food service knife to poke an extra hole in my belt already, and for weeks on end, no matter how tired, I'd wake at three or four in the morning, sometimes hollering at some shadowy figure over me.

He pulled a pen from his pocket and limped over to the wall to write down a phone number on a card, saying his wife ran a neighborhood clinic if I'd like to try some therapy.

No way could I afford anything like that.

Oh, I'm pretty sure she could work something out, he said. She's good that way. And you should come over to the house to meet her and the kids. My daughter writes poetry, and you might be able to help her with it. We'd pay you of course. . . .

Walt helped me figure out that if I dropped the murderous physics, my grades might score scholarship money, maybe soon as second term. He'd hire me to clean rat and pigeon cages, which would free me from the food service's vile hairnet.

(As he had for who knows how many others, Walt had decided to lift me up. The therapy—when I showed up—involved sitting in a cozy office, trying to look sane enough not to be kicked out. But every now and then I'd blubber about being lonesome for home or scared to fail, and I mostly left breathing deeper.)

Buoyed up after talking to Walt, I set out for my dorm. The cold had polished and clarified the sky into onyx. The stars seemed close enough to scoop up. Crossing the quad, I felt some wormhole into my skull finally get bored. There was an internal click as an actual idea of Cassirer's broke through. The sentence that had so addled me suddenly made sense (in the paperback of *The Philosophy of Symbolic Forms* I still own, the phrase has rockets and fireworks scribbled alongside it):

> *The same function which the image of God performs, the same tendency to permanent existence, may be ascribed to the uttered sounds of language.*

He meant that words shaped our realities, our perceptions, giving them an authority God had for other generations. The indecipherable sentence had been circumnavigating my insides like a bluebottle fly for a week, and at last I got hold of it: words would define me, govern and determine me. Words warranted my devotion—not drugs, not boys. That's why I clung to the myth that poetry could somehow magically still my scrambled innards.

I moved through the lung-scalding air, no longer a misplaced cracker but a by-God symbolic animal who'd puzzled out—over a week's time—the meaning of a hard sentence.

But checking my P.O. in the student union the next day, brushed past by the sons and daughters of the professional class—my down-jacketed (alleged) peers—I sensed a dashed line around me where invisible scissors would soon clip me away. Fair-minded, straight-toothed, impossibly clear-skinned, these kids were nothing if not democratically inclined vis-à-vis the likes of me. They blew pot smoke from their joints into my pursed lips and paid my way to Dylan and the Grateful Dead. They gave me rides in paid-for cars. Their parents steered me under restaurant awnings and through doors where the maître d's looked at my soaking tennis shoes long and hard. They passed menus featuring appetizers that cost more than the whole chicken-fried steak dinners Daddy bought us on paycheck night. They invited me home for Thanksgiving and Easter. They seemed to trust my scrappy climb out of the lower class would allow me to handle on first sight all manner of eating utensil by imitating, chimpanzeelike, their movements.

Their bottomless cool—their cynical postures grown from privilege they were ungrateful for—could make me hate them. Born on third base, my daddy always said of the well off, and think they hit a home run.

But by God, I could outdrink the little suckers, and when the dashed lines around my body felt sharp enough to be visible, I might take up a held-out bottle.

Faced with a boy I had a crush on—a bow-legged Missouri cowboy with the face and form of young Marlon Brando—I eagerly took the tequila his friend handed me. Forgoing lime and salt, I tucked my hair behind my ears and tossed back a shot. As that one went down like bleach, I was holding up my glass for another.

Whoa, Brando said, looks like you've done this before.

Absolutely, I said.

She's from Texas, a kid from my physics class said.

Texas girl? Brando said over his shoulder, before turning back to the two girls who'd presented themselves to him like dinner mints. I threw back another shot, which scalded a little channel through me. The boys cheered. By the third shot, the tequila seemed less poisonous. By the fourth, I felt a cool blue moon rising in my chest.

Though I'd vowed not to drink that week (I had an anthro paper to finish), I'd spied Brando doing shots with his pals and wedged into the group. He cut me a smile before squatting down to unlatch his guitar case, and as he started to strap on the instrument, I saw in the case's blue velvet bottom a weathered copy of Joyce's *Portrait of the Artist,* which felt like a further sign that we were carved from the same wood. That novel was one I innately knew to be unreservedly great, and whose first paragraph somebody started slurrily to recite:

> *Once upon a time and a very good time it was there was a moocow coming down along the road and this moocow that was coming down along the road met a nicens little boy named baby tuckoo.*

Next thing I knew, I was earping onto the frozen earth, then girls were steering me loop-legged to my door. Which was the end of that night and more than a few others.

Come Christmas, I caught a ride to Dallas, then took the silver bullet-shaped bus into the Leechfield station, where Daddy stood in creased khakis with comb marks in his black hair. The neck I threw my arms around had gone loose and leathery. For the first time, he smelled old. He took my duffel bag, saying, You could use a few pounds.

Passing through the greenish neon of the station, I felt

time curve back, and us in it. The place seemed coated with
chicken grease. Even the pinball glass was smoky. A man sat
on his shoeshine box listening to a big transistor radio with
a coat-hanger antenna. In his raised-up chair was a thin lady
with conked hair slicked alongside her head.

Outside, Daddy threw my duffel into the truck bed. The
door he opened groaned with rust, the hollow timbre of it
tolling my arrival better than church bells. For five months,
I'd ached to reenter a familiar slot alongside my fading daddy,
but being there my mind went skittery as water flicked on a
skillet. Even with the window open, the truck was redolent
with Camel smoke and the goop Daddy used to clean oil off
his hands with. There was a hint of cumin from a paper bag
of corn-husk tamales from a roadside stand. And running
under it all like current—what got him up in the morning
and laid him out at night was the oak smell of wood barrels
where whiskey soaked up flavor.

For the first time in front of me, he drew a pint bottle
from under his seat. He put the upended lid in the ashtray,
and before he handed the bottle over, he drew out a corner of
his shirttail to wipe the top with, saying, Want a swig?

As a kid sitting on the bar, I'd sipped beer through the
salted triangle of his aluminum can, but Daddy had so long
and adamantly denied drinking every day that Mother had
long since stopped asking. And he'd sure as hell never handed
me any hard liquor.

Daddy's wink echoed our old conspiracy: me and him
against Mother and Lecia, whose tightly guarded collusions
were traded in whispers and giggles that he and I were meant
to stay deaf to.

The bottle gleamed in the air between us. I took the whiskey, planning a courtesy sip. But the aroma stopped me just

as my tongue touched the glass mouth. The warm silk flowered in my mouth and down my gullet, after which a little blue flame of pleasure roared back up my spine. A poof of sequins went sparkling through my middle.

As he went to screw the lid back on, my hand swung out of its own accord, and I said, Can I have another taste?

That taste started me seeking out more hard liquor once I was back at school, though drugs were still easier to come by even than beer. I did okay at old Lackluster College—in no way a star, but neither the abject flop I'd figured on. Daddy carried my grade reports in his ancient wallet.

But it's a truism, I think, that drunks like to run off. Every reality, no matter how pressing—save maybe death row—has an escape route or rabbit hole. Some drinkers go inward into a sullen spiral, and my daddy was one of these; others favor the geographic cure. My mother taught me to seek external agents of transformation—pick a new town or man or job.

That's why I left college at the end of my sophomore year: I just got this urge to run off, maybe because friends in a band were heading for Austin. Or all the rich kids were going abroad. Or maybe the course work was getting too hard, and I couldn't face losing my scholarships and reentering the hairnet. I floundered and skipped classes that winter till, shortly before finals that spring, I just stopped showing up.

Over a hotfudge malted with Walt at the corner drugstore one afternoon, I tried to make my slapdash bailout sound like a literary escapade prompted by a lack of funds. I'd get some writing done while working to save up. Then I'll come back, I told him—though I intended no such thing.

Shirley and I have been talking about that, Walt said, his long spoon scraping the muddy fudge from the glass bottom.

And you've decided to donate a million bucks to me, right?

If we adopted you, he said, the college would have to let you go to school as a faculty child gratis.

I lowered my spoon. Stunned, I was, and touched. They'd never fall for that, I said.

I think they'd have to, Walt said, signaling for a check. Shirley talked to a lawyer friend of ours.

Lifelong, I'd been trying to weasel into another tribe. Back in my neighborhood, I was shameless about showing up on people's porches come supper, then sprawling around their dens till they kicked me out. Wrapped in a crocheted blanket on a hook rug with the game on and the family cheering around me—digging my grubby hand into their popcorn bowl—I could convince myself I was one of them. A few times it almost surprised me when I heard the inevitable sentence: *Time to go home, Mary Marlene.*

Fishing for his wallet, Walt explained how easy it'd be. He and Shirley had talked it over, and even the kids were all for it. His youngest boy had asked whose room I'd sleep in.

Would I have to change my name? I said. Somehow that would seal my betrayal.

I don't think so, he said. Or you can petition to change it back.

The sun was warm on us through the plate glass, and I stared at the door, wishing with all my might that Daddy would come striding through to lay his claim. He'd shake Walt's hand all nice, saying how he appreciated it, but—he'd squeeze my shoulder—he just had to keep me.

The truth was, if it helped with money, Daddy would sign me over in a heartbeat. I was the one who couldn't bear legally lopping myself off from an upbringing I was working so hard to shed.

So I lied that it would hurt my parents too bad, the same

way I used to tell those neighbors I horned in on—right before I figured they'd throw me out—that I had to rush home for a curfew that didn't exist.

Well, think about it, Walt said. We were at the register by then.

How'll I ever pay you back? I said.

For what? He limped back to leave a bill under the salt shaker.

All these lunches, dinners, jobs. . . .

You're not gonna pay me back, he said. It's not that linear. He pushed open the glass door, and I stepped into spring air.

When you're in my place, you're gonna pick up some kid's check.

The idea that Walt was deranged enough to envision me in the position to buy somebody lunch was maybe a bigger vote of confidence than the adoption offer.

When I asked him to drop me at the health service for the sore throat I couldn't shake all spring, he said, Maybe it's just hard to say goodbye.

I whipped around so he wouldn't see my eyes fill, since I was dead sure I wouldn't make it back up there.

But Walt never took his eyes off me. During the time I gypsied around, feebly trying to establish a base, he stayed in touch. No matter where I had a mailbox, his letters sat inside.

Which is maybe why—months after working retail down in Austin—I came back to Minneapolis, where a friend knew a glitzy restaurant where I could bartend. Even there, Walt showed up with other professors to eat the bar's crappy sandwiches. He always left a book or two or a concert ticket, an article on dream research or memory—subjects he knew I kept up with. He never gave up on me, I only stopped being matriculated.

4

There's No Biz Like Po-Biz

*People should like poetry the way a child
likes snow, and they would if poets wrote it.*
   —A LETTER BY WALLACE STEVENS

In the dim realm of that horseshoe bar, I was boss, credibly lying to wives and business partners who phoned in that my patrons were not in fact sitting before me hours on end, imbibing. Such lies kept my tip jar stuffed. Plus compared to those guys—with their car wrecks and one-night stands, their lost families and jobs—my occasional blackout or sidewalk pukefest was bush league.

Binge drinking disagreed with me in no way. The hangovers that haunted the other restaurant folk tended to spare me. Or the ones that did knock me out gave me an excuse to bail from ordinary commerce and loll around feeling resplendently poetic. I drank less steadily than some kids my age (twenty-one), but now I had an appetite for drink, a taste for it, a talent. Maybe it fostered in me a creeping ambition-deficit disorder, but it could ease an ache. So anything worth doing could be undertaken later. Paint the apartment, write a book, quit booze, sure: tomorrow.

Which ensures that life gets lived in miniature. In lieu of the large feelings—sorrow, fury, joy—I had their junior counterparts—anxiety, irritation, excitement.

But humming through me like a third rail was poetry, the myth that if I could shuffle the right words into the right order, I could get my story straight, write myself into an existence that included the company of sacred misfit poets whose pages had kept me company as a kid. Showing up at a normal job was too hard.

Who knows, maybe I'd still be straining martinis from a silver shaker—it was a nice joint—had I not bought a ticket to a midwestern poetry festival so debauched that it couldn't survive even the extremely low bar of acceptable behavior back in the 1970s. Down the dorm hallways, marijuana smoke hazed lazily. At readings, bottles of syrupy wine were passed around. A poetic Woodstock, I told Mother it was on my call home, regaling her with the circuslike atmosphere she'd have been inspired by.

I actually saw living, breathing poets. Back in high school, I'd fallen in love with the visionary antiwar work of Bill Knott, who'd become a cult figure partly through a suicide hoax. After collecting rejection slips, he'd wound up sending a mimeographed note to America's poetry editors, saying something like, *Bill Knott died an orphan and a virgin.* The allegedly posthumous poems came out under the pen name St. Geraud, a character in an eighteenth-century porno novel who ran an orphanage and sodomized his charges. The grotesque humor of the endeavor won me over, particularly when Knott came out from behind his mask with his second book, *Auto-Necrophilia*, which—it took me a while to puzzle out—referred to masturbation after death.

Knott lumped up to the stage, a hulking bubble of a guy in sweatshirt and pants he might have rifled from a dumpster. His heavy black glasses—worn in a wire-rim age—were lopsidedly held together in the center by bandaids. His fair hair hung in unwashed strings. He drew a poem from a wrinkly paper bag stuffed with pages, and after reading a few lines, he said in a disgusted voice, *That's such shit, stupid moron Knott, asshole.* People laughed nervously, looking around. He wadded up the page and tossed it. The room roared.

That's pretty much how the reading went, one balled-up page after another, mingled with lyric poems of great finish and hilarity. The audience hooted in wild and rolling waves. Guys in the front row started throwing the paper balls back, which made Knott hump even deeper in his oversize clothes as if dodging hurled tomatoes.

At the end, a guy in a tie next to me said, I used to think poets shouldn't get public grants, but this guy really can't do anything else.

When Knott left the stage, people hollered for him to come back.

I sat on the hard floor almost aquiver. Writers had heretofore been mythical to me as griffins—winged, otherworldly creatures you had to conjure from the hard-to-find pages they left behind. That was partly why I'd not tried too hard to become one: it was like deciding to be a cowgirl or a maenad.

In our town, the only bookstores sold gold-rimmed Bibles big as coffee tables and plastic dashboard figurines of Jesus—flaming heart all day-glo orange. Yet I'd believed—through grade school—Mother's lie that poetry was a viable profession.

As a toddler, Mother's slate-blue volume of Shakespeare served as my booster seat, and in grade school, I memorized speeches she'd read aloud, to distract or engage her. Picture a bedridden woman with an ice pack balanced on her throbbing head while a girl—age seven, draped in a bedsheet and wearing a cardboard crown—recites *Macbeth* as Lady M. scrubs blood off: *Out, out, damn spot . . .*

Then social mores had intervened. A distinct scene from junior high flushes vividly back.

Girls sitting out of rotation volleyball in gym class stared at me all gap-mouthed when—of a rainy spring day—I spouted e. e. cummings. Through open green gym doors, sheets of rain erased the parking lot we normally stood staring at as if it were a refrigerator about to manifest food. The poem started:

> *in Just-*
>
> *spring   when the world is mud-*
> *luscious . . .*

As I went on, Kitty Stanley sat cross-legged in black gym shorts and white blouse, peeling fuchsia polish off her thumbnail with a watchmaker's precision. She was a mouth breather, Kitty, whose blond bouffant hairdo featured above her bangs a yarn bow the color of a kumquat.

That it? Beverly said. Her black-lined gaze looked like an old-timey bandit mask.

Indeed, I said. (This was my assholish T. S. Eliot stage circa ninth grade, when I peppered my speech with words I thought sounded British like *indeed*.)

Is that a word, *muddy delicious*? Kitty said.

Mud-luscious, I said.

Not no real word, Beverly said, leaning back on both hands, legs crossed.

I studied a volleyball arcing white across the gym ceiling and willed it to smash into Beverly's freakishly round head.

It's squashing together *luscious* and *lush* and *delicious*, and all of it applied to spring mud. It's poetic license, I said.

I think it's real smart how you learn every word so they come out any time you please, Kitty said.

Beverly snorted. I get mud all over Bobby's truck flaps, and believe you me, *delicious* don't figure in.

As insults go, it was weak, but Beverly's facial expression— like she was smelling something—told me to put poetry right back where I'd drug it out from.

Shortly after this, my junior high principal had actually warned me that any girl aiming to be a poet was doomed to become—I shit you not—*no more than a common prostitute.* And so the fantasy went underground, though in high school I'd still hitchhiked two hours to Houston to buy (coincidentally) Bill Knott's first book, which gave me the dim hope that somewhere, a solitary madman knew just how I felt.

Sitting before a living, nose-blowing Bill Knott made all my writer heroes real. It shot voltage through my own poetic leanings, and inside me, some image of myself as a black-turtleneck-clad poet came creaking back to life. The festival must've had fifty or sixty podiums, and behind every one stood a poet with a teaching job and a book to off-load. They were real, and their ranks looked open.

But how to get there? The small U-shaped bar I tended started to feel like a locked corral I needed to jump out of, but which way other than just *not here.*

At the same conference, an unlikely first teacher showed up—a rusty-handed Mississippian named Etheridge Knight, whose debut book had been written in the pen. He was lumbering and black, with a scraggly mustache and a soul patch under his chin. His jaw was lumpy and uneven, with patches of white skin edged in pink—ragged and tear-shaped, as if acid flung in his face had eaten away his color. He spoke of poetry as an oral art (this was pre-poetry-slam America). Without pages, he half-sang the folk tale of Shine, a porter on the *Titanic* strong enough to swim to safety.

> *the banker's daughter ran naked on the deck*
> *with her pink tits trembling and her pants roun her neck*
> *screaming Shine Shine save poor me*
> *and I'll give you all the pussy a black boy needs—*
> *how Shine said now pussy is good and that's no jive*
> *but you got to swim not fuck to stay alive—*
> *And Shine swam on Shine swam on—*

This language both rocked me back and echoed how Daddy talked. I mean, if he thought I was persisting in something I couldn't get done, he'd say, *You keep trying to thread a noodle up that wildcat's ass*; if he thought somebody was poor, *He couldn't buy a piss ant a wrestling jacket.*

Back in Minneapolis, I took the low-tipping day shift just so I could rathole my notebook by the beer spout and scribble.

Crazed to see my name in print, which would prove poethood, I mailed to hapless editors work bad enough that—in retrospect—I'm surprised the rejections didn't come with a cyanide pill. One snotty bastard commented solely on my failure to hit the space bar after periods and commas. *If you could bring yourself to use standard spacing after punctuation, we would find it most helpful.*

Two nights a week, Etheridge held a private poetry workshop at his house, charging young writers like me a pitiful hundred bucks to sit for four months in his living room while he conducted our discussions from the sagging trough of a chenille armchair.

The green and imploding house he shared with his poet-wife, Mary, and their two kids (adopted from Africa back when it was odd) stood out amid the tidy tract houses. Everything about Etheridge's place was off-kilter. The roof sagged. One gutter was untethered. The front screen door hung from a single hinge. Inside, the wood floors buckled as if frozen mid-earthquake. Add a few cypress trees, a front-porch glider, and a hound dog, and the entire tableau could have been picked up by tweezers and used as a set for *Uncle Tom's Cabin*.

Mary, a smart, curvy blonde from Oklahoma, drew paychecks as a social worker plus writing and fighting against apartheid, but even if she'd cleaned from dawn till dusk, I believe that from whatever spot Etheridge occupied, chaos would've spread out like kudzu vines, for he was an addict of the first caliber. Allegedly sober, Etheridge ran his own beer- and marijuana-maintenance program. While he spouted lines from Dickinson, he kept a forty-ounce of Colt malt liquor between his knobby knees.

Back then, in magazines like *The New Yorker*, stories were mostly about ex-Yalies wearing deck shoes. (Ray Carver was about to change all that.) By contrast, Etheridge lectured wearing a string T-shirt and dark pants of a stiff material that I swear to God looked prison issue. He turned his plaid house shoes into slip-ons by stepping on their backs. The Free People's Poetry Workshop, he called us.

What I wrote was mostly unintelligible, except for one bit about a suicidal dog. The first line went, alliteratively enough, *Don't do it, dog.* The stuff I was fighting to avoid sometimes slipped out in vague disguise: a kid raped, a lost father, a woman on the shock treatment table. But because I refused to use sentences—just strung phrases willy-nilly—nobody understood it anyway. The word *cerulean*, I believe, was used.

It's experimental, I argued to the baffled readers arrayed on Etheridge's furniture.

It's in-fucking-comprehensible, he shot back.

Still, the first poems of mine that ever saw print were sent out under Etheridge's aegis, in envelopes he paid postage on. Thrilled to see my name in type, I told my pal John, who'd wallpapered his bathroom with high-class *New Yorker* rejections. His response? *Just as there's a woman for every man, no matter how ugly, there's a magazine for every poem.*

Etheridge's blessing also helped me to snag a job as a poet-in-residence for the city of Minneapolis, the most dubious post I ever held. The city had scrounged up some grants to promote the arts. Some fifty or sixty poets and painters and dancers—hell, we even had a mime, the Mime Laureate of Minneapolis!—got hired to do . . . well, what?

We weren't sure. It was the seventies. Enrich the outer landscape.

Why they hired me, I can't fathom. Age twenty-two, I maybe lied that I had a degree, and I did boast in the interview about three community teaching jobs, two of which were fibs: I'd filled in for a pal working with seniors at the Jewish community center. There I'd befriended a stately holocaust survivor who showed me you could live like an intellectual whether you were in school or not. He loaned me a translation of Dante's *Inferno*, which I left on a bus one drunken night, baldly lying it was stolen—what mugger says, *Hand over the Dante!*

Walt and his wife also hooked me up running a weekly class for severely disturbed kids, but I couldn't handle it. A few months in, I'd had to restrain a psychotic girl in my lap, making my body a living straitjacket, crossing her arms across her chest and wrapping my legs outside hers. Ten and bird-boned, she was. I never went back.

My real teaching job involved a group home for fairly functional retarded women. Once per week after their factory piecework, I showed up with a canvas tote bag of poesie. Only a few could read a little; others just signed their names—the vast majority, not even. They spoke their poems while the staff and I wrote them out. At the end I'd read a handful, then type them all up to copy and pass out the next week.

To say the women changed my life may be a stretch, but only just. I'd been worrying the bone of whether to go back to school for poetry. Or what? Sell kisses at the train depot? Some days all I did to be poetic was wander the public library in black clothes and muddy lipstick. Hell, I'd even moved to England for a spell, tramping around the hills looking at sheep and daffodils. How to go forward was otherwise foggy.

Maybe the girls in my gym class had been right all along, and poetry was a trick on smart people—a bunch of hooey, fawned over by whining fops of the most stick-up-the-ass variety.

The way an uncertain believer might stumble onto proof of God, the women at the group home fully converted me to the Church of Poetry.

That first day I stood at the window of a dayroom looking down as the bus disgorged them. Shedding their coats and the clasped-on mittens that flapped from their coat sleeves, the women bumbled out. They dropped hats or pencils or keys or lunch boxes. One trying to find the end of her scarf turned around in a circle like a slow-motion cat chasing its tail. This halted the women behind her, a few of whom bumped into her and each other.

As staff people herded them in, I felt my armpits grow

damp. The faster ladies spilled into the room around me like kids lining up for a pony ride. A flat-faced woman with the severe and snaggled underbite of a bulldog stood introducing herself with a handshake before she sat. I'm Marion Pinski, she said. P like Polack Pinski. She wore a brown beret flat atop her head like nothing so much as a cow pie.

Alongside her squeezed other women, whose heads seemed small as dolls'. Under narrow shoulders, their bodies went mountainously soft. And they were mushroom-pale, as if they'd been grown underground. It's a shocking thing to face all at once so many kecked-up, genetically disadvantaged humans. In a country that values power and ease and symmetry, velocity and cunning, kinks in their genetic code had robbed them of currency.

Somebody touched my foot. Looking down, I found a sandy-haired woman tugging on my boot buckle. Katie Butke, she introduced herself as. Katie was solid as a fireplug and clean as a boiled peanut, affable but unimpressed by the likes of me. Looking at her, I felt smart all of a sudden, also lucky. You could talk these women out of their bus tokens. Still, glad I'd dodged the bullet they'd caught almost implicated me in their handicap. (At the time I saw only their difficulties. Now I also marvel that they could with verve hug an individual they'd just gotten off the bus with, and that total strangers shampooed Katie's red hair and rubbed lotion on her freckled arms.)

I started off with Pablo Neruda and a thinly disguised Neruda imitator. Good poem vs. cliché. The staff people had warned me the ladies could get distracted and bored, but the Neruda snapped them to attention. *Walking Around* begins, *It so happens I am sick of being a man . . . I am sick of my hair and my eyes and my teeth and my shadows . . .* At one point he says,

> *Still it would be marvelous*
> *to terrify a law clerk with a cut lily,*
> *or kill a nun with a blow on the ear.*

Kill a nun! Katie Butke called out—whether in outrage or enthusiasm, I couldn't tell. The poem ends with wash on the line *from which slow dirty tears are falling.*

Once I stopped, there was a collective sigh, like the pneumatic sound of an engine giving up. A big silence held us. Then applause broke out. Feet were stomped. A few ladies got up to hug each other again. If there'd been pillows, they'd have all started whacking each other.

What did the guy feel who wrote it? I asked. Every hand shot up, but Katie Butke slapped the side of my boot. I pointed to her.

Happy? she said. A few ladies agreed. But a forest of white hands kept flapping.

The recalcitrant Marion Pinski crossed her short white arms across her front, but I called on her anyway.

The shirts, she said in a murmur. The shirts are crying. Sad. The shirts are dirty. The shirts didn't get washed right. The shirts are crying. The man doesn't want Monday.

We broke into small groups, and as I copied down their words, they marveled at my pen's passage across the lines. That's me? a lady named Dawn asked, touching the letters. That's my name?

I kept a copy of the poem Katie Butke wrote that day. It's called *Monkey Face.* Every poem Katie wrote was called *Monkey Face*—a phrase no doubt imprinted on her in ways I hate to think about.

Far away St. Paul
People like robots
Wash their tables
Scrub the floor
Bored things
Washrags on the window
Put it away now
Look at your leg
Tie your shoe. Look
At yourself. A monkey.

One line of Marion Pinski's still pricks me with fresh envy: *I get to dance with the deep boys and the day boys.* (A Buddhist friend would later tell me that Marion was a bodhisattva sent to show me how comical my artistic pretentions were.)

When I gave a local poetry reading—in addition to the Minks and a few local writers—the women came on a bus, and Katie Butke leaped up, shouting with a gospel singer's conviction, *You a monkey face.* (To date, my truest review.) They clapped wildly after every poem. Katie Butke even stood up a few times, taking an operatic from-the-hip bow.

The unchecked emotion they embodied was exactly what Etheridge was trying to drag out of me for my poser's pages. It drove him crazy how I'd stick in fancy names and references I thought sounded clever.

Etheridge used a pen to poke the fedora back on his head. Looking at me with bloodshot eyes, he asked with frank curiosity, Now, why is a little girl from Bumfuck, Texas, dragging FriedrichNietzsche—kicking and screaming—into this poem? Like you're gonna preach. You ain't no preacher, Mary Karr. You're a singer.

When I bristled that I'd been a philosophy major in college, he said, And that's all you're telling anybody. What you took in college. You're pointing right back at your own head, telling everybody how smart it is. Write what you know.

But according to you, I don't know squat.

Your heart, Mary Karr, he'd say. His pen touched my sternum, and it felt for all the world like the point of a dull spear as he said, Your heart knows what your head don't. Or won't.

He wanted me to picture a woman climbing five flights in a Harlem apartment building in summer heat, then having to go back down with armloads of garbage. He said, If you're standing on the corner of 116th Street poeticizing, what could you possibly say to help her climb back up?

This prospect of actual readers flattered me less than it scared me. He kept pushing me to go back to school. Also, long before seeing shrinks helped me to reconcile my warring insides, Etheridge fought to import Daddy onto my page. In one poem, he picked out some feeble old guy whose hands shook as he tried to bait a hook and said, Your old man's knocking on your door, and you won't let him in.

Etheridge spoke to the pool-shooting, catfish-gutting, crawfish-sucking homegirl I was trying to squelch.

Such an unlikely savior. Etheridge sometimes banged on my apartment door at three a.m., trying to mooch money for dope. Mary once caught him in the bathroom—with his kids in the next room—a hypodermic in his jugular.

He talked to me about this new kind of graduate writers' program in Vermont—low-residency, they called it. You show up a few weeks at a pop, twice per year, for lectures, readings, workshops, intense tutoring. A poet tailors a curriculum with you, and for six months you mail manuscripts and papers he or she works over. What did I think? It was either bogus, or I'd never get in.

Meanwhile, I cobbled up an experiment with the ladies

to see whether the poems I brought had sunk in at all, for the scene was part spelling bee, part revival meeting. Each week, I'd pit two poems against each other, a great poem and a crummy one. With an accuracy that rocked me back, they'd boo the crap stuff, then hallelujah the Yeats. Walt talked me into keeping a running tally to see how consistent they were, which I did on an index card taped to my closet door. Over two years, some 80 percent of their choices were as good as most book critics'. Even hard pieces by Stevens and Apollinaire, they'd go crazy for. The sole exceptions? If both poems were average or okay, or if one poem was plain speech and one ornate—in those cases, no predicting what they'd go for.

At the symphony one night when Shirley couldn't go, Walt pressed on flaws in my method, asking, Any way you're swaying them?

You mean I'm unintentionally signaling them somehow? I said. Maybe intoning the gorgeous ones in some hyper-approving way?

The violins were tuning up, the different bows trying to find the same note. It was that instant before a concert when I always wanted to bolt, because what if I didn't like Beethoven, which I'd never heard? Maybe I should beg off and say I'm feeling sick. At home, I could make a hoagie and turn on the tube, rather than stay captive in an overheated hall in a seat that made your legs sweaty with a stranger on one side hogging your armrest.

Walt's face had that expectant air, though, he maybe knew the music was so magnificent that even a plebe like me could hear it. He said, Let's say the women do have some innate taste, despite lacking any analytical tools they could articulate. What's that mean, you think?

I can't remember how I said it—and we both knew I cared too much about the outcome for my little test to pass as science. I told him I wanted to believe in quality the way I had as a kid, when a great poem could flood me with certainty that there was something good in the world. Or somebody out there knew who I was even if we'd never met—or never would meet. Which made poetry one of the sole spiritual acts in our mostly godless household. Just because the ladies never went to school didn't mean they couldn't tell the difference between Beethoven and *The Hokey-Pokey*. Awe was okay with them, possibly their natural state. No really crap teachers had ruined their native taste by preaching what they were supposed to like.

Such a small, pure object a poem could be, made of nothing but air, a tiny string of letters, maybe small enough to fit in the palm of your hand. But it could blow everybody's head off.

Which was what the symphony did that night for the first time, me sitting alongside Walt while the soft timpani mallets with the dandelion-puff heads banged loud enough for the dead, deaf composer to rouse from the distant German dirt.

Afterward, Walt and I didn't say much, just walked through the parking lot exhaling steam with the crowd, everybody's eyes glancing in opposing vectors, brushing off each other but meeting, too, with that soft recognition you have after being drenched awhile by the same orderly chaos. We were like swimmers walking out of the sea. Every ten paces or so, headlights flipping on would turn shadow figures into full-fledged human units. Unlocking the car, Walt brought up my half-assed experiment again, saying, How're you sure you know which poem's best?

I slid inside, saying, I just do.

Which—ignorant though I knew I was—the ladies had proved to me in some way. And the next day, at Walt's urging, I sent away for that graduate application.

5

Never Mind

You wear a mask, and your face grows to fit it.
—GEORGE ORWELL, "SHOOTING AN ELEPHANT"

My first therapist's name was—I shit you not—Tom Sawyer. What are the odds. A grad student Shirley Mink supervised, Tom must've been cudgeled into seeing me for the measly five bucks a pop I paid months late, if at all. With his runner's lanky form, he was usually clad in jeans and hiking boots. His fox-red beard was tamed into the same shape as Freud's— the color so at odds with his streaky blond pageboy that I wondered if it hooked over his ears.

Twice per week, when I deigned to show up—three times if I'd broken up with some beau or been drunked up enough days in a row to wonder was I finally going insane— I whined to Tom about who to date or whether to go back to school or why nobody published my (infantile, unintelligible) poems.

Let's go back to your mother, he said for the hundredth time.

Lord, don't be so Freudian. Soon I'll find you in a tweed vest and bow tie, those little wire rims.

Your complicated mother. Your absent father.

We've been over all that, I said. She's not like that anymore. I mean, she drinks and takes pills more than we'd like. There are the benders still.

Tell it again.

In language more glib and jokey than I'm capable of now, I crankily told Tom the story for the umpteenth time. How Mother doused our every toy with gas and tossed on a match. Much of the night's a blur but for her standing over us with a carving knife.

Tom said, You still have nightmares you've murdered her.

Usually, my daddy does that with a cleaver—wouldn't old Sigmund eat that up, so to speak. There's a Bill Knott poem, *I've recently killed my father and will soon marry my mother. My problem is, should his side of the family be invited to the wedding* . . .

You joke a lot, but you're carrying around some very powerful feelings.

Oh, I feel bad enough, awful even, just not about Mother and Daddy.

Let me ask you something. Whose fault was that night?

We've gone over this. I don't know. Probably mine, like I said. I was a pain in the ass. My sister's to blame maybe a little, but she was older and way less trouble.

For a mother to be expected to show up sane and reliable is the least any kid deserves.

I heated up to defend her. And there, infuriatingly, the scene in the therapist's office and with my mother just cut out, went blank, like undeveloped pictures accidentally slid through an X-ray.

Which kept happening—therapis interruptus. Whenever Tom probed toward my folks at length, I suffered these dramatic erasures and snapped awake, zombielike, leaving the office for the bus stop, wet face stinging. What had I been blubbering about? Not a shred of the session stayed with me, the same person who found long stretches of movie dialogue or yards of doggerel running through her head.

Once when Walt met me for lunch, I asked if these nonalcoholic blackouts were definite proof I was crazy. Just tell me straight, I said, upending the sugar canister into my coffee. Don't hold back.

The brain sometimes has a hard time incorporating certain memories, he said.

I liked that he talked about it in physiological terms, to make it feel less like me, more like a car we were staring into the engine of.

So it's not me—just my brain?

Are you your brain?

Don't try to trick me into learning something, I said.

Your level of functioning contraindicates serious mental illness.

Only intermittently. I keep setting fire to my life.

Interesting image, he said, knowing my incendiary backstory. Maybe if your mother comes in with you for a session the way Tom's suggested, you'll get new data about her hospitalization.

He's theorized that she's manic-depressive.

Will she come if you call?

She'd go to a dogfight to get out of Leechfield.

Which was true enough—not that I prewarned her by

phone that her florid psychosis was our upcoming topic. Actually, I dreaded her coming, since she might freak out and threaten to hurt herself, as she tended to when pressed toward her walled-off past. She'd been a big one to lock herself in the bathroom with a firearm.

But Mother never showed for the session, and—here's the kicker—neither did I. Our excuse? We forgot, both of us, two sessions plus a rescheduled third. Just slipped our minds, the event she'd expensively flown up for. Papa Freud would've said, There are no accidents.

After she'd gone back, I sat across from Tom Sawyer in a tub chair swiveling side to side, and he was—in a quiet, stiffly midwestern way—pissed. Unless I'd commit to getting better, he wouldn't treat me, he said. I had to fly down to Texas and make her talk to me.

She's not gonna kill herself, he said, seeming impatient. You can call me if she starts making those noises. He scribbled out his home number on a card.

Standing, I slung my purse over my shoulder, then I spat out a curse I hadn't heard since seventh grade: You, Sparky, can take a flying fuck at a rolling doughnut. Then I stalked out.

Only looking back, after decades of shrinkdom, do I realize how radical to the point of bizarre his position was. He was either the genius Shirley Mink thought him to be, or a little wobbly sending me down into the lion's den to confront Mother.

(In case you haven't read my early version of the passel of lies my family was built on—yours for a pittance—the broad outline of it needs going over. If you have read it, skip over this part.)

After a conciliatory session with Tom Sawyer—who was

blasé about the rolling-doughnut comment—I flew to Texas on cheap standby, in a cargo plane whose pilot wore a World War I flying cap with flaps like Snoopy wore.

At my folks' house, digging around in the attic, I routed out four wedding rings from a trunk. After days of my relentless nagging, plus a pitcher of margaritas, Mother owned up to having married a few times before Daddy, like maybe about four.

She doesn't date, she marries, her mother had said of her. Age eighteen—not even knocked up before she'd wed at seventeen—she'd given birth to my brother, Tex, followed a few years by his sister, Virginia. Mother's engineer husband could afford a nice place in New York, where she pissed him off by taking classes at the Art Students League. Her bohemian streak didn't suit him. His mother moved up to help with the kids, and one evening Mother came home to find the house cleared to its baseboards, the babies gone. It took her years to track them down in New Mexico, where they were happily in school and calling another woman Mommy. Single, broke, scared, Mother had—on the spot—torn up the custody papers she'd brought along.

Then came her marrying spree, as she looked for a husband who'd help her get those kids back. By the time she got to Daddy—who was willing to take them in—they were grown, Tex training for a stint in Southeast Asia.

So my sister and I had reignited that preexisting loss. That was why Mother had gone nuts, not because I kept asking her to make grilled cheese or give me fifteen cents for the *Weekly Reader*. An old spark had already been burning down the fuse toward her explosion.

After her breakdown, we'd bobbed on unsteadily till I was in grade school, when she inherited a bundle of cotton and banking money from her supposedly middle-class mother, and she divorced Daddy, this time bringing Lecia and me to Colorado. She'd married a Mexican bartender, husband six, buying a bar to boot. Less than a year into that, having spent what may have been a million bucks, Mother had gone back to Daddy, who became the only husband to sign up twice—husband five and seven.

During a handful of stable years, she'd reenrolled in school and wound up teaching art in junior high. But her lost kids never stopped haunting her, she said. Her own mother—my now-dead grandmother—had blamed her.

Once the secret had poured out—the rough patches were gone over—Mother got to wondering about those children. So Lecia hired a Pinkerton detective to track down Tex and Virginia.

My half sister turned out to be a blowsy L.A. blonde with such a taste for pills that I'd bust her eating Daddy's back-pain meds straight from his bedside drawer. I bought her a bus ticket back to San Diego then, and I never saw her again, though she and Mother talked sometimes by phone.

But I took to my easygoing brother, Tex, right off. He was slim and wiry with hair dark as mine. Finding Mother explained to him the artist streak his engineer father had shipped him off to military school to get rid of. After the service, Tex had gone on a tear with drugs and alcohol, but he'd been in active recovery some decades. It tantalized me to think his sobriety might spill over onto Mother, especially when he decided to relocate his photography business to Texas.

Daddy greeted Tex like a lost army buddy, but he'd grown tired of the story long ago, so—after a few hours sitting around the living room catching up—Daddy drifted off to watch some game.

In movie versions of traumatic secrets, the family walks arm in arm into a field of poppies while the sun paints them gold, which scenario I had faith in. With Tex there, a lot of infection drained off pretty fast. Into the night, Mother sat in the rocking chair in her studio, poking at the wood fire, reviewing the tale for some shifting configuration of Lecia and Tex and me. With each version, a new detail emerged—the snow in her hair as she came into the cleared house; the photo of Tex in a sailor suit she'd hoarded; how thick the custody papers were as she tore them—her hands were sore for days.

For decades we'd watched her portraits start with fluid ocher streaks, marveling as each layer of paint drew from the violent slashes a particular shrimp boat, say, down to its last bolt. So for a week or so, with every retelling, Mother herself got more real. Before I left after ten days or so, she'd moved way closer to the front of her face.

Back in the Midwest, I bounced into Tom Sawyer's office like somebody who'd thrown down her crutches to start tap-dancing. He'd been so right. It wasn't my fault, Mother's madness. Cured, I declared myself.

Not long after, the low-residency grad school in Vermont I hadn't believed existed took me on probation, no doubt due to puffed-up references from Walt and Etheridge. I kept living in Minneapolis, teaching there. But twice per year I went to Vermont for a few weeks—poetry camp, I called it.

Age twenty-three, I walked into a decrepit mansion on a campus approaching bankruptcy. (The college would officially fold the year I graduated.) The chintz sofas were faded. The French-pleat drapes were missing a few hooks. The white wine came from a gallon jug and left the taste of pennies in your mouth.

To get there, I'd drawn from a grubstake I'd cobbled together trucking crawfish from Louisiana for my sister's newly acquired farmer husband—the Rice Baron, I called him.

Back then nobody had heard of the teachers whose red ink so bloodied the poems and essays I turned in. Bob still worked construction in the summer to feed his four kids. My thesis advisor, Louise, baked ornate pastries at home, then sold them in local shops or restaurants. Heather had one slender volume and was better known for her wicked pool moves. Frank played jazz piano in a Boston bar on weekends. Ray had almost won a big prize for the dog-eared paperback of stories I'd been hauling around, but he still crashed in a sleeping bag on my floor when he was in Minneapolis. Two brothers, Toby and Geoffrey, hadn't published their memoirs yet. A poet named Ellen Byant Voigt had gathered up this crew about five years before they started dragging Pulitzers and presidential awards and genius grants in their wake.

Easily the least prepared person to study with this august —if not yet anointed—company, I drank like a fish during residencies. Classes ran all day. Parties went till dawn, and I got to hear storytellers of the first order practice their craft. Ray described how the bankruptcy lawyer he'd stiffed of a fee had taken him to small claims court to try to get custody of Ray's dog. The outraged judge had said, *You're gonna take this man's dog?*

Back in Minneapolis, the only way to shovel through the heaps of work was to stay sober, which meant living like a nun. Going nowhere booze was served, I slid as if on a greased track between apartment and library and whatever teaching I could scrape up. No more bartending—the temptation to drink would've kept me blotto—no more pogoing to punk bands. The one art opening I slipped into for a glance around turned into a three-day binge.

After a few years' work, I'd reached the final meeting

with my thesis supervisor—the Resident Genius, I called her—in a chic French restaurant I'd saved up to take her to. She was an elegant woman with a ballerina's slim poise and the ability to run a demitasse spoon around a china cup without looking callow. I felt like a charwoman but tried to play it off as if we were equals, telling her all I needed was the right publisher. (How did I dare? I now think.)

I swear, I said, it's like the magazines installed a machine at my post office that recognizes my address, yanks the poems out, then stuffs them in the return envelope.

Count yourself lucky, she said. You're still promising until your first book's out.

It was dawning on me how uphill a poet's path was, and I confessed to her that if I had to be the choice between being happy or being a poet, I'd choose to be happy.

Setting her spoon down, she said, *Don't worry. You don't have that choice*—which either knighted or blighted me, I'll never know which.

PART II
Flashdance

"So, Papa, are you feeling good now that you're in my hands?"

"No," Papa said, "I'm feeling bad."

Then Semyon asked him, "And my brother Fyodor, when you were hacking him to pieces, did he feel good in your hands?"

"No," Papa said, "Fyodor was feeling bad."

Then Semyon asked him, "And did you think, Papa, that someday you might be feeling bad?"

"No," Papa said, "I didn't think I might be feeling bad."

—ISAAC BABEL, "THE CHURCH IN NOVGOROD"

6

Inheritance Tax Summer

We picked on down the row, the woods getting closer and closer and closer and the secret shade, picking on into the secret shade with my sack and Lafe's sack. Because I said will I or wont I when the sack was half full because I said if the sack was full when we get to the woods it wont be me. . . . If the sack is full, I cannot help it.

—WILLIAM FAULKNER, *AS I LAY DYING*

The young poet I'll wind up marrying tours my grad school for a week. Rumor has it, he'd been the star of genius Robert Lowell's last class at Harvard. Drawn by his shy smile and decorous bearing, I right off start getting to the cafeteria early so as to slide my tray next to his and sit in the scent of detergent he gives off.

Afternoons, we walk through the woods to a sandy stretch of beach alongside a green river, and one day we find inner tubes impressed in the sand as if placed there by wood nymphs. Given the golden aura of ease Warren moves in, I figure this kind of crap must happen to him all the time. His quiet formality counteracts the grungy, drunkenly proffered offers from pierced boys I've shrugged off in various punk bars of late—waiters and turnstile-jumping musicians.

Do you think it's okay if we borrow them?

The hot rubber is warm in my hand as he asks, for I'm greedily rolling what I instantly decided was my inner tube to the water's edge.

We'll bring them right back, I say, impressed to have met such a stand-up citizen.

The inner tubes plop into the green swirl, and we wade in behind. Arms and knees hanging over, we let the current take us. Occasionally, deliciously, my foot brushes his muscled calf, which makes me go all creamy in my center like a stuffed chocolate.

He seems vaguely stirred by my blue-collar credentials, that I paid my way through schools with all manner of unsavory tasks and now hold down community teaching jobs.

That night I call my sister to make my crush official.

Well, he's Ivy-educated, so he's not an idiot, she says. What does he look like?

Superman.

Her silence on the phone is passive doubt.

I swear, like that actor. Very patrician-looking, cheekbones out to here, square jaw. Also those long dimples, very fetching—deep enough to hold a dime.

Is he short?

Six-five, I say.

Height—ours and our boyfriends'—is a running contest

between Lecia and me. If I tell her good news about myself, she's liable to say, *I'm five-nine* and hang up.

You'll have to stand on a step to kiss him.

He rowed crew, I tell her. (Not really his sport.) Plus, he can recite more Shakespeare than anybody not paid to learn it.

Shakespeare meets Superman? He might as well walk out with his hands up.

A few nights before the residency ends, he asks where I'd like to have our first solo dinner, and I say—provocatively, I hope—Montreal.

I hope you don't mind chipping in on gas, he says.

Among young poets, this is standard, even on a date—is this a date? I gnaw my thumbnail.

Before we hit the freeway, Warren stops for an oil check, though his car—a recent graduation gift—still has the dealer's sticker on the rear window.

What's your dad do? I ask as Warren squeegees off the windshield.

He's a lawyer, Warren says. I don't ask what kind of law because who knew there was more than one.

Buckled into the driver's seat, he adjusts the rearview with microscopic precision before even cranking the ignition—a care that opposes my haphazard plowing around in an uninspected Vega, its heater pumping out enough monoxide to give passengers a metallic-tasting headache.

The mountain road hairpins under us, and the green valleys that open up in the windows can't stop my fixation on his regal profile. Trying to impress him, I quote a new translation from Swede Tomas Tranströmer.

Warren counters with "*Season of mists and mellow fruitfulness . . .*" And watching his unkissed mouth shaping those plush syllables is the libidinal equivalent of a studly crooner mouthing a love song.

Wordsworth? I say.

Keats's "Ode to Autumn."

Dang, I say with a Gomer Pyle grin—my mask in grad school, where I'd posed as a redneck aborigine just to warn everybody up front how far behind I was before it blatted out like a fart. Once there, I started burrowing nightly into the library to look up references everybody else nodded in recognition over.

As a result, I've taken in a gnat's portion of American and European poetry, but our banter—Warren's and mine— includes his modestly correcting me on the English tradition. By the time we cross over into Quebec, I've scrawled a long list of books to wade through, impressed he can teach me so much. There's a low-slung fingernail of moon in the orange sky, and I pretend to interpret the local license plate slogan— *Je me souviens*, I remember—as *I am a souvenir.*

He smiles. You're kidding, right?

Not even I am that primitive.

You're not at all primitive, he says.

Don't lie, I say. But I secretly hope to pass for a girl he maybe went to prep school with, though I could've impersonated a baboon closer.

In the restaurant, we give our names as Wally and Holly Stevens, a poet and his editor daughter. At a tiny candlelit table, I smell the red wine on Warren's breath. As he passes over my menu, his hand touches mine, and the pulse in my chest grows so thunderous I fear he'll make it out. This has to be a date, dammit. When he starts to quote Yeats's famous love poem, *When you are old and gray and full of sleep/And nodding by the fire take down this book . . .*

I leap in to finish: *And slowly read, and dream of the soft look Your eyes had once, and of their shadows deep . . .*

And if there'd been a chaise longue nearby to land on, I might have stood up and swooned.

The night before I graduate, he shows up at a bar where I dance with him all night while my putative suitor buys our drinks. In the wee hours, Warren quotes the famous pastoral proposition poem, *Come live with me and be my love . . .* The sixteenth-century version of *Hubba, hubba, sweetcakes.* My heart's banging bongos. And four months later—after he's driven cross-country to see me several times—he asks me to move to Cambridge with him. Three years after that, we'll get engaged.

But before any of that, I have to meet the family, and boy am I eager, facing the task with a peasant girl's bouncy determination to wow people not overimpressed by much. The final miles Warren's tiny car putters, I hold a compact in one hand and a mascara wand in the other, globbing on lashes. (Little did I know my mother's advice—*You can never wear too much mascara*—is, in this company, deeply wrong.)

We pass through wrought-iron gates, and I look up, wand in hand, to ask, Is this a subdivision?

This is my house, he says.

It's a testament to Warren's reticence that he's failed to mention the place is posh enough to sport a baronial-sounding name without seeming ridiculous: Fairweather Hall. There's a separate wing for the live-in staff, severely reduced now that the six children are gone. If I remember right, the gardener even grew up on the estate since his father had been Mr. Whitbread's valet in law school—sounding like a Chekhov serf to me.

After Warren parks, I gawk my way from the car, jaw unhinged, about to burst out with a ghetto *goddamn.*

Why didn't you tell me about all this? I ask.

Tell you about what? he wonders, completely sincere, for he's never less than sincere, which partly informs my devotion. I already know how Warren shrinks from show. When people ask where he went to college, he'll avoid dropping the H-bomb as long as possible, though I'd have tattooed it on my forehead.

That ivy-scribbled house has a fairy-tale quality, with gardens sprawled around it and long, vaulted windows you could drive a Buick through. Plus a door bigger than my daddy's bass boat, with a bronze knocker, even. The uniformed Irish maid waits outside to help us with our bags, which Warren refuses, partly because she's at least seventy and no taller than five feet.

They call her Kelley, though it's her last name, and I'll later find out she was deputized to take Warren trick-or-treating when he was a kid, with a sheet over her head and a bag for her own candy. Odd, I thought, my parents hadn't taken me around, either. (Though the Whitbreads' offhand parenting style was light-years from my family's, both Warren and I grew up yearning for a warmer home than where we'd started.)

I don't have the sense not to hug whoever greets us, so I try to throw my arms around Kelley, and she flinches away, straightening her apron. Facing the big house, I'd like to say I'm neither wowed nor panicky, but I feel like a field hand called out of the cotton.

Would you like some tea? Kelley asks.

Yes, please, Warren says, closing the door.

The foyer, a crystal chandelier like a sparkly jungle gym hangs from the two-story ceiling. Two dogs waggle around us, which Warren pats and baby-talks to while I stare. Cloudily mirrored alcoves hold Chinese vases. The staircase curves grandly enough for his older sister to have descended for her debut into New York society on it. At some point, Warren gently uses his hand to close my jaw.

For something to say, I ask the dogs' names.

The mutt is Sammy, Kelley says, and this grand old man—she ruffles the ears of the golden retriever—is Tiger.

Tiger Three, Warren says. He explains that the death of Tiger One so traumatized the family twenty years back that his father kept buying new pups and stapling the old name on.

Tea comes in the formal library, Kelley lurching in under the weight of a silver tray. A dozen cookies circle a linen napkin, and following Warren's lead, I take a single measly cookie the size of a half dollar, eyeing the rest with the same appetite that keeps Tiger panting openmouthed nearby. In that house, you have to practice not wanting.

The living room has about fourteen chintz couches and a fireplace big enough to roast a pig, plus polo trophies and embossed silver cigarette cases. Also a baby grand nobody's used since Warren left for prep school.

I ask where the TV goes in that vast space, and he drags aside the drapes to reveal the portable set his dad infrequently rolls out for viewing golf. Warren tells me if his father poked his head in the living room and found Warren and his sister before the TV, he'd never fail to say, *Hello, idiots.*

Which shocks me. In my house, personal freedom is all, amusement so hard won in that town that the right to scrabble for it is inalienable. Also in my house, cruelty was rarely so deliberate, more often the haphazard side effect of being shitfaced.

I plop down at the keyboard to play the only chord I know, but Warren mentions his mother naps after lunch. He sits next to me with a wry smile. In the car he'd told me how he'd chosen poetry over his family's penchant for law, partly to escape that preordered hamster wheel he was bred for. He's opting for a game only history can measure his success in. (He didn't mention how his father came home from Wall Street and read Homer in Greek and Virgil in Latin.) How clear Warren's green eyes are as he restates those to me noble convictions, and then he bends to kiss me with a mouth tasting of anise seed. Poetry will deliver him from his stultifying fate as it will me from my turbulent one. We're sealed in that unlikely covenant already, with the vast house spread out around us as the dogs circle, tags clanking.

Afterward, Warren leads me meandering through the scented rose garden and alongside the neat rows of vegetables. I think of Daddy's pride at tomatoes staked in paint buckets on the porch under the clothesline sagging with dishrags.

The tennis courts were razed for a huge pool. At the old stable—empty of horses—we feed carrots to the gray-muzzled donkeys. Once bought to keep the thoroughbreds calm, they're fat court jesters who've taken over the place now the royal family's died off. The family's history is linked to horses. In my hometown, they're used to cut cattle. As a kid, Warren and his sisters rode with their father before breakfast in the mornings. You had to make the high jump to get an extra serving of roast beef at dinner.

Crossing the wide pantry, I spy the saucer of cookies and ask, Your mother still upstairs?

Why are you whispering, sweetie? he asks, adding, Take another one if you like.

How can you only eat one cookie? I say, biting down on one, then thumbing the fallen crumbs off my lip.

My father's always on some diet he can't adhere to. It must've affected the rest of us, he says.

Evening finds us seated at the long glossy table, half the length of a bowling alley, where his parents sit at opposite ends—his father portly in a tweed jacket with patched elbows; his mother blond and thin as a greyhound, smiling.

Thank Mary for the Burgundy, Mrs. Whitbread says.

You brought this? Mr. Whitbread holds his glass up. (In fact, I'd called the old bar I used to tend to find out what to bring.) It's excellent. He takes a sip, adding, My own children think I'm rich enough to buy my own wine.

I could never find one you liked, Warren says.

Which prompts the first of many silences I'll sit through at that table. Silence rolls across us like a gray sea fog. Ice crystals form around our faces. Forks freeze in place. The salad plates are cleared. Warren sits straight enough to be lashed to a stake.

Kelley comes in hauling a massive tray where two capons lie prissily on curlicues of kale. Mr. Whitbread rises to carve. I study the stiff painting over the massive sideboard—Mr. Whitbread in full riding gear atop a horse. I feel a stab of tribal pride that in the cracker-box house I grew up in, Mother's blazing nudes assembled with swashbuckling brushstrokes show way more sensibility.

So, Warren, his father finally says, will you row this year?

Warren says, I'm not in college anymore.

I shoot my eyes to him, but he fails to meet my gaze. How, I wonder, if you pay tuition, is it possible not to know whether the kid's still in school?

Mr. Whitbread forks poultry slices onto a plate, and no one says anything till after Kelley settles it before me. He says, That's right. Nancy's at Harvard.

Nancy's getting ready for law school, Mrs. Whitbread says.

I'm working in the library, Warren says.

Right, his father says.

The Harvard library, his mother adds, wreathed in a smile I can't decipher. That stamp on Warren's job invokes the family's appetite for excellence, how expected it is, demanded, devoured. It strikes me then how a house so large might feel like cramped quarters.

To their credit, they all read so much they seem to accept Warren's poem-making—he's just starting to publish in journals—as a worthy enterprise despite its fiscal impracticality. Still, they say little about it (and it's the not saying, I later learn, that matters).

Widener Library? his father asks.

Lamont, Warren says. There's a recorded poetry archive there.

He's remastering these great lost recordings, I say. He found one of Tennyson. And these amazing Nabokov lectures.

The arctic wind blows over us again, for my bragging has breached some protocol too delicate for me to understand yet. One does not brag; one does not need to. Mr. Whitbread pours me more wine, a sympathetic gesture that feels—no doubt unintentionally—like a pat on a dog's head.

Kelley comes in with a vat of asparagus she goes around dishing out.

Mr. Whitbread keeps looking for one of the standard social connection points—to explain who the hell I am, I guess—till Mrs. Whitbread mentions that I'm friends with the writer Geoffrey Wolff, whose memoir of his con-man father had made a splash the year before. One of the few writers of any stature I know, Geoffrey happens to be married to Warren's first cousin.

It's a frail link, and Geoffrey's being Jewish maybe undoes most of its value, but I try to capitalize on it, saying that he and his brother, Toby, taught at my grad school.

Mrs. Whitbread perks up. You went to Princeton? Our son-in-law went there.

Warren explains I hadn't gone to Princeton but to a hippie school that just went belly-up.

With that in the open, we fall to sawing our food. The cutlery weighs about a pound—a heft that sends some ineffable message.

And what are two young poets reading? Mr. Whitbread asks.

I babble on about the memoirs of Chilean poet Neruda, for ballast throwing in some pretentious French philosophy I've never so much as held in my hands.

Mr. Whitbread asks for more asparagus, and Kelley vanishes with the bowl.

How about you, Warren?

Warren—having barely touched his food—dabs his mouth before saying, A biography of Samuel Johnson.

Boswell? Mr. Whitbread says. I loved Boswell. How he described spying on Mr. and Mrs. Johnson through the bedroom keyhole in flagrante delicto *like two walruses.*

Mrs. Whitbread ducks her head, and I try not to snicker, for any talk of sex in those environs seems particularly wanton.

This is by Walter Jackson Bate, Warren says.

Bate's a campus luminary you can see sashaying through the library stacks wearing a little porkpie hat like Art Carney in *The Honeymooners.*

Kelley returns to say there isn't any more asparagus, and the cook bellows from the kitchen, *Tell him if he ate like a normal man, there would've been enough asparagus.* Which holler blows invisibly through the room. Again Mrs. Whitbread covers her mouth with her napkin, and Warren's eyes aren't beaming over at mine. The Whitbread talent for ignoring the ugly obvious is a quality I covet.

Before we leave the table, we're supposed to give our breakfast requests to the cook via Kelley. Mrs. Whitbread finds it odd that I won't have at least a poached egg. But in the tract houses I visited as a kid, you declined food, presuming a spare larder made any offering a polite show.

You'll starve into a little chicken, Mrs. Whitbread says, standing and placing her napkin on the table.

Over port in the library, I manage to sip daintily—having swilled enough wine at dinner to keep pace with Warren's father—while I flip through portraits. In the small solitary time I'd had with Warren after tea, I'd tried to drag out some explanation of the house, the family's history, but he'd dozed by the pool instead.

Sitting in their library, the Whitbreads are only slightly more forthcoming. So I pore over the photo albums like a scholar trying to decipher the rules of the realm. With each flip of the page, I tune in more keenly to what the sloppy shoe box of photos in my homestead holds: Mother's cousin Henry drunk in Mexico, dressed as a matador; Daddy and his brothers with alligators they'd killed for the hides strung from a tree.

How would the society page editor chronicle my lineage for this historic visit to Fairweather Hall? At that time my family is broke out in the kind of misery common to share-croppers in Faulkner novels. Just that month Daddy had suffered a stroke. While drinking at the VFW bar, he'd toppled off a bar stool. He's still alive but paralyzed and speechless, barely aware that Mother's popping valium like Pop-Tarts.

But the Whitbreads' photo album bulges with enough presidents to fill a high school history book. Both Roosevelts practiced in the family firm. Here's Great-grandfather in the old touring car with McKinley right before he was shot.

Warren gets quiet during the stories. He was bred in quiet

and carries quiet in him but elegance also. Even picking burrs out of Tiger's tail he can pull off with gravitas. But he can also drift far from me into himself. Sitting across from him, I can't meet his eyes. Maybe he's patiently irritated with how awed I am by the posh household he's fleeing. Or maybe I'm breaking rules of comportment subtle enough to resemble the minuscule gaffes you get demerits for in precision diving contests.

Warren's grandfather—in riding gear circa 1930-something, holding a polo mallet—is Warren's exact double. Here's the cover of *The New York Times* that falsely reported his death after a fall. Mr. Whitbread stares into some decades'-old distance, saying, The old man was on a horse again the next morning. Infuriated my mother. People in New York were sending wreaths to the house, and he was galloping across a field.

Effortless, excellence has to be. Tossed off, reflecting the ease you're born to, which opposes what little I've garnered about comportment. I'm bred for farm work, and for such folk, the only A's you get come from effort. Strife and strain are all the world can offer, and they temper you into something unbreakable, because Lord knows they'll try—without letup—to break you. Where I come from, house guests have to know you've sweated over a stove, for sweat is how care is shown. At the Whitbreads', preparations are both slapdash and immaculate. You toss some melba toast on a plate next to a fragrant St. André triple-crème cheese, or on Christmas Eve, half a pound of caviar casually flipped into a silver urn.

It's taken me so much *effort* just to do as medium-shitty as I've heretofore done. Just to drop out of college, stay alive, and have my teeth taken care of.

I take another sip of port, which slides down as if greased.

Warren seems thousands of miles away, and why has he kept all this from me?

Here's Mrs. Whitbread in her dress for Queen Elizabeth's coronation. Some polo connection? They've stopped explaining why they were various places. Here's Mr. Whitbread flanked by briefcase-carrying aides, striding confidently up the steps of the Supreme Court.

Warren says, I remember sitting behind you, and you pulled out some notecards.

You were there? Mr. Whitbread asks.

Mrs. Whitbread looks exasperated. Of course, darling. I thought they should experience it.

Warren goes on, And your client said, *What are you doing*?

Mr. Whitbread tosses some nuts into his mouth, saying, I suppose I told him I was preparing my argument. And he said, *Now*?

(Working for *The Washington Post* at the time, Geoffrey Wolff—that frailest of bridges between Warren's parents and me—later claimed Mr. Whitbread was the only man he ever saw talk *down* to the Supreme Court.)

At dinner, I'd seen my lover's fine jaw flex as he studied his plate, and I'd felt the liquid warmth of our time together evaporate as he braced himself for his father's scrutiny. Now I long for some definitive gesture to free him, to throw my port glass into the fireplace and stalk out with a poor kid's piety, riding off with him in his Mazda into a life with nary a polo divet to stomp. But the house's disabling comfort saps resolve.

And by the time we're in the library, I've begun to breathe in the parents' gentility. The conversation is so adroit—the nonchalance so juicy—I lap it up as Tiger did our fatty scraps, steel bowls rattling on the kitchen tiles. I want to believe I'm at home with these composed individuals. They're liberal in their politics, after all. From where I sit on the low settee wedged among needlepoint pillows, I can see a whole shelf devoted to the egalitarian writings of Thomas Jefferson. Surely they recognize my native intellect. At some point Mrs. Whitbread says casually, What religion does your family practice, Mary?

Which I take as interest in my strangely compelling history. I think of my mother, who studied every faith and—with her husbands—committed to none.

We're not anything, really, I say. But I find myself dredging up a few childhood visits to the Presbyterian church, for I know a joke punch line about Episcopalians being Presbyterians with trust funds.

But I catch Mrs. Whitbread's unmet glance toward Warren, and it dawns on me that had he brought home his classmate Caroline Kennedy, her being a Catholic might have been a mark against her.

In a mind shift, I'm a schoolgirl again in summer, and my half-Indian daddy has just come in the back door at dawn with grime under his nails from a double shift. How carefully he draws five one-dollar bills from his weathered billfold to give Mother for two pairs of school shoes—one for me, one for Lecia. While I wait for her to bring the car around, he slips off his shirt, showing a chest pale as paper where his worker's tan runs out. He steps out of his khakis, and jutting through his baggy boxers, his legs are knobby and thin. One thigh's pronounced hunk of shrapnel is royal blue. The long scar up his right shinbone where a horse he was breaking threw and dragged him looks freshly scabby. He sits down on the bed's edge, staring at his brown forearms. *Daddy*, I whisper, and that greedy call for him snaps the connection to the past. The voltage drops, and he's gone, reabsorbed into the shriveled form in my mother's house, tended days by a male nurse we can't afford, nights by Mother, who resents it.

In an instant I'm back in the Whitbreads' library, and Daddy lies uninsured, half paralyzed.

On the mantle, sits a recent Christmas snapshot with all the siblings before the fireplace, glossy-haired and tidy. They actually *match* like the gorgeous silverware. Not resemblance but precise replication. I think, *Tiger One, Tiger Two . . .* (I'll come to believe that the WASP genetic code imperially squashes the other parent's contributing DNA in offspring. My own son, blond and blue-eyed, will bear so little of me that ladies in the park will think I've been hired to push his stroller.)

Just as we're saying good night, Mr. Whitbread inquires whether, as a Texan, my father's in oil, and I tell him he was, adding—wittily, I think—up to his elbows twelve hours a day. Which fact they take with a preoccupied air. I could speculate on what they thought, but they're unreadable as granite.

That night, lying in Warren's narrow bed, where I've sneaked from his sister's flowery boudoir to make love, I ask him, How'd I do?

He cups my face. I love you, he says. Leafy shadows move over us. (How young we were.)

Do you think they heard us just now?

Don't be silly, he says. I doubt they'd care.

Their room is in another wing, which includes—among other mysteries—Mr. Whitbread's own dressing room, padlocked from the outside. Not even the maid is allowed to clean in there.

Warren is lying on his back, and his face mesmerizes me—the patrician nose, Germanic jaw.

Do they like me? I say.

You want everybody to like you, he says.

You don't? I say.

Only you, he says. And Tiger.

Not Sammy?

Sammy's *common*, Warren says, referring to something his mother said about a cousin's wife.

I'm common, I say.

I always fancied an affair with a scullery maid, he says. I'm propped on an elbow studying him. He fails to open his eyes, as he says, Aren't you even a little sleepy?

I'm pouting, I say. Can't you hear me pouting with your eyes shut?

He reaches up a hand to pinch my pouting mouth with two fingers. Okay, duck lips, he says, rolling over. My father thinks you're smart and funny—both uncommon virtues. My mother thinks if you keep jogging, you'll damage your female organs and fail to reproduce.

Do they think I'm cute?

He's half blind. She wants to dress you in hot pink or lime green.

Tell me they like me and I'll sneak back to your sister's room.

As much as they like anybody, he says. Don't worry about it, sweetie.

The next morning I'm wide-eyed before dawn, half waiting for some Inquisitor to roust me from the ruffled covers of the type Little Bo Peep probably slept in. I bathe with French-milled soap and brush my short hair.

In the library, I find a copy of Matthew Arnold's poems autographed to some illegible forebear. I'm perusing when a voice from the stair causes Tiger Three to rise shakily on his ancient hips and trot out. Mr. Whitbread says, *I fail to see why you couldn't greet them when they arrived, for God's sake.*

Once the front door has opened and shut, Tiger slinks back in and slumps at my feet. After a while I smell coffee and bacon, and a while later, I see a wizened, disheveled old woman balding under her black hairnet. Slippers slide her up the hall across from me to the wet bar. (I'd later find out she's the cook.) She opens the fridge and draws out a carton of eggnog, pouring herself a small punch cup full. How sweet, I think, they keep eggnog in the summer. Then she unscrews the top of a bottle of dark rum and upends it with both hands. She takes two long draws, then shuffles off.

7

The Constant Lovers

The myth they chose was the constant lovers.
The theme was richness over time
It is a difficult story, and the wise never choose it
because it requires such long performance,
and because there is nothing, by definition,
between the acts . . .
      —ROBERT HASS, "AGAINST BOTTICELLI"

It would've been a vintage personal ad. *Scared, provincial girl desperate to escape family insanity seeks quietly witty, literate gorilla. Profound loneliness a must. Belief in poetry must supersede belief in capitalism. She: abrim with self-loathing, incapable of chilly silence. He: won't yell, wag firearms, or leave.*

Were Warren laboring over this story, I'd no doubt appear drunkenly shrieking; spending every cent I could get my mitts on; alternately crowding his scholar's home with revelers, then starting to vanish nights into a kind of recovery cult—none of this entirely untrue. I would've preferred that my ex vet this manuscript and correct the glaring flaws. Wisely, he balked—I'd have hated to see his version, too.

How to write it without self deceit? I set out to forge a family, but it fell apart. Know any divorcée who ever stops weighing fault for a marriage's implosion on some divine scales?

There's also a psychological phenomenon that messes with my ability to depict our nuptial collapse—the normally crisp film of my memory has, in this period, more mysterious blanks than the Nixon tapes. Maybe the agony of our demise was too harrowing for my head to hold on to, or my maternal psyche is shielding my son from the ugly bits. Or I was too shitfaced at the end.

Whatever the case, those years only filter back through the self I had at the time, when I was most certainly—even by my yardstick then—a certain species of crazy. But inside that was a girl starving for stability and in love with a shy, brilliant man fleeing the aristocracy he was born to.

Decades ago, I trained myself to mistrust that girl's perceptions. No doubt she projected as many pixels onto the world's screen as she took in. So while I trust the stories I recall in broad outline, their interpretation through my old self is suspect. Forget reporting the external events right, try judging them when you're an alumna of custodial care. When I reach to grasp a solid truth from that time, smoke pours through my fingers.

Yet driving east with all my belongings wedged into Warren's small white car, I feel swept off my feet as any storybook maiden by her champion. It's Thanksgiving weekend, and the holiday burger taken at a roadside diner is a feast.

We move into a bleached-out neo-ghetto apartment, which we pack with books and our two rickety desks laden with separate typewriters. December, a potted fern going brown gets hung with cardboard angels we cover in foil. On their heads I glue faces torn out of newspaper or off postcards—the Three Stooges, a poet or two, movie stars. On one, I fix Cary Grant, for that's who Warren is to me—the pre-occupied professor in *Bringing Up Baby*, ignorant of how his patrician profile could make Katharine Hepburn trail him down the street in her convertible, holding her hat on with one kid-gloved hand.

The weak spots in our union are there from the git-go—aren't they always? But every difference lures me, for if I can yield to Warren's way of being, his cool certainty can replace my ragtag—intermittently drunken—lurching around.

Like any traveler from a ruined land, I try to adapt to the new customs, part of some ineffable mystery that compromises the man whose photo I carry in my wallet like an amulet against the squalor I was born to. I yearn for transformation, and Warren is its catalyst. What I don't understand, I try to yield to, though I'm genetically disinclined to follow instruction.

Like we never, ever discuss finances. Some tiny trust pays his half of our meager rent and keeps him bobbing at the poverty level. How much was it? I'd never know.

We keep separate accounts and split bills. I try to absorb his reticence in this as I try to mimic his gargantuan work ethic—how early he rises to write, the number of sit-ups he grunts through at night. Without a paying post at first, he volunteers afternoons in the poetry library with its archive.

For my part, I'm rebuffed from any pseudo-literary job I catch the faintest rumor of—part-time teaching or poets-in-the-schools. Hell, the dudes working the registers in the bookstores have Ph.D.'s. At a chichi restaurant, I take a job busing tables at lunch—a steep fall for the former poet laureate of Minneapolis. On day one, a particularly snide waiter scoffs at my ignorance of a fish knife, along with how sloppy I am at embossing the tiny butter terrines. He's a waspish guy who—at regular wine tastings for the staff—makes such phony remarks that the other waiters fight back with goofy comments, such as: *Fruity but not screaming;* or *A surly adolescent wine that loiters in your mouth.*

One day I take a double shift, and a famous novelist I'd been passingly introduced to in grad school—the bone-breakingly handsome John Irving—appears as if lowered by butterflies into my station. After filling his water glass once, I hide in the kitchen or bathroom for much of the remaining shift, derangedly imagining he'll recognize me.

At shift's end, the manager threatens to fire me for malingering, so I quit, for which gift he pumps my hand like I've given him the winning lottery ticket. In the glass window behind him, snow starts down. Soon as he leaves the dining room, I set every single place with knives, one silver blade after another, while through the sliding glass and across the night sky, the wind sends slim white stitches.

The dining room lights dim just as I clock out, and I make out strains of some symphony piped into the bar. My head cants like a blue tick hound's. Maybe I owe myself a drink.

I've been dug in on Warren's one-or-two-beer policy, part of re-forming myself to fit him. As for doing with so little alcohol, so safely squirreled away do I feel in our book-lined rooms, undergoing my willed overhaul, that I could almost subsist on his breath alone.

In my old life, I never kept liquor in my apartment, for—
while I could go without for weeks—I never knew when I'd
wind up draining anything around. And around the punk
bars where I hung out in grad school, if I got lured into the
alley and offered cocaine, I could snuffle up the stuff, but
I lacked both the money and the recklessness to be a bona
fide cokehead. Only once did I incur a debt, and having to
sell a TV to pay it back curbed future coke binges. At a few
all night parties, I sat among half-strangers in a screaming
sweat on a sagging couch—jaw clenched, eyelids stapled to
my forehead—while some leering dealer suggested I go back
to his place. A small point of pride: I never said yes. The scene
scared me. I scared me.

I wouldn't call my pre-Warren drinking out of control
because I had control. So long as I didn't leave my apartment,
I didn't drink.

In Cambridge, that person no longer exists. With an invisible eraser, I'm internally rubbing hard at the core of her,
and Warren's steady, unwavering gaze is lasering away her
external edges. Soon she'll be mist.

I stand at the bar, its tiered bottles like a shiny choir
about to burst into song. With only five or six dollars in tips,
how much trouble can I get in? Warren will pick me up soon,
and the bar's on the cusp of closing early. At one end, a man
in evening clothes with long gray hair swept back sits behind
a sherry glass. On the stool next to him, a tipped violin case.
Across from him is the despicable waiter, cradling a brandy
snifter. His normally pony-tailed hair's undone. The waiter
says, Buy you a farewell cognac?

I say thanks and settle in with coat covering my
grease-spattered uniform. The waiter downs his own drink.
Standing, he slides spare bills across the bar, adding—before

he flips his cashmere scarf around his neck Lautrec-style—At least I've helped you to master the fish knife.

I hold the glass globe in my hand as the dim yellow lights slide off its perimeter, and boy, does that drink slide down like scorched sunshine. I'm just draining it when the manager—no doubt eager to see me leaving—flies up and buys me another. And right before Warren comes, I ponder a third. What the hell, right? I'm unemployed, with school loans I can't pay, an invalid dad whose nursing I need to start chipping in on.

When I lift my index finger, the barman wipes his hands and refills my snifter. I'm the sole customer—the barman having just covered his olives and cherries with cling film—when he nonchalantly slides a white slip of paper to me. I nonchalantly flip it over. The bill comes to twenty dollars.

Hold it, I say, those two bought my other drinks.

I'm well buzzed by then, wavering.

I know, he says. This is for the third one.

I cling to the edge of the bar and say, That cognac was twenty dollars?

He nods.

I drank sixty dollars' worth of cognac just now?

His nod is stiffer this time. The bar itself starts a slow swim around me, as if on a hydraulic pole. I explain that twenty dollars is approximately one tenth of my rent. The shoes I have on probably cost ten if they were sneakers.

He says, I can go get Patrick if you want to dispute it.

I'm too drunk by this time to dispute anything with any-body. Can't they take it out of my check? He tells me that he personally has to level out the till.

Even though Warren, who probably has twenty bucks, is en route to pick me up, I instinctively know he'll cringe at my begging a loan. Before we left on our camping trip, he'd been horrified to find out I had just a few hundred bucks in my account. If I remember right, he'd been ripped off by an alleged pal in a trip across Europe, and his life's goal involves living sparsely enough never again to be forced to ask his father for money.

So we always split even the smallest breakfast chits. If anything, I have the poor girl's need to prove solvency that makes me an inveterate check grabber. Age about seventeen, I stopped counting on my parents for rent and food. (I need to go to the dentist, I told Mother once. To which she said, Ask around on campus, I'm sure you'll find a cheap one. Translation: Shift for yourself.) Among the artists I dated, chivalry seldom figured in.

In Cambridge the barman stacks glasses, glancing up like I'm a shoplifter. Pretty soon Warren comes in wearing a down jacket, looking tall enough to offset my busgirl scumminess.

I draw him aside and explain, perhaps slurrily, why I need a twenty, just till the next day. I want to pay off the glaring barman posthaste.

But Warren stares in disbelief, saying, When Tom and I drink with his friend for four hours, the whole bill isn't twenty dollars.

By this time the manager has set his coffee cup on the bar alongside his keys.

Warren says, Why didn't you go to the machine?

I haven't gotten an ATM card yet, I say.

Where's your credit card?

I lost it, I lie, for I couldn't tell him the one I'd used to pay for a hotel once had long since been snipped in half at some cash register. This debt wasn't just recklessly come by, being due to last-minute plane tickets when Daddy had one stroke after another.

You're not out of money, are you?

I'm not. Though I'm within a month of it.

Warren opens his wallet and draws out the twenty, handing it over like a radioactive item with tongs. The mild unease I expected is (did I imagine this?) the scrutiny a thief draws. Since our romance started, I've gone months devoid of shame, maybe even deceiving myself that I've been cleansed of it, till its icy bucket dumps over me from scalp to foot soles.

Outside, we walk a cobbled sidewalk toward his car, the snow spatting on the hood of my parka. Along the curving streets of Cambridge, the silence carries us past the tightly clipped hedges. The colonial houses in white and canary yellow and smoky blue with lacquered black shutters are like magazine houses—clean places I want to disappear into the safe bricks of. When I can't bear the weight of Warren's silence anymore, I burst out with, What's the big deal? I'll pay you tomorrow.

He shushes me and looks around.

I tug his sleeve so he faces me, but he's looking over my head for spectators. I say, Who'll hear us? It's an empty street.

He takes his arm from me and walks on. At the car door, he says, My cousin owns that restaurant.

Which I'd forgotten.

Nothing deflates a righteous drunk like the pinprick of reality. The air rushes out of me as I climb in the car. He buckles in, and I remind him the cousin doesn't even know I worked there. The job came through a college pal on the waitstaff. Warren cranks up.

Sitting alongside him, I sense that his finger is fixed to some invisible eject button about to vault me from his side. If I close my eyes, I can almost feel myself spinning away, growing smaller and smaller. I shrink like a spider on a coal.

The snow spits on the windows and slides off. Warren's gloveless fingers, so long and finely shaped, grip the wheel.

What I did, I don't exactly know. Maybe I reached for his hand. Maybe I gave him shit for being conventional. My methods for clinging to him were varied and pitiful. Eventually, I needed him badly enough that I said whatever I had to, push him away. Counterphobic, a shrink once called it, meaning I run fast toward any event I suspect might be excruciating.

I'm not preppie enough for you, I say.

His silence holds as we drive. I amplify my rhetoric and volume. Maybe I should be wearing a kilt with a fucking gold safety pin, I say.

He parks the car outside our apartment. As he's locking up, he says—color blazing high on his flared cheekbones—And you quit your job. With your school loans and your father sick. Are you crazy?

This is a buzzword with me, since deep down I know I'm crazy, my chief fear being that everybody'll find out.

So I do the only thing I can think of: I run. I run onto the sidewalk and drop to my knees, sobbing like a banshee. A bratty move, but Warren takes the bait and comes to help me up. Then a few things happen in an order I can't recall. He asks me please to go inside. I start to vomit in the snow— three cognacs in those days being a heavy dose. A policeman shows up to check out the seedy scene, and from Warren's arms, I jabber, I'm fine, Officer, just too much to drink. My boyfriend's taking me home.

Back in the apartment, I lie in bed next to him, circled by the night's chaos as if by gnats. Our fight's antithetical to Warren's penchant for order and routine—his alphabetical file folders and meticulously typed drafts, the paper clip al-

ways in the same spot. (How like my daddy that was.) If he
hates a book on page one, he'll nonetheless finish it, for he's
made the commitment. And I hope he'll commit to me that
way and be as loath to leave me undone.

I lie there pondering his fiscal prickliness, wholly mysterious to me. Back home, nobody had any money, so we
swapped the same few bucks back and forth with open hands.
(Those without money don't grasp right off having to discipline yourself against sycophants.)

Listening to his even breath, I sense the oppressive
weight of my old self inside me pressing to run wild again.
My old mother I'm trying to keep in. Snow pecks at the window screens.

And then the sound of our upstairs neighbor playing the
ukelele—*plunka plunka plunka*. There is no instrument goof-
ier nor more insidious. The guy can play for hours, and while
I can sack out during a train wreck, Warren heaves over and
swears. He reaches his arm out and flips on the white noise
machine that blocks all sound. It makes a cocoon of rushing
noise meant to mimic an air conditioner or waterfall. To me,
it sounds like the sucking of a dentist's drain. Warren needs
absolute silence, absolute dark to sleep, and with the entire
racket in my head, I know myself to be an inadvertent force
for pandemonium.

For a long time, I lie studying in the blue dark Warren's
angled jaw and ski-slope cheekbones. It's shallow, I confess,
but the architecture of his face never fails to transfix me.
It's the kind of face people on the street invariably asked for
directions—the face of the army officer, the team captain, the
star professor.

Without Warren's hands cupping my own face, I'm almost faceless. I need his body in bed and his books on my
shelves anchoring me to the planet. I need him ahead of me

to complete a two-mile run, else I give up and light a smoke. I need his editing skills. When he draws his pen through clunky lines, I cut them. I need his unbudgeable integrity. I mean, when a big-deal magazine requested changing some of his poems, he pulled them rather than compromise. I'd have typed mine backward in Urdu to see them into print.

Underneath the worries with Warren and money and how to live runs a humming current of hurt—Daddy lying wordless, eyes cloudy. They said he wouldn't live off the respirator, but it's over a year now. He's being calcified, his empty shape pressed into the sheets like a fern in lava. Ask him if he wants more juice, and he might shout out, *Bacon!* Part of me believes I should catch the next bus down there to start spoon-feeding him—that's my fantasy—a daughterly sacrifice I lack the maturity to pull off, for my patience with bedpans and bent straws rarely lasts an hour. Carrying the warm jar of piss his catheter linked him to, even the short distance to the caged hospital bed set up in my girlhood room, felt like bearing death itself.

Lying alongside Warren that night, I again resolve to generate income, really get serious about it, to chip in on Daddy's nursing and still meet school loans, without ever pestering Warren again, lest that gap between our backgrounds yawn open. Money can finalize my change, I tell myself. Also, I have to never, never, never drink hard stuff. Long as I stick to beer or wine, I'll be fine.

In the morning, when Warren stirs, I've already gone to the bank. The mug of coffee I bring him has a twenty-dollar bill rubber-banded to the handle.

If we talked about the night before, I don't recall it, which isn't fair to either of us, for it doesn't show our reasoned selves paring away at our scared ones. But it's a neurological fact that the scared self holds on while the reasoned one lets go.

The adrenaline that let our ancestors escape the sabertooth tiger sears into the meat of our brains the extraordinary, the loud. The shrieking fight or the out-of-character insult endures forever, while the daily sweetness dissolves like sugar in water.

Not long after, though, some of his doubts about me leak out again, and again the topic's a disparity in how we want to live. We've jogged five miles around Fresh Pond and are stretching out when he says, You know what my sister noticed about you first?

I cling to the fence and am bending my knee to loosen the quad, wheezing out, My rapier wit?

Warren's quick smile skids past my joke. He says, That you had really nice luggage. She warned me that a girl with such fancy luggage might expect to live higher on the hog than a poet would.

The irony? It had been Lecia's Hartmann luggage from the Rice Baron before they'd divorced—borrowed so as not to be embarrassed bringing an army duffel bag to his parents' house.

A week or so later, we unwrap our brown-papered Christmas gifts decorated with crayons and string—homemade gifts all. I'd stitched up a giant pillow to serve as a faux headboard, stars on a background of deep blue. He'll spend Christmas with his family, because otherwise he'd never see his far-flung siblings. To me their cool exchanges mirror chatter at a bus stop. My pending visit to Daddy is an event on a par with cyanide.

Warren stretches his legs in front of the red leather club chair appropriated from his parents' attic. He picks at a moist banana muffin I'd made from scratch—black bananas being cheapest. I unwrap the small packet of audio tapes he made me—recordings of some lost lectures on the epic by an un-known prof.

Some girls pine for jewelry, but for me the tapes are like an invitation into Warren's monastery, since his devotion to poetry has a monkish quality. I'd spent way more years wor-rying about how to look like a poet—buying black clothes, smearing on scarlet lipstick, languidly draping myself over thrift-store furniture—than I had learning how to assemble words in some discernible order.

I slide the cassette into the tape deck and press play. The old recording is scratchy enough to conjure a time before we were born. The professor's first sentence brings me up short, for it sketches a football field-sized hole in my reading. He notes there's as much distance between Homer and Virgil as between Chaucer and us.

I press stop, saying, Isn't that like a thousand years?

Around that, Warren says. He peels the paper from the muffin.

Since grad school, I'd felt as stuffed full of knowledge as a Christmas goose. Suddenly, a thousand unknown years of poetic history yawns unstudied before me. How little I know panics me.

I say, I'd always figured those toga-wearing guys hung out around the same time.

His smile is soft. You always know what poets wore.

I say something like, Baudelaire tweezed his nose hairs and wore the floppy black satin bow. Dickinson wore white like a virgin bride. Warren Whitbread wore Brooks Brothers shirts, button-down, oxford-cloth. Jeans and khakis. He was long of limb and lean in a blue bathrobe.

He says, And Mary Karr?

Black black black. Plus loads of mascara. Spike heels.

He reaches among the wrappings on the floor and holds up the eye-fryingly pink sweater his mother picked up for me in Bermuda, saying, You're not ready for this yet?

Grotesque as it looks, in some ways, I want nothing more than to look right occupying it.

8

Temporary Help

I work in a giant building:
forty floors and forty cubicles
per wing, four wings per floor,
one person and one personal
computer per cubicle, a labyrinth
in which everyone's goal is to stay lost.
— JOHN ENGMAN, "TEMPORARY HELP"

Come January, as part of clawing my way into the white-collar classes I mock, I sit behind the receptionist's desk of a telecommunications firm that helped build and maintain the internet. In this age, faxes are big news. Operators still plug callers in and out of switchboards. Crawling with horn-rimmed MIT geniuses, this place is, and they're marketing (unsuccessfully if you can believe it) the very first e-mail program. They're almost growing too fast not to hire me, so soon

I move up from receptionist ($12K) to a secretarial job I suck at ($13K). Since I need the overtime, I take up nighttime data entry for accounting.

It's staring into one of those green screens, doing corporate budgets, that I notice how high salaries rise in marketing. Also, they spend hundreds of thousands on trade shows each year, and my product-manager girlfriend informs me that nobody pays attention to the budgets. So in the company library, I read a bunch of trade magazines and essentially retype what they said needs to happen into a proposal for managing that budget. Poof, I'm a marketeer.

Riding the six-thirty bus to the company in my cheap suit with my briefcase on my lap, I can pass for a normal citizen—except for scribbling poetry in a black notebook. I never thought of myself as competent in commerce, particularly, and striding through the doors lends me a new bearing. I join a corporate women's track team, lured by the sweet prospect of fitting in as we lope around the pond at lunch hour. Me, belonging somewhere. Sliding the company credit card across a hotel desk, I radiate bourgeois integrity. For a girl bred to yank peanuts out of the ground, any desk job gives off an urban sheen. And this is the go-go eighties in a company where they slap up new cubicles every week.

Meanwhile, Warren's volunteer library job has morphed into a full-time assistant curator's position, so we've moved to a tree-lined suburb where the noise quotient disturbs his work and sleep less. Financially, I'm not exactly out of the woods, but with the first health insurance I've ever had, I track down a therapist. Night terrors still wake me screaming twice a week, and if I have a few drinks, an image of Daddy warping into fossil form can set me on a crying jag.

Every month we scrape together enough to eat out at a

cheap fish house—mussels in garlic and white wine. Once, at the next table, a similarly steaming bowl is lowered in front of a Polish Nobel laureate in poetry whose public lectures we've been religiously going to, all goggle-eyed. We marvel at his high forehead, like that bust of Beethoven you always see.

Don't stare, Warren says.

But I can't stop looking at this laureate's gray and diabolical eyebrows, projecting above his light eyes like a ram's horns. He practically speeds up my heart.

Do tree surgeons gape at great examples of tree surgery? Do line cooks get misty eyed seeing a well run café pump out orders? For me seeing this guy gives an almost sexual thrill— like a horny teenager faced with a centerfold. Or more like a devout altar girl seeing a saint.

Please don't, Warren finally says in a voice barely audible. He places an empty purple shell in the bowl between us.

What? I say.

Don't introduce yourself, he says. Admit you're thinking about it.

It's true that my former grad school professor Bob translates the guy at Berkeley, so we connect at some small nexus.

Warren and I both pick at our mussels till I say, Why not? It's something I can tell our grandkids about. I touched the hand that wrote those words.

I don't want to be here for it, Warren says. He raises a finger for the check. Behind his napkin, he says, You don't have to meet every famous poet.

In his view, my appetite for social activity is voracious. I remember seeing an invitation to his college reunion on the kitchen table that year. The choices were:

> I can attend.
> I hope I can attend.

I cannot attend.

He circled the words to read *I hope I cannot attend* before sending it back.

You're at Harvard every day, I say. You record Seamus Heaney lectures (Harvard's own Nobel-anointed poet). He was your teacher, even. You host poetry readings twice a month.

The Greek waiter drops off the check, and I rifle my briefcase as Warren goes over the math. He says, Seamus is plagued by toadies. I don't want to be one of them.

I snatch the check from his hand, saying, I'm the boring stiff in a suit who comes in late to the reading and nobody talks to at the reception. I live in a business gulag.

He says, Nobody thinks of you as a wallflower, Mare.

I glance over at the Polish luminary, adding, I just want to shake his hand.

Warren looks as if he'd like to sink through the floor, so I say, Go ahead. I'll meet you at the car.

As he slips on his coat, I say, Not speaking to Seamus is not treating him like a normal person, you know.

He pulls on his stocking cap with a grimace.

Seconds later, I shake the great laureate's hand, and it shames me to say I'm so desperate to enter the world in which he's lord that I get a shock of electricity doing so.

We're driving home when Warren says, You'd sit in his lap if he'd let you.

He's eighty, I say. I just wanted to touch him and see if he was real.

Cambridge can make history come alive to you with its parade of big-deal writers. At MIT, we see blind Borges right before he dies. And if we bicker over our social differences, still a steady current of book talk flows back and forth.

Through Warren's library job, I visit the special collections, and together we bend over the silver reliquary a pope once wore that holds a lock of John Keats's hair. Next to my face, breathing frost on the glass, Warren's mouth whispers a sonnet. Together we read Keats's letters to his lost beloved about how the stitches on a cap she made him went through him like a spear. I lace my fingers with his. The average non-poetry devotee may think the intensity around this stuff off-kilter at the least, but for us, it's like digging our hands together into a secret vat of pearls. In that realm only we are rich as any royalty.

9

There Went the Bride

> This is hell,
>   but I planned it, I sawed it,
> I nailed it, and I
>   will live in it until it kills me.
> I can nail my left palm
>   to the left-hand crosspiece but
> I can't do everything myself.
>   I need a hand to nail the right,
> a help, a love, a you, a wife.
>   —ALAN DUGAN, "LOVE SONG: I AND THOU"

Weddings had ahold of Mother—not in a good way, not in the girlish way of ordering orange blossoms and trawling for china patterns. She's more like the old Vietnam vet who—seeing the ceiling fan whir—throws himself on the floor to scream *Incoming!* Any ceremonial assemblage of families tends to set Mother off.

On the occasion of Lecia's—at a justice of the peace in El Paso—Mother got walleyed drunk and cussed out her rice-farming son-in-law, calling him an ignorant Republican hillbilly. She'd also torn up the only Polaroids of the event, at which point Lecia and I blackmailed her into temporarily giving up the sauce by threatening never to see her again.

Lecia's marriage to the Rice Baron didn't last—her divorce coincided with my engagement—but our uproar with Mother bought us several heavily medicated years in which she moped around the house, occasionally threatening suicide. What did I want for her then? Good cable and some downers—in other words, to keep her quiet so she didn't incinerate anything. In a poem of mine, I noted that she aimed the channel changer like a wrist rocket at the last reality she could alter.

The occasion for her falling off the wagon is the afternoon of my rehearsal dinner at the Ritz in Boston, where my father-in-law-to-be had kept a tab since law school. To make us appear even more fractious, Lecia is living like a squatter in two rooms behind her insurance office with her toddler son and the Salvadoran couple who left the Rice Baron's employ to help raise the boy.

Before the rehearsal dinner, I'm lying in a shampoo chair with my head in the black sink, neck arched upward in a perfect position to have my throat cut, and I catch a distant whiff of marijuana.

Mother, I think. With that single word, an unease comes shimmering into my solar plexus.

My stylist, Richard, who's been vigorously scrubbing my scalp, twists my soapy hair into a unicorn horn, saying, Maybe you should wear it like this down the aisle.

I interrupt him, rising up. Do you smell that? I say.

What? he says.

Pot, I say.

Lifting his nose in the air, he gives a stuffed-up snuffle, then says, Allergies.

It's dusk, and I've warned Richard and his beautician colleague Curtis in advance not to offer Mother and me their usual convivial glass of wine. Twice.

Reluctantly, I lie back down, but some engine of vigilance has been kick-started in my middle, and it's starting to rumble. I say, Curtis wouldn't give her marijuana.

Curtis can't *afford* marijuana, Richard says, adding, It's probably floating up from the alley.

And with that, I tell him how—visiting me once at college—Mother got gunched out of her brains with my pals. In my twenties, she sat in on a poetry workshop with Etheridge, and afterward, I found her on his back step sharing a blunt with him and a bunch of young brothers. Which embarrassed me at the time, since she flirted like a saloon floozy, but also since her lack of maternal posture always unconsciously felt like some failure of mine on the child front.

By the end of the Mother stories, Richard's finger-combing through the suds in my hair with warm water has sent an ease from the scalp down my spine and along my limbs.

She's in good hands with Curtis, Richard says. He's wrapped my hair in a towel, and I sit upright.

And there's nobody else here?

We closed the shop for you two. Very exclusive, Richard says, adding, we have caught kids getting high in the alley before.

Not long after, Curtis swans in, giving off an odor of patchouli oil as he rifles a drawer. He says, Your mom's a riot. I'm gonna visither in Texas. She knows a place I can buy ostrich-skin cowboy boots.

I'm sure she does, I say.

Some time later, when Curtis presents her, I see he's jacked her hair up into a concoction only a drag queen could relish. Her eyes are glassy, and her neck has that bobblehead swivel.

Mother! I say.

Don't I look precious? she says, hands on her hips.

You look high!

Do you think? Curtis says. She made me do it that high.

Mother tips her head coquettishly, which, with the giant hairdo, has the effect of a topiary starting to topple over. She says, We smoked a little maryjane.

Then we're in Warren's tiny backseat. As he navigates the river road traffic to the Ritz, I'm violently trying to de-escalate her hair.

Why now, Mother? I say, almost in tears. Why'd you have to start now?

Ow, she says. She's holding her ears as I tug. Don't ruin your mascara.

You reek of marijuana, I say.

The city of Cambridge is sliding away behind us. At the boathouse, we pass somebody hauling a lone scull from the water.

I apologize to Warren as I work at the vast rats' nest of her head.

I don't smell anything, he says. With Warren, you can never know if this is impeccable denial or politeness. Maybe at all those heavy-drinking WASP country club events, he'd learned to ignore the average soused-up human.

I stop yanking at her hair and notice the buildings of Harvard—carved from various fine types of stone—slipping by like a kingdom I'd never gain the keys to. The whole city is so profoundly Caucasian. One of the city's signature food items is a slablike whitefish devoid of the southern paprika and varicolored peppers that might make such a thing edible. Even its basketball team is thick with knobby-jointed midwestern farm boys whose pasty torsos evoke the aforementioned fish.

Nobody ever wants me to have any fun. What's the big deal? Ow, she says.

This is payback for all those Tonette permanents you scalded my ears off with.

Mother tries to catch Warren's eyes in the rearview, saying, Warren, you've gotta come to Texas and see the pictures, of your wife. Do you think I look bad?

You got in the back so quick I couldn't see you, he says. His eyes are fixed on the lights of Boston.

Master of diplomacy, I say. A compliment, this is, since— without such detachment—I still get whiplash from my own family's turbulence.

Warren, can you hand me my purse? she says. I'll find the Shalimar.

Can we stop and buy some Visine? I say. And some mouthwash, maybe?

It'll make us late, he says.

And I need some cigarettes, Mother says, rummaging through her purse. She stops suddenly and looks at me. She touches her mother's cameo at my neck, saying, I'd like to paint you like this.

The road's lights steamroll over us.

I can see the sweat break out on Warren's temples as I beg him to stop, though he hates being late. I've mostly tamped down Mother's ash-white hair, and I'm using my fingers to comb through its natural waves, saying, You do have the best cheekbones, Mother.

I can't tell if there are tears in her eyes or she's just high as she says, I don't want to go if I'm gonna embarrass you.

Warren pulls up outside a bodega and leaves us in the puffing car. Seeing his runner's form in the unfamiliar structure of a suit brings a surge of ardor. Soon as he's out of sight, Mother says, Harold and I share a glass of wine every now and then, when we go out dancing—Harold being the somewhat prissy young man of color hired to help care for Daddy.

This gives me a sick feeling in my chest. I look toward the door Warren disappeared through, his presence an antivenin to the snakebite of Mother's disarray. Our family's so inadequately small compared to the profligate Whitbreads. My own daddy's so out of things, he probably doesn't actually know I'm getting married.

Inside, I keep trying to squash down the image of my blear-eyed daddy, since a buried part of me longs for him to be reborn all tall and sober, to loop my arm in his, to wrap my hand on his biceps, then squire me to Warren's side. A father walks his daughter down the aisle. Such a wholly unoriginal wish could dismantle me if I permit myself to dip into it. In my head, I shoo it off like an insect.

Warren gets back in the car, handing me a small paper bag over his shoulder. I fish through it for the eyedrops. Mother has her Shalimar out and is studying the cap for where the nozzle is. I tell her, They'll be unfailingly polite. They always are.

She squirts behind her ear, and the scent of rose attar touches some reptilian area of my brain, where lies whatever faint recollection of beauty I have.

Warren, she says, you know what they say a mother-in-law's job is at a wedding?

I don't, he says, pushing his glasses up his nose.

Just shut up and wear beige.

He actually snorts at the prospect.

Mother takes my hand in her scented one. My heart was thumping so bad in my chest. I was scared to take another valium in case there was a toast or something because I'd fall into my plate.

I take no comfort in sharing anxiety with my once towering, powerful mother, for any ways we favor each other feel distinctly unbridal. I show her my throat, adding, Make me smell like you. Then we draw up into the gilded light of the Ritz, and the doorman helps me out.

We enter the paneled bar to find the Whitbreads plural— six siblings, two daughters-in-law, one son-in-law—scattered among the low tables. Taken together, they're the tallest people in the room, and possibly the best looking. My chic sister and her lawyer boyfriend have been chatting equably with them over drinks when we bluster in. There's the hubbub of shaken hands, and I can see Mother's turned out nice and smiling. The martini that lands before me gets tossed down.

Drinking to handle the angst of Mother's drinking— caused by her own angst—means our twin dipsomanias face off like a pair of mirrors, one generation offloading misery to the other through dwindling generations, back through history to when humans first fermented grapes.

The next thing I know, Lecia's grabbing my arm as we stride up the stairs to the table, saying, What is she on? Then we're seated at enormous tables draped with enough linen to clothe a convent.

Sometime after the first course, Warren turns to me, asking if we can speak privately in the foyer. I rise on numb legs. The pre-wedding joke Lecia kept nudging me with was this: Soon as the Whitbreads met Mother, the wedding would be off. From across the room, my sister's eyes lock on mine, brows raised. I shrug at her, and her napkin seems to wipe off her own smile.

Walking behind Warren, I'm approaching execution, till he stops and draws from his breast pocket a small blue velvet box. It holds a platinum ring with a sapphire the size of a chiclet flanked by diamonds of equal size, which—with all the drinks in me—makes me wobble. He slides it onto my shaking finger, saying, They're family stones. Mother had it made. I joke I'll need a bodyguard to wear it in public. When I lean back to stare into his green eyes, I resist the urge to kiss him—a public display he'd hate. But our gazes are so interwoven, I feel neither Texas trash nor WASP-itude can touch us.

It doesn't matter that my mother-in-law sobs through much of the meal, not—I'm guessing—from joy. Warren's brother Dev says with genuine puzzlement as we head down the grand staircase, *She was crying?* And I think How do they block this stuff out? Nor does it matter that Mother offered to paint Mr. Whitbread in the nude and quote *fix anything you need fixed* close quote.

The next day, at the inn we took over for the wedding, I swallow enough expensive champagne to float me effort-lessly to the altar, toward the only lover I've ever both adored and admired. Around us, the green lawns of New England spread away into a fresh geography. Warren slides my moth-er's mother's rose gold band on my finger next to the blinding platinum and jewels from his, and it's a transforming sen-sation. The ties of both our families unloose us. We are, by my measure, free of them all, our disparate homesteads. Our small family circle will be impenetrable.

10

Bound

He remembered poor Julian and his romantic awe of [the rich] and how he had started a story once that began, "The very rich are different from you and me." And how someone had said to Julian, "Yes, they have more money."
—ERNEST HEMINGWAY, "SNOWS OF KILIMANJARO"

When two hearts beat as one, there are in-laws to bond with, or, in my family's case, outlaws. But for our first years Warren and I never go to Texas, not once. (Later, I'll resent this like hell, but I don't recall arguing about it much.) Daddy's dying in the house I grew up in, while Mother begrudgingly nurses him. Yet Warren's sense of duty to his own family is a virtue I so hope will tether him to me that I try to take on his obligation as my own. Plus if I didn't go with him, we'd wind up with separate holidays, and I have some daytime soap-opera notion of what it means to be wifely. Besides, Lecia and Mother visit us a few times per year in the way Warren's far-flung siblings never would, and I fly home to see Daddy plenty alone.

Yet for every conceivable holiday—from Easter lamb to Christmas ham—our tin-can car crunches up the drive to the Whitbread estate, which lures me in some ways and yet always saps me dry. This isn't meant to sound peevish, for the Whitbreads are never not nice. But from the second I haul my bag up the curved stair, the place drains me of force like a battery going rust. Maybe it's all the fine wines I take in. Of those many visits, I remember absolutely nil. Beyond sitting at a table while plates appear and get swept away, I can't recount one damn thing we did.

The estate sits spitting distance from New York, and those first years, I show up with clippings of art I want to look at or friends' bands I plan to hear. We never—not once—go into the city. One doesn't venture outside estate walls. Even the clawed furniture seems dug in to the deep nap of ancient rugs.

But that doesn't explain the lethargy that overcomes me there, the anesthetic effect of luxury. Instead of jogging, we read by the pool or walk down to feed carrots to the donkeys. The paper is meticulously studied, also *The New Yorker*. I sometimes poke around the attic or unused bedrooms, opening the ancient chests of drawers to catch whiffs of cedar or lavender sachet.

It's a readerly tribe, and I can slouch in a leather chair drinking with a book in my lap for hours as well they can—my one affinity. But no sense of connection ever evolves into closeness. Outside each other's company, Warren's parents refer to each other as Mr. and Mrs. Whitbread, so I'd never presume first names.

Only once does Mr. Whitbread ring our house. It's Warren's birthday, and I answer as Mr. Whitbread says, *This is*—long pause as he contemplates what to call himself, uncomfortable saying either Dev Whitbread or Mr. Whitbread—*Warren Whitbread's father.*

I put down the phone and announce to Warren, Your father's on the phone.

What does he want? Warren says, not even rising from his desk.

I suppose to tell you happy birthday.

The light reflecting on Warren's glasses transforms his eyes into white rectangles as he says, Ask him if it's important.

On our regular visits to the big house, I'm all too eager to inject myself into the clever table conversations, which cover history and great novels, sport and politics—all with an ease I struggle to keep up with.

But smart as the conversation is, it has a strangely repetitive quality. You never know anybody better—the talk never deepens, but neither does it show the slightest strain, and I'm nothing if not strained to the gills virtually every second. You enter that place and live suspended in amber like characters in a Victorian novel.

How're your parents, Mary, I'm asked. How's your father? And I say the same and that it's sad, and everyone agrees, and then the character of my pretzeled daddy is dismissed like a servant whose health has been respectfully inquired after.

For four long years, Warren never meets the dying man whose care, or lack of it, occupies my thoughts waking and sleeping without relent. Dreams of Daddy haunt me. In one, I scoop his scrawny frame into my arms like he's a baby, and his limbs begin to snap off as if they were a leper's as I fight not to drop him.

In fairness to Warren, I often have to fly down expensively at the last minute for some bedside death watch Daddy winds up surviving. Or maybe I've struck some unconscious deal to shield him from the cesspool of my birth, or I'm eager to win some blessing from the Whitbreads that they're no doubt not even interested enough to withhold.

So the day I move Daddy out of our childhood home, I've flown in alone. Lecia has a meeting in Houston that day for her insurance business, and Mother hides sobbing in the garage.

There's a big financial argument for keeping Daddy home, of course. But the florid bedsores in his heels have begun to fester beyond what I can stand thinking about. The only day nurse we can afford is the kindly but sometimes stuporific Harold. At night Mother fails to turn Daddy often enough to keep the sores at bay.

So I arrive alone alongside Daddy's home hospital bed. There's the bleach from the sheets and the air tinny with iodine. Under the air conditioner grind, his breathing is labored. Honeysuckle vines cling to the window screen, and a chameleon hangs by its claws.

My hand grasps the aluminum bar Daddy's hand holds on to. He is clinging hard, and the bewilderment in his face tells me that all the explaining I've done about the move has rolled through his head like tumbleweed. I say, You're going for a simple hip surgery, then in a few days, Lecia will ride with you to a facility where nurses can take better care of you than Mother.

Yamma?

Mama's heart medication has been doubled, Daddy.

A dozen times I've been over this, but for the first time, his expression goes quizzical, his head cants.

Yamma? he says.

Mama's not here, I say.

Yamma, he says, and a silly grin splays across his face, and he lets go the bed bar like a man relinquishing his hold on a life rope. Then he grabs my hand through the bars.

Garfield, he says. He says this word a lot. Mother and Harold take it as a reference to the orange rascal of a cartoon cat from the funnies. Daddy has an orange cat coffee mug he can't drink out of, and a plastic figurine that nonstop bares his teeth in a snide grin.

Garfield, Daddy says.

Maybe this is the day I figure out that Daddy never gave a shit about an orange effing feline in the funnies, which he used to flip past on his way to the scores. Garfield's the name of our own street. What dimwits we are. How often did he tell me I couldn't leave home by saying, You're staying right here at 4901 Garfield.

Garfield, he says. Which means Home. Safe. Stay. How little we ever wanted, the creatures in my family, and how hard we struggled in one another's company not to get it.

Looooo, he says, which means both *hello* and *I love you.*

I love you back, I say. I love you more cause you're bigger.

But in my mind are other sentences, which I've spoken to enough licensed professionals by now that I can let them stream through me without a scalding lava burn. *I love you harder cause I need you more, you leathery old galoot. Did my absence hurt you into this? How dare you cease to daddy me so soon. . . .*

And when the ambulance driver shows up with his stretcher, he and the attendant have to pry Daddy's large-knuckled hands off the silver bars of that bed. Daddy's eyes lock on mine. He says one word to me, and it must meander through his skull a long time, searching through the ruined brain to find the perfect monosyllabic curse.

Bad, he says to me. They've taken his teeth out, and tears river down the crow's feet of his tough Indian face. Bad bad bad.

I talk to the ambulance driver. I look through Daddy's wallet for his social security card, which I can't find. What I do find is my first college report card—straight A's for the only time since grade school. Also, there's the copy of the first poem I published at age nineteen, with the stains of many beers where it had been spread across the damp surface of many bars, a page smoothed out for men no doubt too bleary to read it.

We loved each other this way, Daddy and I, from afar. We're like totem animals in each other's foreign cosmologies —like islanders whose ancestral gods favor each other. Each of us represented to the other what little we knew of love inside that family, but whoever I've turned into has wiped away who I was as a kid, whoever he once loved. Age about twelve, I'd ceased to shoot pool and scale fish, stopped tuning in to the Friday night fights after Ali and Liston, nor did I follow the Yankees with the intensity Daddy thought their due.

My very last visit when Daddy was still upright and continent and unparalyzed, he'd squired me to a New Year's dance at the American Legion club, a place so skeevy neither Mother nor Lecia ever—to my knowledge—set shoe leather in the joint. I dressed for the occasion as I might have for Sunday school or a job interview. Daddy steered me by my elbow through the threshold onto the sloping floor of scarred sky-blue linoleum, inside the boxy paneled walls with imitation knotholes that could—with sufficient liquor—make you feel

stared at by all the veterans who'd drunk themselves into
early graves in that place.

Folding chairs were drawn around small tables whose
treacherous wobbles required matchbooks, and the matchbooks advertised kits you could write away for so as to finish
high school and become an artist or beautician or drill press
operator. The women's room had the shocking dead-meat
smell of a butcher shop and a mirror whose crack left it in the
shape of Louisiana.

And since January first was Daddy's birthday, he'd joked
that the party was for him. One after another, I'd danced
with the men he'd worked on oil towers with and caught bass
with, guys who'd built the garage studio for my mother one
blistering summer. Two elementally nicknamed Red and
Blue, men monosyllabic in every way. One named Buck, one
Bubba, one Sweet. Not one didn't have a union card in his
wallet, and their faces were weathered as dried fruit. *Your
daddy's so proud of you, how smart you are and your writing and all.* The Texas two-step we did, the cotton-eyed Joe,
swing dancing I could barely keep up with.

At the end of the night, the ladies' room sink was plugged
up with puke, and two disputes had been taken outside—one
over a pool game, one over Lord knows what. By the time
Daddy grabbed my hand for the last dance, the floor had
begun a slow tilt-a-whirl around us. His squinting bloodshot
eyes stared over my shoulder as he glided me around to *The
Tennessee Waltz*. We listed through the song. I don't remember midnight.

At the truck, I yelled myself hoarse trying to get his keys
away from him.

A passing cowboy said, Dang, Pete, give the girl your keys.

And Daddy said, Mind your own business before I stomp
a mudhole in your ass.

And I remember the fog we drove in, how it billowed up over the road from the bayou on either side till the road narrowed to smoke. The biker bars I'd been in, skinny-dipping drunk in a lake miles wide, hitchhiking: Never had I felt closer to death than with that old man feeling his drunk path on and off the road shoulder through that smoky miasma.

The day I moved Daddy to the hospital, he grabs my arm as we cross the lawn. I'm carrying his piss jug again. The checks I sent home never paid down the guilt I tote today for having disappeared from the place he's dying in, which is—in turn—a place dying in me. My life with Warren somehow excludes my daddy. The me Daddy knew doesn't exist in Warren's house, which is maybe why my husband didn't come down on this mission—*down* being the operative word. Where I came from is a comedown.

Daddy's last upright public appearance was on the bar stool in the VFW, where one final shot of whiskey felled him the way German snipers had failed to. In an increasingly skeletal form, he kept breathing, though each week he's sanded closer to the bone. But he'd been floating farther from me, starting when I'd left him—he'd left me? I never could decide—more than a decade before.

The ambulance door seals me inside with him. Daddy's good hand wipes his wet face then swats my hand away.

11

In Search of Incompetence

I wanted to be a rain salesman,
carrying my satchel full of rain from door to door,
selling thunder, selling the way air feels after a downpour,
but there were no openings in the rain department,
and so they left me dying behind this desk—adding bleeps
subtracting chunks—and I would give a bowl of wild blossoms,
some rain, and two shakes of my fist at the sky to be living.
—JOHN ENGMAN, "WORK"

I don't drink every day, but I find myself unpredictably blotto at inopportune times.

Like the night before my thirtieth birthday: I lie fully dressed—albeit shoeless—in a charcoal business suit in the bathtub of a Silicon Valley motel, sipping whiskey from one of those minibar bottles that makes you pucker your lips into a doll's pinhole mouth. On the shag rug, the legal pad with notes for my all day corporate presentation tomorrow holds a single x and y axis drawn into an L-shaped graph. To say I'm ill prepared understates the problem. My sole plan is to: (1) stride into the boardroom; (2) smile like a monkey as I briskly shake hands. Then I imagine a diaphanous veil falling across the rest of my presentation.

I lie in the empty tub as in a tomb. From the outer hallway comes a ruckus that works on my brain like an eggbeater. Much of the Loyola men's basketball team is running hither and yon, playing some game with a tennis ball. Every now and then they hurl the ball against my hollow-core door. This is not an accident.

Earlier tonight, with rabid expression and possibly some spit spray, I told the team they had to keep it down or I'd call the front desk. They froze and stared as if some bog creature had reared up from the mud. The instant I closed the door, the game resumed at full decibel level.

The rusty old clerk who came to rescue me had a dowager's hump that kept him bent over at ninety degrees. He kept glancing over his shoulder at the ballplayers arrayed behind as he said, We're full tonight. I can't move your room. Then he turned on his heel and hightailed it through the gauntlet of giants back to the elevator, which two looming guys were holding open.

Against the hotel door, the tennis ball occasionally whams, shaking the door earthquakelike on its hinges. If they could bust in, they'd throw me on a bonfire and torch me, I know it.

They must sense the pitiful failure I'm mired in: turning thirty, far from home and family, making it up as I go. Worst of all, I've failed to publish a book, which means my ancient fantasy of being a writer has abraded off like the name on a wind-worn tombstone.

I unscrew the tiny bottle of vodka's red lid and suck a

few drops. Every asshole I know has published a book. Over six years, I've collected rejections for my manuscript, sometimes the occasional nice note for second place. So a sheaf of dog-eared pages curling at the edges lies on my desk like drying roadkill, though every dang poem in it has come out in some literary mag, which is—as Warren points out—not nothing.

But unless a book publisher stitches them into a volume, I'll never land the teaching job that'll let me shed snakeskin-like the business suit I wear like an unwilling drag queen. It's an old dream. Age about seven, I started posing for the jacket photo in the bathroom shaving mirror. When my sister caught me wearing the baleful, heavy-lidded pout I figured would look snappy, she'd cackle like a magpie, then holler to Mother I'd stolen her beret again. My response? I'd pinch my index finger and thumb together over and over and go *psss psss psss* like a puff adder. Somehow I'd figured out that this gesture drove her batshit.

By age thirty, I'm not writing squat, which I blame on my ramped-up consulting schedule, knowing full well my favorite poet was a full-time insurance exec. Warren keeps urging me to deal with my complicated family on the page, but that seems too damp-eyed, though even I know the crap I crank out referring to Homer and Virgil is pretentious before Warren carefully pens *pretentious* on page bottom.

The bathtub I'm lying in feels like a stone island I've shipwrecked myself on. My pantyhose have twisted around, and the black unwashed soles gross me out. I'm a hack, a hired ghostwriter who gins out reports on Swedish telecommunications companies, or phone technology, or packet switching and deregulation.

Oh, and reviews of assholes who've actually published poetry collections, in a magazine my husband edits. Which, if he didn't revise my prose with a hacksaw, I probably wouldn't get in to.

Bam bam bam. The door rattles. I holler out, You grisly fuckers! If I had a firearm, I'd hunt each of you down like the dogs you are.

Now I've taken up a weensy bottle of Scotch, J&B in the green bottle. What moron designed these bottles so small? And why a mini-bar when a maxibar is clearly what's called for?

Today on the phone, the big-deal consultant who got me into this business said, Your having to give this presentation in my stead is a little like going to work in the hospital as a janitor and winding up performing brain surgery.

Don't remind me, I said.

Think about it, he mused. Your whole business career has derived from a series of flukes. . . .

While he talked, I stretched the phone cord and dexterously slipped the small fridge key into its slot. I said, Aren't you supposed to be finding flights?

My travel agent's going to ring the other line, he said.

He was a captain of industry, this guy. Once the thirtysomething president of my old company's e-mail subsidiary, he'd left to consult for big bucks, promising me enough subcontracting work in ghostwriting and market research to hang out my own consulting shingle. I could double my salary while freeing up intervals for poetry.

On the phone to me, he said, You can write the next great business best seller. First there was *In Search of Excellence*, Mary Karr brings us *In Search of Incompetence.*

He was rich enough to be jovial about this, but I knew if I screwed up the presentation and lost this client's fat retainer, I'd be dead, for without this expert's benevolent referrals, I had zero credential.

Can you help me with my notes? I said.

But through the phone's overseas hiss, I heard another phone start ringing, and he said, Maybe this other flight came through—

Then the dial tone went retreating across the Asian oceans, and I resisted the impulse to pound the phone receiver on the first solid surface.

Toward dawn in the hotel room, I pick up the legal pad and try to envision my solo presentation. Standing at the grease board, I'll draw a horizontal line—an x axis—saying, This line represents your spending. It goes from spending zero on the left to shelling out shitloads of money on the right. My vertical y axis measures returns on that money—from getting back zero at the bottom to making zillions at the top. I'm gonna tell the president of Company X and his minions that they need to spend as little as possible while making shitloads in return. The question is, how to stretch this expensive advice into a nine-hour meeting?

I never have to find out. The next morning Mr. Consultant skids into the boardroom sideways from a flight I never knew he got on. He takes the laser pointer from my hand, and I sit sweatily at the conference table. Other than taking notes, I'm free of the babble floating over us. Free, that's how being a poet looks to me, like freedom from the grind among pencil-necked office guys in clip-on ties.

Sitting there, I fantasize about the birthday dinner my grad school guru planned in San Francisco before I catch the red-eye back. He'll talk about translating the great Polish Nobel dude and about the ballads of Wordsworth and about his own drunk mother whose loony-bin demise he managed to live through. He knows the botanical names of plants and how to do carpentry work. In my mind, I picture his curious, becalmed expression the way certain saffron-robed acolytes do Buddha. His very stare will rebaptize me a writer, despite my business suit.

But he doesn't make it. (Later, I'll find out his bloody divorce had just started.)

On the verge of missing my flight, I lug my garment bag back to the rental car and weave drunkenly through the fog to the airport, where I toss down enough cocktails to note how costly my rising tolerance is. Eventually, I call Warren from the pay phone. The phone rings and rings, and I hear my own voice on the machine, and I say, Pick up, pick up.

He listens patiently, for he is both patient and a listener. And he reminds me his book isn't in print yet, either. It's the work that counts. I feel my mouth slurring words as I ask him to pick me up at the airport in the morning for my birthday—the only present I want.

I thought you wanted that party we're having, he says, with your sister coming for a week.

This party—our first—was long negotiated. He's noting the traffic to and from the airport, the hours of writing he'll lose. Should I offer to cancel the party in order to be picked up? When he hangs up, I feel confident that I'll see him at the gate.

Having touched down in Boston at dawn, I wander through the airport with an inner plunging sense—no sign of Warren. When the magic doors glide open on the empty taxi stand, I feel the regressed terror of a kid lost in the glass cubicles of a department store because her manic mother has just wandered off—maybe on purpose, maybe not. (Crazy to admit this, but true.)

How do you get past it, I ask my shrink, when you never got that sense of acceptance and security as a kid?

You've got to nurture yourself through those instants, he

says, recognize the source of the misery as out of kilter with the stimulus. Realize you're not lost. You're an adult. Warren didn't hurt you on purpose. You were perfectly capable of getting yourself home.

Nurture myself. Now, there's an idea I can glom on to. I say, Like I could have a drink when I got home?

If that calms you, he says. One drink.

Just what I hoped he'd say.

12

Bent Bender

"Well, if God doesn't exist, who's laughing at us?"
—FYODOR DOSTOYEVSKY, *THE BROTHERS KARAMAZOV*

One day Lecia rings me up. Tawdry, she says.

An adjective meaning crude or trashy or otherwise unseemly, I say. Talk to me.

Mother's sleeping with Harold, she says, meaning Daddy's pill-popping nurse, crashing of late in the spare room.

Never happen, I say. That man has got to be gay.

Happened, she says. They showed up drunk last night, talking about the hustle contest at Get Down Brown's.

Lecia lives two hours from our hometown, but her former secretary saw Mother and Harold necking. I wonder were they doing this with Daddy in the house!

Who knows? Lecia says. Daddy's so out of it, he may not have twigged to it anyway. If anything, he likes Harold better than Mother.

Harold's nicer, I say. Way nicer.

And he used to work at the jail, Lecia says. I wonder if they practice safe sex.

We both went quiet till I add, She needs to get an AIDS test.

Tawdry, Lecia says.

Tawdry, I say, and hang up.

So vivid is Mother's story of her final drunk with Harold—so painterly in its grotesque detail—that I take the liberty of recounting as if I were there, for a good story told often enough puts you in rooms never occupied. The way other families keep wedding videos or log dates in a Bible, mine stores in the genetic warehouse alcohol-fueled catastrophe.

I'm the voyeur as Harold tries to zip Mother into her red sequined top, a close fit on her sixty-two-year-old frame. You need to spray some PAM on me, Mother says. Before the mirror, she sucks in her cheeks and rouges a terra-cotta stripe in the cheekbone's shadow. He tugs down on the blouse hem and she feels her zipper pop midback.

Whoa, she says. I can feel a breeze in here. She takes a sip of Harold's banana daiquiri as he checks her out from behind.

I'll safety-pin it, he says.

After draining the glass, she holds up the empty, saying, And do me.

He opens the refrigerator, on which Mother has painted a bulbous hippolike old woman, nude in a floppy hat.

Hippos are their theme animal, Mother and Harold's. In the months since I've moved Daddy into the home, the old house has sprouted hippos all over. Money I've sent to help out has partly been used for the bloated, nappy furniture they laze on—also for redoing the bath, where Mother painted another cartoonlike mural of twin hippos, which I fear echoes the two of them nude together.

Mother dials the phone while telling Harold to put some britches on. The silky polyester shirt he slides into has zig-zag lightning bolts. Once the buttons are fastened, the front puckers.

In our apartment in Cambridge, the phone squeals, and I holler to my husband, who's typing in the next room, That's her.

Don't answer it, he says. I know he's right. The meetings I've been dipping into for children of alcoholics—at the urging of Tex—suggest I stay out of Mother's orbit when she's loaded. I started consulting Tex when she and Harold took off on this tear a few months back. But rather than steer clear of her like they all say, I'm morbidly compelled to connect with her. Pray about it, those religious morons suggest, for they fancy some bearded giant staring down from a cloud is gonna zap me into shape. But a god I don't believe in can't wave a wand over my mother to stop her drinking. Or wipe away thirty years of fret that therapy has just tamped down.

Harold says I'm smoking hot, like a skillet, Mother says.

Lucky you, I say.

Y'all going out tonight? she wants to know.

Hardly, I said. Warren's working on an essay. I'm ghost-writing an article about the stock market for that business review. I'm on deadline—huge pressure.

Actually, I'm not working on squat. I've been swilling chardonnay on the tiny porch—a back stair landing off our colonial—while headphones pump Mozart's Requiem into my head over and over. However sorry for myself Mozart's howling angels can make me, I want Mother to feel sorrier. This is part of our elaborate economy circa 1984. I send her money, and she lets me blame her for everything wrong with my life. She also intermittently berates me for becoming a corporate drudge. On the phone, she asks what we're doing home on a Saturday night.

You're both sticks-in-the-mud, she tells me. Or is it stick-in-the-muds?

We're working, Mother. We're not out drinking ourselves to death.

Don't start on me, she says.

I was talking about Daddy, I say. But I hadn't been talking about Daddy. I'd been trying to land a small barb through the thick fog around her.

Since you moved your daddy out, Mother says, I feel like a teenager again.

Is your blood pressure any better? I ask, hearing in the background the music from *Flashdance* start up.

I'm so fat, she says, I'm scared to take my damn blood pressure.

You've never been fat in your life, I say. I'll bet he's still wearing his poison ring. One of the ways my sister and I stay convinced that Harold's gay is the hinged ring he carries valium in.

He wears those cheap ass gold chains—she raises her voice in Harold's direction—*that're turning his chest green.*

In the doorway across from me, Warren comes to mime hanging up the phone, and I raise my index finger to indicate I'll be a sec. Why don't I put the phone down? She's ranting about the losers in the damn sobriety group Tex goes to. She says, His daddy told him I didn't want him, which was a goddamn lie. Who does that to a baby? He might not have been an alcoholic without that.

I thought you and Harold were gonna go to some meetings with him? I say.

I went to one, and it was *I went here and got drunk, I went there and got drunk.*

In the background, I hear the blender whir as she adds, I'd sooner dip snuff.

Again, Warren appears in the door, holding up the empty bottle of wine with a puzzled look on his face. I jot down on a pad that I spilled the bottle.

Mother's saying, I'm not an alcoholic, Mary. When you were little, I called the hotline that one time, and they showed up with a six-pack of beer because they assumed I'd be having the DTs. Without seizures, I didn't make the team. They told me, You're not an alcoholic, lady.

Eventually, I hang up to drink my own self into a stupor. And the next morning, when I ring Mother's house to ensure she's still got a pulse, I get no answer and no answer.

Calling Lecia next, I hear her ask am I sitting down. The question takes the bottom out of my stomach like a speed bump, and for the umpteenth time in my life, I feel the cold impact of Mother's death. It's so easy to picture her and Harold reeling down the road from Get Down Brown's like they were in bumper cars.

She's not dead, Lecia says. Dead would be simpler.

Lecia tells me that Harold allegedly propositioned some cowboy in the men's room, and the guy had beaten the shit out of him. Which prompted Mother to draw—from her beaded bag—the pearl-handled revolver so small it could pass for a cigarette lighter. She held the cowboys at bay through the parking lot while she wrangled the pulp-faced Harold into her car.

Once home, Mother poured herself a glass of milk and opened a tranquilizing package of ho-hos. Then she proceeded to tear Harold a new asshole—verbally speaking. He was bloody-nosed already, and stout as a prize pig, blubbering Mother was his soul mate till he corked off on the kitchen floor.

Mother had sat on the counter stool, sipping at the milk and ratcheting up her pissed-off with every whisper sweep of the clock till it came to her Harold needed a piece of her mind. She'd pelted him with a pastry, then kicked him *not very hard*, she'd told Lecia, and mostly in his big fat ass.

Then she got her pistol out again and fired it over Harold's head, and he'd screamed himself awake. Somewhere in there, he'd pissed his pants. She couldn't shift him off the kitchen floor, so she called to Tex, who hauled Harold to detox.

She *shot* at him? I say.

That's exactly what I said. *You shot at him?* Lecia says. So embarrassing.

Lecia's our only family member plagued by a sense of propriety. She belongs to civic groups and the country club. She'd that morning taken from Mother's house every gun she could rustle up. Do I know of any little pistols laying around? I don't.

It's like the old days, I say. Remember her shooting at Hector? (Lecia and I had draped ourselves over our stepfather's semi-supine form while Mother brandished a firearm.)

Daddy, too.

When did she shoot at Daddy?

You were too little to remember. I know I told you about it. One Christmas. You never saw the bullet hole in the kitchen tile by the stove?

I thought Daddy was cleaning a pistol. Why'd she shoot at him?

The better question is, Lecia adds, why'd she shoot at anybody?

There was a pause, and we said in unison, *To get their attention.*

Which had been her standard explanation over the years.

I know a lot of people, Lecia says. I know a lot of people who're drunks. I even know a lot of drunks with guns—and grudges. Our mother's the only person I know ever shot at anybody.

It seems a nasty side effect of sleeping with her.

In fairness to her, Lecia says, she sounds contrite.

Maybe we could check her in the same place as Harold, I say. They could go in on the buddy system, like the navy.

Later, Tex calls to announce he's shepherding Harold through the hospital's recovery meetings, with Mother visiting every day (such loyalty makes me wonder if she makes her alleged weekly visits to Daddy in the home—though they no doubt barely register on him.) Tex can't keep the bemusement out of his voice when he adds, You'll never guess what she wound up doing this morning?

Going to one of those supportive-wives' meetings?

Yes, ma'am.

Like a witch in church, I say.

Some lady put her off by talking about wiping her husband's ass, and Mother claimed she got sick to her stomach. Anyway, Harold and I were in the meeting across the hall with all the drunks. Everybody laughing and raising hell. So she wound up crossing over.

She went to a meeting of sober drunks?

She did.

Will wonders never cease, I say. If this winds up taking, I owe you big.

She's going to another meeting tonight.

You're expecting too much, I say. She's only there because he is—

Don't be too sure, he says. They give out these white chips to anybody sober a day. Desire chip, it's called. Looks like a poker chip. She raised her hand and stood up in front and got herself one. She raised her hand and said, I'm Charlie, and I'm an alcoholic.

Tomorrow she'll wake up and say, *I'm Charlie, and I'm the fire chief.*

Tex says one of the lecturers at the detox was the very guy she'd called thirty years back, the guy who said she wasn't sick enough to be an alcoholic.

I'd like to give that bastard a piece of my mind, I say.

But cynical as I try to sound about Mother's stab at normalcy, I hang up to dial my sister, and together our tough talk gets thinner, the pauses in the conversation longer. We're starting—reluctantly—to hope.

Afterward, I go into Warren's study and lean on the door frame, saying, Mother's getting sober.

He glances up, saying, I never thought she drank that much.

I gape at him, and he says, I know when you were little, she was bad.

Later, Mother calls, sounding chastened, and I scold her and hang up, for when she's in no immediate danger of killing herself, I get to spill onto her the black bile I feel.

Eventually, I get drunk at her again, driving to the liquor store for a bottle of Jack Daniels like my poor old daddy used to drink (no scrap of awareness in the similarity), and I drink it in the garage while flipping through my wedding pictures, where Mother looks walleyed and very pleased with herself. I could drag her behind my car, I think. Instead, I drain the poison that I hope will kill her.

13

Homesick

. . . Mind like a floating white cloud,
Sunset like the parting of old acquaintances
Who bow over their clasped hands at a distance.
Our horses neigh to each other
as we are departing.

           —LI PO, "TAKING LEAVE OF A FRIEND"

               (TRANS. EZRA POUND)

Two years after the wedding—five years after we met—Warren meets my invalid daddy on a summer day when the humid Texas air is saturated from the local oil refineries with a fluorocarbon stench that could peel paint. It's their sole encounter.

I lead Warren into the urine-drenched air of Daddy's nursing home with a bluster I don't feel, hugging the nurses on duty as if we're long lost sorority sisters. But inside, I'm ashiver with anxiety. For what? What could I expect to go right or wrong between two men with such gulfs between them and such silence inside them—Warren bred to it, Daddy broken to it.

Amid the other patients in the dayroom, Daddy is sitting with a thin pink blanket over his legs when we walk up. When he sees me, his face tries to brighten, but the dead half of it hangs down. He's shaking his head with a stiff, persistent fraction of a smile. Truly, he's a man split in half, neither fully dead nor fully alive.

His eyes are black as a crow's, though, and they sparkle and go wet when he sees me.

Mur, he says, Murr.

That's right, I say. It's Mary. I kiss his whiskery neck, asking does he want me to shave him before I leave.

But he doesn't register the offer—a relief, since I whinge at inflicting the slightest razor nick.

His good hand grabs my left hand, grips it with the old iron he had in my youth. I stand next to him while Warren waits off to the side.

A little old lady in cat's eye glasses with hair woven atop her head wheels up to me. She says, Are you his wife?

No, ma'am, I say, wondering if maybe Mother doesn't visit as often as she's told us, else this old bird was also too out of things to remember Mother.

His sweetheart?

No, ma'am, I say. I'm his daughter.

Thank goodness, she says. I'm his girlfriend.

Daddy lets go my hand a second and waves over toward the lady. She wheels to his other side, then puts her hand on one wheel of his chair protectively, saying, He buys me Cokes. He stays with me all day, so I never have to wonder where he's at.

He's good that way, I say.

He's never lied to me, not once.

From the half of Daddy's face I can see, his old smile is perfect. His eye glances off mine in cahoots. I can, for an instant, see him as he'd been all tall, kneeling down to me, saying, *Don't tell your mama and sister. You and me'll sneak off for a strawberry freeze . . .*

I start to move away, and he grasps my hand with a lobster grip. I wave Warren over. Daddy, I say, this is Warren.

Daddy glances at him.

Is that your sweetheart? the lady says.

Yes, ma'am.

Daddy studies my hand as if it were some codex that needed to be deciphered somehow. He looks up at me, and from a great distance—tens of thousands of miles, decades—it's as if he's been fast-forwarded into our presence. Our glances click, and his claw of a hand clings to mine. *Murrr,* he said.

That's right, Daddy.

He shakes his head and purses his lips. He looks around the room as if for help. The lady says, You're making him mad, little lady. She pats his hand again. Honey, she says—honey, can I get you a Dr Pepper?

He half nods.

All right then, she says and wheels around.

My chiclet engagement ring's still loose, only held on by the wedding ring I had fitted. Daddy wiggles the ring on my knuckle. He says, *Murrr . . . murr.*

Married, I finally say. I'm married. Yes, to Warren. He's my husband. I reach for Warren and draw him over. For a second there, I hold each of their hands, standing like a conduit between them. I'm still looking only at the good half of Daddy's face. He gives Warren the up and down scrutiny he'd bring to a horse prior to auction, then he glances back at me and rolls his eyes as if to say, jokingly, *This yahoo.*

Then he lets go my hand to shake Warren's, and I take that in.

And that's it, that instant. My life as I've shaped it includes—for that instant only—the daddy I once loved more than beans and rice. The lady wheels back with a Dr Pepper. I help her flip the tab, and she slides a bent straw into it.

We take turns buying, she tells me.

Daddy takes a sip and winks at her. Then he looks over at me, saying, *Looooo.*

I love you, too, Daddy, I say.

At the end of the visit, Warren calls him Mr. Karr and says he's glad to meet him. And Daddy takes my hand in his and looks down at it and up at Warren. His eyes meet mine, and in a stiff nod, I get his last blessing, since within the year, we'll come back to bury him.

14

The Inconceivable
Meets the Conceivable

*There was earth inside them, and
they dug.*

*They dug and dug, and so
their day went by, their night.
And they did not praise God,
who, so they heard, wanted all this,
who, so they heard, knew all this.*
— PAUL CELAN, "THERE WAS EARTH INSIDE THEM"
(TRANS. MICHAEL HAMBURGER)

The call comes on the ancient black rotary phone in the middle of the night at the Whitbreads' Rhode Island beach house. Daddy's dead. Five years after we'd refused both breathing apparatus and feeding tube, he'd gone on blinking.

He hadn't wanted to die, which was contrary to all his stoic-sounding predictions about infirmity. On the back porch one night when I was home from college, he'd issued a long and drunken disquisition about how—if he became bedridden—I should never let some machine pump his lungs with air. He'd said, Don't you let me linger.

Frogs were keeping time in air drenched with honey-suckle.

Your mama and sister won't do this, but you do it. Get you a pillow and lay it over my face.

I sipped at my Lone Star beer, which he'd doctored with salt so it was akin to sea water.

Don't you feel bad if I struggle.

I probably agreed just to get him to shut up. But whatever death he'd expected to slump into, he'd fought off.

On the dawn plane flying to Texas, I feel furious relief that he's finally gone curling over me like a cold green wave, and in the backwash of that, icy shame. Wave after wave, I'm drenched and shamed that way till touch down on the tarmac between palms and razor grass.

Daddy's dead. I no longer have to wander the corridors of corporate America feigning an expertise I in no way have, solely to pay for the bedpans and catheters and the slender white worms of gauze they pack into the bedsores on the backs of his heels as the bones try to cut their way free of flesh.

He's dead. They nailed him in a box, and a long conveyor belt rolled him into a flaming oven even before my plane scraped down.

At the funeral home, I help up the steps my farm girl aunt, Daddy's sister, who believes that in the final Rapture our graves will split and our bodies arise clothed in healthy flesh. She's the only relative I felt kin to at a cellular level, and she holds out her shaking, bird-boned hand for me to steady herself, saying, *Take me to him.* Her milky blue eyes stare through gold-rimmed spectacles bought before Eisenhower.

Holding the one hand, I explain about the cremation, and her free hand—clutching a thin hankie imprinted with violets—flies to her gaping mouth, and she cries with an agony worthy of Job, You burnt my brother! (Ignorant, I was, till she cried out, of the trick Mother and Lecia had played on me by dispatching me to explain the cremation to Aunt Gladys.)

After the service at Mother's house, I'm lowering to the table a bowl of mustard greens salty with hunks of fatback. Lecia asks, Where's Warren? She's upending a Tupperware carton of fried chicken onto a platter.

He's gotta be in the bathroom, I figure.

Not long after that, my cousin Jim Ed—wearing, I believe, the same blazer from our granddaddy's funeral when I was in sixth grade—asks, Where's your good-looking husband? I'd like to shake his hand.

Jim Ed has retired from coaching football, and he talks about how Daddy had taught him to catch the pigskin two-handed.

My favorite cousin, Peggy Ruth, says, That man of yours oughta try these biscuits I brought.

I know—as my husband does not—that you thumb a hole in a cold biscuit and fill it with a stiff smidge of creamery butter and a lolly gob of cane syrup and bite down so your chin is not spared the squish. And I know that the maple syrup Yankees favor is a paltry stand-in for the burnt-sugar taste you squeeze from sugar cane, whose white inner pulp is sheathed inside purplish-brown bark I can peel with a pocketknife.

And where is Warren, anyway?

Outside, the hundred-degree air is sopping. But someone had seen him in jogging clothes, so I look up and down the road edged with bleached oyster shells. Under mimosa trees,

I cross the neighbor's yard, past the garage where I was raped as a child. I come to the culvert I had on the night of the assault imagined my blue corpse floating in (not because the neighbor boy who was the culprit might have thrown me there, but because part of me knew I was already over).

My silk blouse is wet at the pits, my pencil skirt at the waistband. I long to peel off my pantyhose. Shielding my eyes from the sun, I scan the landscape for Warren's tall form: he's nowhere. I'm not so much pissed that he's vanished, just left town, which—given Mother's penchant for flight—seems feasible even for Warren.

Eventually, we call Lecia's house, and her housekeeper says she let Warren in to shower. He didn't have a car to drive back to my mother's so he stayed on. Hours later, when we come in, he's on the sofa alongside the basketball playoffs with the remote in his hand.

(Did we fight about this? I can't dredge it up. I'd started to mistrust what I wanted, since my therapy at the time involved sifting reasonable wants from the nutty ones rearing up from the past.)

On the plane, Warren and I fly back in a silence that I've learned to copy from him, and since birth offsets the agony of death like nothing else, I carry in me the feverish craving of a woman wanting to lodge some luminescent bubble of baby in my middle.

I take his hand to ask if we can start trying.

We're not really in a financial position yet, he says. Maybe if I wind up taking over the curatorship in a year or two.

He pushes his glasses up his nose and fetches his book from the seat pocket, but I push on, saying, I'm teaching part-time now—a better schedule for a baby. The editing stuff I can do at night.

We haven't even started saving for a house yet.

Why can't your dad help us with a down payment? I ask.

Warren looks out the plane window at the arctic of floofy clouds.

I mean, he could take it from whatever you'll inherit, no?

I doubt I'll inherit anything, he says. There are six children. Just drop it, Mare.

I can't accept the fact that Warren's family ethos reflects Andrew Carnegie's old saw about how inherited money has to be held back at the risk of withering ambition, but I sit in silence.

The plane flies on, carrying us in its hull. Warren stares off into the distance the rich enter when talk of money comes up.

But a woman whose third eye has begun to stare at some invisible baby is incapable of dropping the subject. So at the Labor Day clambake in the Rhode Island beach house—itself four times the size of what I grew up in—after intermittent nagging from me, Warren walks up to the white wicker chair containing his father and asks the old man about helping us when I get pregnant. Only on the drive home will Warren even say aloud that the talk took place. But any details about it stay sealed in that head of his.

He'll help us, Warren says.

The car passes a long stretch of beach roses in bloom.

How? I say.

I don't want to go into it. It's private.

I'm your wife, I say.

At a stoplight before the freeway, he puts the car in park and stares at me, saying, You got what you wanted. Now get off my back.

(Don't think he spoke to me this way often. He didn't, which is why—unfairly—it sticks.)

At that instant, I stop drinking cold turkey. I don't re-member it being hard. In fact, it's the last easy quit I'd have. I give up liquor and cigarettes to purify myself for the baby taking cherubic shape in my head long before my body gets to it.

In some ways, I believe conception will be hard for me. *One of God's little prototypes*, Hunter Thompson once said of some ne'er-do-well pal—*never even considered for mass pro-duction*. I pore over books about getting knocked up as if it weren't standard order for every creature from cat to cock-roach. Warren knows I'm logging my morning temperature, a sharp rise being a sign that you've dropped an egg into the chute. The first slightly overheated morning, it so happens that Hurricane Gloria has ripped down the phone lines on our block and shut down the library. Warren takes the bus home early like a man summoned to battle, and a month later, I miss my period.

Already? he says, staring at me across the huge steaks I've splurged on, the half-empty bottle of nonalcoholic wine.

You're not excited, I say.

He considers the burgundy fizz in the glass. Tastes like grape syrup.

Not about the wine, you bonehead, I say. About the bun in the oven.

Baby Otis? Warren says. It's great.

Pouring him more nonalcoholic wine, I say, You're upset. You're not excited.

He stares across the candlelit table.

No, he says. I mean, yes. It's just . . .

I've Ziploc-bagged the telltale pregnancy thermometer and stuck it in a vase between us, tying it with a ribbon like a daisy. He touches it with a finger as if it might be hot, saying,

How reliable is this? I mean, should you go to the doctor or something?

Despite his slight remove, I think what a perfect dad he'll make, tempered as he is by gentleness. He once quoted to me Henry James's three rules: Be kind, be kind, be kind. I've observed him with his sister's kids, patiently tossing the whiffle ball underhand. They climb into his lap for stories.

But few men—no matter how tenderhearted—go so gaga over the unborn as an inseminated woman will. At night I read one baby book after another, and most spare weekend hours I spend pawing through garage sales for cast-off cribs and baby clothes. And so begins what I see as his slow fade from me. We talk less and less, and since we both grew up in houses schooled to letting people vaporize into their own internal deserts with alacrity, we each let the other get smaller.

At Christmas, his father says he knew I was pregnant when I said no to wine, and many toasts are drunk to my health and the baby's. My mother-in-law promises to ante up all the baby clothes and linens, and Mr. Whitbread says he'll cover my half of the rent. But driving home, Warren's silence fills the car.

What is it? I say.

Nothing, he says. It's nothing.

You're looking at me so sternly, I say. And truly staring at him, I see in his green eyes that some metal doors seemed to have slid shut.

Buckle your seat belt, he says. You need to start wearing a seat belt.

The car continues down the snowy and narrowing road.

I eat: french fries with gravy. Liver with greasy heaps of onions. Dried strawberries smudged with gorgonzola cheese, crackers slathered with fig jam. Stepping on the scale, I hear my doctor admonish that I'll gain fifty pounds if I don't slow down, but I couldn't care less. How proud I feel shoving that giant globe of a belly through the subway turnstile.

But the more heft I have, the more elusive Warren seems to become, the more transparent, retreating into a void I stare into, studying him while he reads, repeatedly poking my head into his office the weekends he works.

Maybe he's having an affair, Mother says. That's how some guys react to fatherhood.

Mother! I say. Warren's not like that.

Has he started drinking more? she asks, adding, His daddy could sure put it away.

Not everybody's a sot, I say. More than two drinks and Warren gets pukey.

One night he leaves a message not to hold dinner, he won't be home till ten. The car pulls into the garage, and he finds me sitting on the back steps.

Where were you? I say, reaching for the stair railing to pull myself up, belly first.

He unfolds from the hatchback, arms laden with books. School, he says.

What school? I say. For what? (Had we really not discussed this? Surely we did, but I don't recall it that way.)

I told you I was starting school for my master's. It's paid for through work.

I thought next fall, after the baby came, I say.

You shouldn't be out here without a coat, he says.

Don't you think it's bad timing? I say.

You're one to talk, he says, gesturing to my belly.

Can you at least not take summer classes? The baby'll come in June.

He sighs. Maybe this year. But I want to get it over with.

During the week, he leaves at eight in the morning, and three nights a week, he gets in after ten. Weekends, he always seems to be working on papers or that literary magazine he cofounded.

Lying next to him, my body swells as if hooked to a bicycle pump, and with each inch of girth, he floats further, and I began slowly to shift my gaze away from his back. I start to stare inward to the pearlescent mystery I'm carrying. Some nights I tell myself the birth will bring Warren back to me.

(And maybe—in his version of events—he'd report that I'd studied baby books with a Talmudic intensity, hardly reading anymore the poetry he was devoted to. The bigger I got, the lower my IQ, I swear. It's not politic to say so, but hey. Maybe Warren was telling himself the birth would bring me back to him.)

One day, as I meticulously fold and refold minuscule T-shirts and onesies in the trance of the deeply unprepared, the phone rings. And a woman's voice says the sentence I've been waiting to hear for so long, I'm almost deaf to it. So obsessed am I with the upcoming birth that she has to repeat it several times.

I said that we'd like to publish your book of poems.

Okay, I say, having become a farm animal at this point. With the phone to my ear, I slide the top off a box of chocolates my sister sent and start poking them in search of caramel.

What do you mean, *Okay*? the editor says. We'd like to publish your book next year.

That's good, I say, poking as one piece gushes white goop, so I pass over it.

You don't sound very excited, she says.

I'm having a baby, I say dreamily. And truly the notion of a book has grown misty.

Right this second?

Soon, I say. At that instant, my fingernail punctures chocolate and hits caramel. What does she need from me? The names of anybody dumb enough to blurb it. A dust-jacket photo laying around.

I chew my caramel, satisfied as a brood sow in a mud wallow. Neither good nor ill can reach me.

15

Journey of the Magi

Who is there?
I.
Who is I?
Thou.
And that is the awakening—the Thou and the I.
— PAUL VALÉRY

Women in my bloodline don't pop out babies like pieces of toast. We're narrow-hipped. Birthing tends to drag on— long days of false labor followed by a good twenty hours of exorcism-quality dismay. We're less known for patience than drive, and being flat on our back is anathema. Lecia's own son took so long to find daylight that his father—during a grisly period called *transition* that involves much howling— excused himself, sending Mother into the room as backup. Lecia had been cursing him and God and most of the nurses.

Mother stood bedside a few minutes, then—as Lecia huffed for air—held up her handbag, saying, Look at this cute little purse I bought.

At which, my sister screamed, Get her the fuck out of here!

Mother, later outraged at Lecia's overreaction, said, I was just trying to take her mind off it.

In my case, delivery takes a full twenty-two hours—forty-four if you count the false labor that kept me manically rocking in a chair all night like some bulbous figure in a horror movie. At the hospital, they inject various mickeys into my IV, telling me I'll be asleep in a minute, but that's only one of many lies—like banning the word *pain* in favor of *discomfort*, conveniently reducing the hospital's need to deal with it while treating the mother like a piece of furniture.

In natural childbirth classes, with women sprawled around the room on wrestling mats, the men had seemed mystified by the process. One night in the car going home, Warren said, When are we supposed to learn the stuff that stops the pain?

We already have, I said. That's what the breathing exercises are.

My God, he said, that won't accomplish anything.

Almost two days into my own marathon, I enter the half-drugged, hallucinogenic state that causes the room I lie in to bulge like a fishbowl around me. Staring at the calico curtains hung against the vomit-green walls to make the birthing room look *homey*, I keep echoing Oscar Wilde's last words: *Either this wallpaper goes, or I do.*

The big disappointment? The needle painfully jabbed into my spine to block pain quote-unquote *didn't take.*

This is the breezy parlance of the anesthesia dude. He stands in the door with clip-on sunglasses flipped up from his specs. He's clearly on his way out.

Whaddayou *mean*, I roar at him, whaddayou MEAN it *didn't take!*

I'm incapable of speaking without exclamation points and italics and any available typographical inflation. In between cogent sentences, the nurse with the tiny white head and gargantuan blue eyes—real crocodile-sized peepers—leans over me, saying, *Breathe . . .*

Warren's head appears alongside hers, his face bulging forward like a drop of water squeezed from a turkey baster. *Breathe . . .*

I holler, DO IT AGAIN!

The nurse is telling me it's too late.

You didn't say it *might not take*, I say. You said . . . You *promised . . .* You PROMISED I'd be *numb* from the WAIST DOWN!!

I bang on a thigh. My LEG is like a *rump roast!!*

Not much later, Warren's face leans down through the haze, saying, I need a sandwich.

WHAT! I say. A *fucking SANDWICH?*

It won't take long, he says. He's gone for what seems a long stretch but can't be even an hour.

He comes back just as they start wheeling me spread-eagled and undraped down a public hall, with me saying, *No man gets to see this who hasn't bought me dinner*—a joke the doctor doesn't get, followed by, to Warren, *Where the everloving fuck were you?*

Sleeping, it turns out, on the front lawn of the hospital after a turkey sandwich. He's now loping alongside my gurney toward the delivery room, his face masked.

An eternity later, I feel a cataclysmic movement, and—in one massive thunderclap of pain—all my innards seem to exit. I feel abruptly vacated. Warren shouts up at me, It's a boy. I lie there throbbing while some space bar in the action gets hit, and there's an interval of quiet, then the baby's throaty cry. All the attending humans seem busily focused elsewhere till they hand Dev to me—short for Devereux—a family name of the Whitbread's. This new Dev is squinty and crimson, and they've stretched a little white knit cap on his head.

As he leans over me, Warren's face is damp, too, and his ocean-lit eyes fixed on me with wondrous attention, and in that interval I first hold our bundled son, I feel us all stitched inside a glorious tapestry, breathing the same antiseptic air, cool as pine—a rare atmosphere conscribes us—the family I've pined for, an end to the perennial estrangement I've powered through the world running from. Warren and I both address Dev in coos and smooches and clicks.

Dev squints up with dark blue eyes as if trying to make us out through smoke, and from the instant his gaze brushes by me, some inner high beams flip on. Never have I felt such blazing focus for another living creature. I can't stop looking at him. Joy, it is, which I've never known before, only pleasure or excitement. Joy is a different thing, because its focus exists outside the self—delight in something external, not satisfaction of some inner craving. I feel such untrammeled love for these two beings.

Back in my room, the nurse hands Dev to me again, and boy, is he hollering to blow the hair off your head.

This one has a set of lungs, the nurse says, and a strong opinion.

But soon as I open my seersucker gown to his velvety face, the crying snaps off. Dev nuzzles toward the only spot on my body soft enough to accommodate him, and blessed silence ensues.

Look at him latch on, Warren says.

My hand cups the duck-fuzzed head—such a strong pulse against my hand, faster than my own, but they syncopate somehow like tom-toms from far off villages.

The pediatric nurse says, This one's what we call a sucky baby.

I finally ask, What do you think he's thinking?

You know the static channel on the TV? she says.

It's almost like he knows you, Warren says.

The nurse says, I think they can smell their mothers.

I smooch his little hand, cooing, You're my crème brûlée, my chocolate shake, my bear claw. You're my—in a flash, I think of my daddy snuggling the white cat he once so spoiled—boon companion.

With Dev tucked under my arm, I set to staring at him as if to emboss my gaze on him, to seal him in the safe bubble of it, and so also to sear into my own head every iota of him.

Warren comments that he does look an awful lot like Winston Churchill. Put a cigar in his mouth . . .

Bite your tongue, I say. At some point the woman in the next bed comes over to show us her boy, and when she peels aside the blanket to reveal his face, I have to stop my own recoil, for that is one unfortunate-looking baby.

He's cute, Warren says.

This kid has a face like a caved-in squash. His full head of hair lends him a werewolf aspect. My plump, pink-cheeked, bald-as-a-bubble infant sets the standard against which all others will come up short.

I sit there with a smile welded on my face till the werewolf baby starts to sputter neurasthenically, *Ehh . . . ehhh ehhh . . .*

The woman looks up at us, saying, Time to nurse.

If Dev, who wails like a freight train when hungry, made no more noise than that, he'd starve.

I'm tired, Warren says, though his handsome face holds nary a crease. Bone-weary, I let him peel my clingy hand off his biceps to extract himself.

16

Postal Partum

*Let him be happy from time to
time, and leap over abysses.*
—WISLAWA SZYMBORSKA, "A TALE BEGUN"
(TRANS. STANISLAV BARANCZAK)

You think having a baby is a big dang accomplishment, and the nurses smile, and the doctor seems distractedly glad, and you're lying there not even minding overmuch how you're torn from stem to stern because you're so proud to have laid your egg, then the nurse comes in and hands you a round plastic pee catcher shaped like a matador's hat—itself piss-yellow in color—to sit over the toilet seat, for really, all anybody in the hospital wants you to do is pee. Forget the baby, that's all anybody's waiting for: You pee, you go home.

I couldn't. It's an indelicate thing to have to confess, but the long labor had distended my bladder or hurt my urethra's muscle tone or blah blah blah. They give me a pee bag and a catheter, but since the gallons of IV fluid they'd pumped into me over more than a day had seeped into my tissues, I stay swollen like a prize pig. People on the ward ask me more than once when I'm due, which shocks me, for without my baby bump, I feel lithe as Miss America, puzzled when my old skinny jeans can't shimmy over my dimpled knee.

The doctor stares at his clipboard, saying, It happens with incompetent labor.

Or a doctor's incompetent delivery, I snap.

Mare! Warren says.

Why can't you stick up for me? I burst out. I'm tired and sore, and my abruptly massive boobs have hardened into bricks as the milk floods in.

Mare, *incompetent*'s a medical term, not personal disparagement.

Spoken like a man who went home and slept all night, I say, dabbing at my eyes.

The doctor predicts it might be a day or two until I can pee, and they'll keep me till then. He shakes Warren's hand and leaves the room, and Warren announces—almost in passing—that he's taken his paternity leave that week. Problem being, when the baby and I come home, I'll fly solo.

All right, I say—what choice do I have, and so besotted am I with the baby, I almost don't care—I'll get Mother to come.

At the bank of elevators, Warren pushes the button. I sit in my wheelchair with the geriatic pee bag taped to my leg and our squinty son in my arms. The silver door slides open.

Hold the elevator, a voice cries out, and from behind us skitters up a couple from our natural childbirth class.

Warren moves aside while they get on. The new mom has

a paper cone of roses in her lap, and the grandmother holds the baby while the grandfather videotapes the whole thing.

Wave goodbye to your first home, Spenser, Grandpa says.

The grandmother flaps Spencer's limp paw.

While Warren holds the door for them, I ask him when he'll be back.

Tomorrow about five.

The doors begin to close.

Wait, I say. Why so late?

The elevator door's black rubber bumper stops mid-bounce against Warren's hand.

He says, Visiting hours are five to seven.

Not for dads, I say.

But the silver doors have shut him away. And I know Warren will come religiously from five till seven—never a minute longer. (To be fair to Warren, not yet thirty, he must've been shocked, as men often are—and the younger, the more shocked—by the dreamy looks their previously income-generating wives get when staring at some dumb hunks of baby.)

With Dev, my every practical impulse has snapped off like a spigot turned tight. So what if I'm invisible to Warren or he to me? My rent's paid. I have my boy. In six weeks, I'll start to teach three days per week, three or four classes per day. No other fact sinks in.

Sitting in my room the next night, after Warren's brief, distracted visit, I feed the baby out of some gleaming core inside. It's you and me, Dev, I say, which solitude is—in some ways—familiar. At least now I have a small sack of infant to cuddle with, a boy molded from silk and cream whose howling cares vanish soon as I take him in my arms.

For seven days, I stay catheterized in the hospital. In seven days, the Bible tells us, God made the world, but I fail to release my pent-up urine. Eventually, the insurance company starts to squawk, and while the doctor doesn't like sending me home with a bag strapped to my leg, they figure I can get up every morning after breastfeeding all night, load the baby into the car seat with diapers and changes of clothes and miscellaneous crap. I can drive to the clinic, get on the table, have the catheter taken out, then wait, breastfeeding in the hall, till four to see if I can relieve myself of urine before then getting recatheterized— a length of flaming skewer slid into my body's rawest corridor.

Warren seems hardly to register any of this, sleeping every night unperturbed downstairs. Every hour and a half or two, Dev squawks, and I stagger to his crib, change his diaper, latch him to one breast then another, burp him, swaddle him. Then back in my solitary bed, steal an hour or two of sleep before Dev eats again. Born three weeks early it's as if he's trying to catch up, he just needs to be bigger than my scrawny body could tote. (He grew at twice the normal rate, and I'd have been smarter nursing him in the bed, but I'd been warned—ironically—that it'd ruin my marriage.)

Maybe I don't resent Warren more because he's the only author of relief for me. He walks in the door like clockwork every day at six, the hour Dev inexplicably begins to holler as if being bullwhipped. And only Warren loves him enough to advance toward that flaming shriek.

What's wrong with him? Warren says, taking him from me, handling him like rare glass.

He's clearly unhappy here, I say.

As Warren folds the boy to his body, I enter the only certain stretch of rest in my day.

Hold his head, I say. It's damp. Maybe tuck this blanket around him. Bring an umbrella in case it starts to mist. And when you change him, use the white cream.

I've got him, Mare. Just let me do it.

I plod back up the stairs and pitch forward, imploding in a black-brained sleep.

Around eleven, the door swings wide, and Warren lays Dev in my arms before tiptoeing downstairs to his pallet in the living room, where the white-fog machine throws up each night a wall of noise beyond which we don't exist. He's working, going to grad school full-time. I have to breastfeed anyway, the argument goes.

Then Mother flies up to help, a sober mother who sees frying chicken and assembling lasagna as a way to mend all the chaos she'd brought in the thirty years prior. All my life, she lived in a state of irritation predicated on either drinking too much or not having drunk enough. Never (is this true?) did I lie in bed and have her cook for me. As a child, when I got measles and chickenpox, she'd announce, I just don't like sick people, leaving me feverishly staring at the TV's flickering grown-ups.

On this trip, Mother is transformed. She goes with me to the clinic every day, helping me load the baby in the car. Most evenings she brings my dinner steaming from a tray—doughy dumplings in oniony broth, chicken collapsed off its bones, turnip greens with fatback. Afternoons, she lies in bed with me, the baby between us kicking his covers off as I gaze at him.

Mary, I believe you're gonna stare the skin off him, she says.

Sober she might be, but she's still capricious as a cat. After about a week, when I've gotten used to counting on her, she disappears one day. I'd run out of diapers, and she'd rushed heroically off to the store. Her first hour away, I figure she got lost. An hour later, I decide she's had a car wreck. An hour after that, I know she's dead or stopped at a bar somewhere, so I wrap Dev's bare ass in a towel held together by duct tape and lug him to the market in a stroller, finding no sign of our car in the lot.

Late that afternoon Mother prances in with brochures for tours of Russia and China. She is—miraculously enough—cold sober. But she met a man at a travel agency next to the grocery store, and he took her to lunch and to see the glass flowers at the Harvard Museum. By then she's built up enough goodwill during the visit that I let it slide.

My therapist later reminds me that, however sober, Mother will forever be a haphazard fetcher of necessary items. Treat her more like a five-year-old, the therapist says, which method starts shaping expectations to the right size.

Meanwhile, the catheter that's been in place for weeks has chafed till there's blood in the piss bag, fire running through my ripped-up undercarriage. After a full month of daily drives to the clinic, I insist they teach me how to catheterize myself—it's not rocket science, after all. They send me home with a bottle of betadyne and sterile gauze and a bag of glass catheters. Within a day or two—maybe after a respite from the nonstop irritation of the catheter—I start relieving myself like all the other girls.

Which is Mother's cue to leave. Why? She's sick of it, no more complicated than that. Right before she takes off, she walks in on me sobbing. Aw, she says, and she sets down the tray and takes my hand in her silky hand, asking, What is it, baby?

I don't have enough milk tonight. I got up and worked on my classes for fall, and maybe I didn't drink enough water today. But he's still hungry.

Dev's starting to twist his head alongside me, building up to burst into wails, I can tell.

Let me give him a bottle of formula, Mother says. You need the break. He might even sleep a little longer tonight.

I start to cry full throttle at the mention of it, for the bottle is a badge of failure among young mothers.

Let me keep him tonight, she says. Please. I'll keep him down with me in the dining room.

The thought of uninterrupted sleep glows in my head, and while my better instincts say she's inclined to all manner of caprice, I make her swear she'll wake me if there's any need or he won't quiet.

Then I sail off into a sleep that unrolls in my head endless bolts of black velvet.

My boobs wake me up, leaking breast milk. I lie in the damp they'd made. Across my legs is a fresh river of sun. In the elm trees off our balcony, loud black crows caw. I right myself and get my bearings in the sunny room. I hear noise downstairs and feel my way to the stair landing where I can hear the baby's morning squeaks.

I tiptoe down the carpeted stairs, then peek in to see Mother cradling Dev, saying, Old Blue Eyes, that's what Grandma Charlie's gonna call you. And when you get ready, you come down. You ain't never had no fun till you get to my house. . . .

In some way, that tender tone obliterates decades of psychic carnage between us, though Mother's pending departure recarves an ancient ache in me. She tells me our family threesome will never really knit together till she clears out and Warren comes back to our bed. However polite their exchanges, he absents himself more with her here.

She's at the grocery store one day when Warren is sponge-bathing the baby in a little rubber inner-tube tub in the kitchen sink. Before, I've supervised the project with the hovering posture of a vulture over a carcass. This time I've been warned off, but I nonetheless busily fold the warm laundry in the kitchen within sight. While ladling warm water over the baby's belly, Warren recites a goofy limerick he's written, using the husky tone he'd previously reserved for a retriever:

> *There once was a boy named Rotundi,*
> *Who sailed into the Bay of Fundi*
> *Said a fish by his side*
> *My goodness, you're wide,*
> *He said, Yes, that's cause I'm always hun-gee.*

That's darling, I say. Did you write that?

He says yes, and I listen to Dev's feet kick with spastic flailing. His pudgy arm flies before his eyes, and he tries to focus on it, puzzled. *Whazzat?* his look says.

Is the water too hot? I say.

It's body temperature, just like you said.

Don't yell in front of him, I say.

I'm not yelling, he says, I'm trying to take care of my son without you hounding me.

Dev's arm flies by his face again, and he startles as if thinking, *There it goes again!*

You really adore him, I say.

Warren looks at me. Of course, I do, he says, he's my son.

(Was this tone matter-of-fact or territorial? Did I—in my postpartum weariness—impose the most negative slant? Toward me, he tightened every line, which opposed the shining face he brought to the baby.)

I'm leaving you a warm towel here, I say. It's got a little hood.

For God's sake.

Well, you have to keep his head warm.

Goddamn it, Mare. Just go upstairs.

On the stairwell, I overhear another of Warren's compositions:

> *I really like my mother.*
> *I wouldn't have another.*
> *My father is a very special guy.*

Dev makes a chortling noise.

> *My head is made of rubber.*
> *My body's made of blubber.*
> *When I step into the tubber*
> *It's high tide.*

That night before supper, I ask Warren again when he plans to move back into our bed. He says, Once he's on a regular schedule.

He's on a regular schedule. He's up all night. I'm up all night.

I can't be up all night and work all day, he says. Classes are starting.

I miss you, I say.

I'm here every second, he says—every instant I'm not at work, I'm here.

Here but not here, I say.

At one point, at wits' end about not sleeping, I call up Mrs. Whitbread, who'd after all raised six children. What did she recommend?

It was so different in those days, darling, she says.

When she speaks, I clutch the black receiver, for her voice conjures clipped lawns under maple trees, the easeful life of

Scott Fitzgerald's Daisy—men in linen suits and women in billowy pastels, pitchers of lemonade on silver trays. I wasn't entitled to any of that, of course, but the whiff of it lent me glancing courage.

She says, Everybody had help. If one of them wouldn't sleep, I'd let the nurse take the baby home till he got on a good schedule. Or, she says thoughtfully, I'd give them a little phenobarbital.

Shortly before Mother takes off, she comes creaking up the stairs early one night with two bottles of beer and a frosted mug. They do not yet glow for I've been off the sauce for a year and am so besotted with Dev that drinking's been forgotten.

She pours the golden mixture down the side of the tilted glass, saying, This'll help your milk let down.

I say, I thought you were anti-booze.

Even my religious cousin Delores, she says, drank beer when she was nursing. She actually had to pinch her nose to get it down.

The fizzy sip tastes of roasted grain, tidy fields waving in wind. By the second or third sip, I remember the slosh of lake water against a boat Daddy had rented, how I sipped from a metal can of Lone Star while he picked through lures alongside me. Thus starts—for healing purposes, of course—my daily beer or two.

Within weeks, I stop breastfeeding, partly because I know three or four or five beers could affect Dev's milk supply. Warren's at school, so he must miss these escalating beer guzzles.

And that's how—in some cosmic accounting of our family's rampant dipsomania—Mother's recovery dovetailed with the start of my own years' long binge, for from that day forward, I drank in increasing amounts, as if our gene pool owed the universe at least one worthless drunk at a time.

17

No Mom Is an Island

I was always waiting, always there.
Know anyone else who can say that.
　　　　　　—FRANZ WRIGHT, "ALCOHOL"

Through the baby monitor comes a single raspy cough. It barely pierces the heavy sleep that wraps my skull in sodden layers of papier-mâché. Static follows, then a tinny whimper. I fold one pillow over my head. Another gets tucked in my concavities. The husband's long body unrolls. The white noise machine he's installed to block out all disturbance makes the brain-sucking racket of a dentist's drain. It vacuums all consciousness from my head. Sleep.

Till a doubled cough punctures my head like two shots from a nail gun. I blink my eyes open to the room, immaculately black as he likes it, but for the faint luminosity of the upraised clock hands (2:50) and the tiny red snake eye of the monitor. I fix on it to stop my mind's inward roiling vertigo an instant—a marble looping around a barrel.

My head is grinding out bad news: *That bruise on your shin is bone cancer. . . .* But one glance at the husband's profile, and I flash on my only happy thought for weeks, the smooth moonstone of an idea. If I had a rubber bladder under my pillow—the kind that cartoon characters whip from their sleeves—I could muster the strength to rear up and whack him vigorously about the head. My mouth creaks toward a smile at the prospect, since his sleep has been unbroken now for almost a year. I gaze at him from under the pillow like a rattler under a rock.

A swerving comet's tail of silence issues from the monitor. I let my eyes seal shut, then inwardly tumble back down the black tunnel of oblivion that's my one aspiration.

During my teetotaling pregnancy, when my hormonal stupor must've helped me sober up cold turkey, I envisioned these night wakings as if sprinkled with fairy dust. Hearing baby gurgle and coo, I'd leap up to float—smiling and moonlit and brimming with breast milk—in frothy gown to the crib in the next room,

Three gasping coughs in rapid succession, rat-a-tat-tat. I blink at the clock hands (2:58). Silence.

I'll get up, my husband says. His muscular arm starts to feel around the night table for his glasses.

To which a sane woman with classes to teach tomorrow would've said, *Thanks, hon*, as she sank back into slumbering meadows. He offers again, and again I say no, which is not—as I mean him to think it is—concern for his obligations. Nor is it maternal love for my blond and improbably blue-eyed toddler, just old enough to be lurching around the coffee table, chortling with every stumpy step. I tell the husband

I've got it because it ticks another plus sign in my column in this game of shit-eating I have composed my marriage to be. Whoever eats the biggest shit sandwich wins, and I'm playing to justify the fact that I'd rather drink than love.

The times Dev's spiked a fever, I shook Warren awake and—fearing meningitis—we tore to Children's Hospital. With medicine, it'd take Dev a week or so to stop coughing himself awake most nights. Then a week to stop nightly wakings, then here came the next cold, invariably flaming into a fever. The doctors agree the infections and fevers are strange but not unheard of. By every yardstick, my strapping son is a developmental champ. His bounce is boundless, but my limbs are filled with lead pellets, and my head has started to scramble like an anthill.

Another series of whooping lands a hammer blow to my sternum, and I jerk upright. It's the reflexive, automatic move from some gore-fest movie—that last scene when the butchered killer you think has finally bitten it jolts up. My arm wheels over to smack off the baby monitor. Then, lacking the will to rise (3:07), I plummet back down like a shot bird.

The cough penetrates my dream with the sandpapered force of a chain-smoking speed freak. It's Daddy's pneumonia-laden cough, Mother's emphysema wheeze. Even without the monitor, I can hear the hacking gasps start. My body's a sandbag, but my eyelids split open like clam shells (3:10). On the table, a tumbler of mahogany whiskey burns bright as any flaming oil slick. Gone a little watery on top, it's still possessed of a golden nimbus.

That's the secret to getting up: the glass talks and my neck cranes toward the drink like flower to sunbeam. My heavy skull rises, throbbing with a pulse beat. I grab the drink and let a long gulp burn a corridor through the sludge that runs up the middle of me—that trace of fire my sole brightness. A drink once brought ease, a bronze warmth spreading through all my muddy regions. Now it only brings a brief respite from the bone ache of craving it, no more delicious numbness.

Slurping these spirits is soul preparation, a warped communion, myself serving as god, priest, and congregation. I rise on rickety legs, dripping sweat despite the air conditioner's blast across my naked chest. Forgoing bathrobe, I pull on a wife-beater T-shirt. (3:15!)

In the next room, my son, stout but saggy-kneed, clings to the crib bars like a prisoner. Menthol steam from the vaporizer has made a ghost of him. His ringlets are plastered to his head, and coughs rack his small frame. The animal suffering that's rattling him throws ice water on me, and I enjoy a surge of unalloyed love for him, followed by panic, followed by guilt.

He sees me rushing toward him and abruptly drops his outstretched arms an instant to say, No pants? His head's tilted with bald curiosity.

Which cracks me up, and he laughs till the coughs start exploding through him again, by which point I've cleaved him to me, both of us sweating. His diaper's sagging from the vaporizer's work, but fresh steam is his lifeline. Carrying him to the bathroom, I crank on the shower.

But before I change him, before I squirt the syrupy acetaminophen into his mouth, I haul him whooping down the stairs to the kitchen. I open the stove where a near empty bottle of Jack Daniels squats like the proverbial troll under the bridge. Needing neither glass nor ice, I press my lips to the cool mouth, and it blows into my lungs so I can keep on.

PART III
Self Help

It would be good to feel good about yourself for good.

—WILLIAM MATTHEWS, "SELF HELP"

Unless a film of flesh envelops us, we die. Man exists only insofar as he is separated from his surroundings. The cranium is a space traveler's helmet. Stay inside or you perish. Death is divestment, death is communion. It may be wonderful to mix with the landscape, but to do so is the end of the tender ego.

—VLADIMIR NABOKOV, *PNIN*

18

Ivy Beleaguered

Monday
Me.
Tuesday
Me.
Wednesday
Me.
Thursday
Me.

—WITOLD GOMBROWICZ, *DIARY*

In my thirty-fourth year to heaven, I find myself at the copy machine of an exalted, ivy-embroidered university, pressing down on the spine of a memoir by Vladimir Nabokov. The green light under my hands slides over the book's face, and the spillage from the edges scalds through my shut eyelids.

It's seven-thirty a.m., and I can feel the corpse tint of my face: Frankenstein-monster green. The machine goes *whap . . . whap* at slower intervals than the throb in my head, which sounds like *thunk*. The *whaps* stab me. The *thunks* make my eyes bulge in their sockets like a squeezed rubber doll's.

It's my first year teaching six classes, which has freed me from the deeply respectable but non-writer-esque telecom consulting I could spend eighty hours a week at. Not a new-mom job by any stretch, that work. The sole vestige of the career? I'm on retainer freelancing for a business mag whose editor has left two strongly worded messages on our machine. I'm late with my article on the new Russian perestroika.

Whap . . . thunk.

The image of my blond three years' son this morning, sob-bing and holding out his arms to me while Warren strapped him into the child seat, is a hot stove I can't stop touching.

Warren drops him off at daycare now for reasons that are complex.

Sure, I need to get in early to copy course materials illicitly—an infraction the secretary, who comes in at nine—warned adjunct teachers about back in the August training session, copies being too costly for the sniveling, no-hope-of-tenure human I am.

Also, on the snowy road here some mornings, I stop to puke out the car door, releasing into a snow bank an acidic coffee bile that stays on my teeth despite brushing vigor-ously enough to bloody my gums, leaving a bile taste no mint can mask. At the daycare center, mommy-vomiting is frowned on.

But even if I didn't want to vomit before I got to the day-care center—which resembles a modest colonial parson's house like in *The Scarlet Letter*—the perky bustle of the place would incline me in a vomitous direction.

The last time I did the morning dropoff was right after

Christmas break. The director had waved me into her office, walls tacked with the bespattered finger paintings of Harvard's budding geniuses. I'd sat on a stiff chair while she told me Dev was so anxious he couldn't fall asleep at naptime.

Is everything okay at home? she asked. She had front teeth like fence pickets, and the reflection on her octagonal wire-rims was my puffy face.

Of course everything was great. I was great and my husband was great. Happiness was the currency we paid to get our kid accepted here.

So I failed to tell her that my husband and I had barely spoken that week, and sometimes, before I made dinner, I considered dousing the oven's pilot light and sticking my head in. Or that—driving to my in-laws' for Christmas dinner—I'd risen at four, ostensibly to bake pies but actually to drive around the local reservoir, finishing a six-pack of beer while listening to Argentine tangos.

Wheeling in tight rings at about sixty around the local reservoir—night smearing across the windows as the tangos unrolled—I'd felt myself circling my marriage and being erased with each rotation. Around and around my head I went. My longed-for circle of family is choking me. The silk bow ties on my cheap business blouses—that middle-class disguise I'd wished for—are choking me. The good family name for my son is a strangle, since it forces me to drive with a restless kid hours in murderous traffic to dine with polite people who never, not in decades, stop being strangers. I'd never have let on when Warren and I married how it tickled me to see our names in the Social Registry, an attitude I now despise in myself, and my sole act of penance had been agreeing with Warren to take us out.

During the war-zone months of early infancy when Warren slept, it was as if every hour of sleep I lost, he'd stolen.

Now I've placed Warren at the radiant center of my misery, no longer comrade but capo. We've devolved into a cold war with a child-centered détente.

Whap . . . thunk. The scanning light casts my face the color of ectoplasm in horror films.

Plus, just thinking about the easeful, educated parents at daycare makes my throat sour. Walking up the tree-lined boulevard toward the center always brings out my inner Igor.

I often run into Wincing Evan, so called because of the flinch—bordering on a Tourette's-like seizure—he goes into whenever he spots Dev and me approaching. Head down, he'll actually scamper across the street to avoid saying hello.

In some ways, Evan is a figure of the type I aspire to cut. He translates (let's say) Gogol. He publishes in *The New York Review of Books* and abroad. Unlike the blocky Boston bankers who abound in Harvard Square, he cruises in for Parents' Day wearing a fluid flannel coat with French tailoring, for he and his professor wife (a comp-lit professor whose easy red-lipped smile could've sold lipstick) summer overseas often enough to use *summer* as a verb.

Their immaculately turned-out son—Jonathan, age under four years—has shining hair and a good start on French and German. He's a chess player with a princely manner. I swear if his voice were a little deeper, he could join the diplomatic corps.

I once saw Dev, whose sandwich that day was, as most days, a peon's peanut butter and jelly, try to urge Jonathan into swapping lunches. Young Jonathan peeled back one corner of his seven-grain bread carefully enough not to break the crust. Dev peered in. Jonathan said, Mine is brie and kiwi fruit.

Dev reached for it, and Jonathan cupped one hand around it. It has less sugar than yours. His next sentence was so remarkable, I noted it down in my journal: I first had this sandwich in Vienna. . . .

Perhaps Evan's flinch stemmed from the day Dev had elected to yank Jonathan's mittens from his coat pocket, bolt up the stairs while Evan and Warren chased after him, and fling them into the toilet.

Warren fished them out with a pencil and offered to launder them. When I got the ziploc bag from my husband, I tossed the mittens into the trash among the potato peelings. I just didn't want to deal with them—or the whole starchy Cambridge milieu.

So the mittens stop me dropping Dev off, or the puking. My head spends much of its day pumping out reasons for not doing what I should the way a magician draws long strings of scarves from a sleeve. Warren drops him now, an act that brings him endless praise. How great, the teachers say every day when I fetch Dev, that Warren drops him off!

And isn't it great that I pick him up? Then spend all day and night with him? I once asked.

From their stunned expressions, I could guess that it wasn't. Not so much.

About once a week Warren asks for the laundered mittens, and I pretend to rummage around before wandering away, giving in to my failure as a laundress—read: mother.

The other couples in the center look so blithe. They plead academic poverty but drive swanky foreign cars and live sweatered in cashmere. They take family vacations in beachy climes with grandparents who plunk seashells into buckets their toddler grandchildren tote while the couple slips off to the local bookstore or bakery to canoodle over steaming coffee.

Our nearest grandparents are assiduously hands-off. Though Mrs. Whitbread had cranked out six kids like linked hot dogs, Warren's upbringing was almost Victorian in its chill. By his testament, he'd been presented from time to time like a petit four, scrubbed up and bathrobed before bedtime for kisses. Otherwise, he'd been banished to a gulag nursery guarded by some icy servant.

During our own requisite holidays at the great house, we spent hours chasing Dev through rooms big as skating rinks packed with costly breakables, which we weren't allowed to move out of kid reach. A sofa lined with antique dolls stared at Dev with insouciant porcelain faces he squirmed in my arms to get at. Once, from exhausted spite, I let him smash one.

As for Mr. Whitbread, he seemed to eye Dev's festive ramblings as he might have a cockroach's. He once made the boy cry by calling him—beyond my earshot, of course—*an ignorant little crud.* Dev's teary response, which Warren reported—*You're a big fat man with a red nose*—proved Dev had enough Texan in him to take the patriarch in a verbal tussle.

Other couples in our orbit had such easeful abundance inside their families. One took a pensione in Rome owned by somebody's aunt who's married to Lord Suck-on-This of the foreign service. Another woman's uncle gave her a house down payment.

It's the most amazing piece of luck . . .

It's not luck! I want to scream. You're rich! You're rich, and your parents are rich. Of course the Whitbreads were, too, and none of them ever had a cavity that ached in the mouth like a rotted cypress stump for weeks on end. Nor did they have to scrounge nursery furniture from a garage sale. The only clothes Dev gets are handed down from my sister's kid.

That Lecia sends her son's outgrown slick leather jackets and that fancy loafers come free never strikes me as fortune.

Nor does my subsidized rent. Nor the fancy Harvard doctors Dev has through Warren's job. Nor the Minks' ongoing calls and letters. I have a gaze that blanks out luck any time I face it, like a black box over the eyes of a porn star.

Whap and *thunk*. I compose my Christmas list for my in-laws, who always give exactly what you ask for—nothing more, nothing less. This year I've asked for a crockpot, but I secretly long for a Smith & Wesson.

The machine jams. I resist the urge to step back five yards and head-butt it repeatedly. By fumbling around on the side, I locate some kind of handle and pull. I stare at the machine's innards. For one thousand years I could ponder here before any useful action cameto me.

There appears behind me a young poet with tortoiseshell glasses and a striped scarf. He's a real professor with the right to get his copies done, so he knows how to clear the machine jam with a few arcane moves. It hums to life again.

Celery-green light starts sliding across my face, and I can feel how massive my pores must look—real moon craters.

Exfoliate, I think. When did I last exfoliate? Buy a scrub or grind up some almonds—was it almonds?

An autodidact from a poor Irish family, yards smarter than I am, this young prof sports the countenance of an choirboy.

You can jump in, I say. But he says I should go ahead before the secretary gets in and runs me off.

Then he asks when my poetry book will be out, and it's like he's bringing up a wart or goiter I've secretly had taken off, since the book came out two years ago, with grossly underwhelming response. Even I barely noticed, being stuck in the muddy trench of Dev's sleepless infancy when the box hit the porch. Tearing it open, I'd lifted a copy, thumbed it, and tried to tell myself it was some worthy stone added to poetry's great mountain. But I hid it out of eyeshot in my study—the sight of it made me sick.

First books rarely get the attention they deserve, the other poet says with a kind look.

I explain that virtually all copies sold were, I'm guessing, bought by my sister, who gave twenty or thirty for Christmas that year.

He tells me the story of a writer who—on finding his own first book remaindered in a used bookstore—opened to the flyleaf only to discover his own signature above the note *To Mum and Dad. . . .*

He gestures behind me, where the secretary is making her way up the hall, and I grab my armload of contraband copies before scuttling off like a burglar with the house silver.

A few people are starting to trickle through the halls, and I seize up, overcome with a sense of inadequacy to teach anybody anything. I simply can't be the only dumb person in this place one more instant. Before I can stop myself, I loudly say, Let's start a contest for who hasn't read the most important book. I raise my hand like a testifying evangelist to shout, I haven't read Spenser's *Faerie Queene*. Who hasn't read a greater book?

A friend pokes his head from an office, yelling, I never read *Moby-Dick*.

Somebody behind me says, I haven't read Byron's *Don Juan*.

A passing scholar corrects the pronunciation to what I guess must be super-anglicized Oxfordese, saying, *Don Jew-wan*.

Pompous effing fop, I think. You should be shot.

Another voice hasn't read a word by Virginia Woolf. Students are starting to gape.

Later, in my shared cubicle along a line of hissing radiators, I spread dozens of copies and start assembly-line stapling Mr. Nabokov's memoir, the sentences I once worshipped now streaming in a hieroglyphic blur off my eyeballs, flooding me with gall.

19

The Mokus Squirreliness
of the Unmet Mind

> *. . . oh how oddly*
> *the drinker seems*
> *to withdraw*
> *from the act of drinking.*
> —RAINER MARIA RILKE, "SECOND ELEGY"
> (TRANS. DAVID YOUNG)

I keep getting drunk. There's no more interesting way to say it. Only drunk does the volume crank down. Liquor no longer lets me bullshit myself that I'm taller, faster, funnier. Instead, it shrinks me to a plodding zombie state in which one day smudges into every other—it blurs time.

Swaying on the back landing in the small hours, I stare at the boxy garage and ghostly replicas of it multiplying along either side, like playing cards spread against the slate sky. Though this plural perspective is standard, I'm surprised by my own shitfaced state. The walkman sends punk rock banging across the tiny bones of my ears. And with the phonebook-sized stack of papers on my lap still unmarked, I—once more, with feeling—take the pledge to quit drinking. Cross my heart. Pinky swear to myself. This is it, I say, the last night I sit here.

Okay, I say in my head. I give. You're right. (Who am I talking to? Fighting with?)

By the next afternoon, while I'm lugging the third armload of groceries up the back stairs, Dev, who's bolted ahead to the living room, shrieks like he's been stabbed, and I drop the sack on the kitchen floor, hearing as it hits what must be a jar of tomato sauce detonating. In the living room, I find Dev has leaped—illicitly, for the nine hundredth time—off the sofa back, trying to land in the clothes basket like a circus diver into a bucket of water. He's whapped his noggin on the coffee table corner. Now dead center on his pale, formerly smooth forehead, there's a blue knot like a horn trying to break through. I gather him up and rush to the kitchen, aiming to grab a soothing bag of frozen peas.

But I step on a shard of tomato sauce jar, gash my instep, slide as on a banana peel, barely hanging on to Dev till we skid to a stop. I tiptoe across the linoleum, dragging a snail of blood till I can plop him in a kitchen chair, instructing him to hold the peas to his head and not move an inch while I bunny-hop upstairs to bandage my foot.

Coming back, I find he's dragged the formerly white laundry into the kitchen to mop up the tomato sauce. I'm helping, he says, albeit surrounded by gleaming daggers of glass while on his forehead the blue Bambi horn seems to throb.

Minutes later, my hand twists off a beer cap as I tell my-self that a beer isn't really a drink after all. So I have another after that to speed preparing the pot roast, and maybe even a third. Before we head to the park, I tuck two more beer bottles in my coat pocket, plus one in my purse alongside a juice box.

Coming home at dusk, I find smoke billowing from the stove door's edges, the alarm screaming. I yank out the forgotten roast, black and unidentifiable as any roadkill. Mary's pot-roast recipe? Drink a six-pack then ring the fire department.

And rather than call for pizza while congratulating my-self that Dev was king of the monkey bars in an arctic gale, I pile a hungry boy into the car for a rush-hour lope through the store for another pot roast, since I'd idly mentioned to my husband a pot roast was forthcoming. Thus ignoring the fact that Warren would forgo roast to find a cheerful spouse and a slice or two of pepperoni.

In the store, I trot through the aisles behind a veering cart, thinking, Isn't Warren a demanding dick to insist on pot roast? My blood-alcohol level is waning, and as my near-starved toddler holds out his arms toward a sugary cereal, his whine revs up till he's baying like a sick calf to be liberated from the cart. I look at his quite prominent—is that his pulse throbbing?—blue horn as the strangers fix me in their sights. (*What a mean, awful mother!*) Dev is hoisted out while he thrashes and arches his back like he's being abducted. We abandon our sundries.

Outside, I strap him into his car seat while he flails, and I shout at him—Goddammit, Dev, you're gonna make me nuts—and tears fill his blue eyes. He covers his face with his hands. While grocery carts veer alongside us, I catch in the rearview Dev's face all quiet and big eyed. So I heft him out of the car seat and smother his face in kisses, gushing regret.

Back home, still there is no pot roast. I scramble eggs while uncorking a new wine, the sweet squeak of the cork releasing the aroma of ferment, and I tell myself, Who wouldn't drink? This is the last bottle. I'll finish it, then start fresh tomorrow.

In a sneaky, insidious process, it's all I really look forward to, and I'd bare my teeth at anybody approaching the glass in my hand with a mind toward taking it.

That night Warren comes in at ten-thirty, failing to thank me for the noodley casserole glop I slap in a bowl. Ditzy with wine and holding a boulder of guilt, I confess to Warren about snapping at Dev in the store.

He blinks. You can't do that.

Easy for you to say, you're not here all day.

But Warren faces me with the piety of a natural parent. Trained to rein in a thoroughbred or wrest a slipper from a teething pooch, he's disinclined to lose his cool.

As he's gathering up household garbage for the dawn pickup, I brillo the blackened pot-roast pan, slamming it against the sink's perimeter, blue suds foaming around nails chewed to the quick.

At one point he holds up a garbage sack of empties, asking, Did you finish a whole case of beer?

Of course not, I tell him.

(How trippingly off the tongue that lie goes. It weighs less than a mustard seed.)

I just bought that beer last weekend, he says.

Well, maybe you're drinking more than you know, I say.

Which is laughable, as Warren is a fount of discipline, a completer of sit-ups, a runner of many miles. We have a rowing machine set up in his study, and at night he pulls against oars for an hour at a pop. He barely uses a whole pat of butter on a potato. He slices turkey thin enough to read through.

If you lie to your husband—even about something so banal as how much you drink—each lie is a brick in a wall going up between you, and when he tells you he loves you, it's deflected away.

On the porch again, I scan the snowy landscape with an irritation almost predatory. The head can travel a far piece while the body sits in one spot. It can traverse many decades, and many conversations can be had, even with the dead. *Daddy* . . . I say, staring off the dark porch into my snowy yard. Before he died, the wordlessness he floated inside during my teen years had become permanent. If he roused at all, his head craned around bewildered, and he handled his dead hand like a parcel he'd been asked to hold for a stranger.

Yet through alcohol's alchemy, I'd swear some nights his shadowy form stands in the yard behind an old push-type lawn mower. *Why'd you keep drinking?* And Daddy, who was a shrugger, a starer into distances, shrugs and stares. *You know* . . . Then he dissolves into the falling snow. I upend the smooth bourbon, trying to achieve the same blunt, anesthetized state that once snuffed him out.

It can't have been sleeting or snowing every second of those years, but that's my memory of it—the hood was always up on my parka, with some weather going *tick tick tick tick* against the waterproofing.

There's snow in my head, too. Wide blizzards of bad news blowing sideways. My few hopes are desperate ones. One key fantasy on the porch—no kidding—is winning the magazine sweepstakes I've never entered. I habitually filch sweepstakes forms from doctor's-office magazines or shopping circulars. Sitting outside by flashlight—*have to change that overhead porch bulb*—I meticulously fill them out, imagining the limo pulling up with balloons and champagne. Such a good story we'll be: two poets win a jackpot. . . .

The night ends with a black smudge, and come dawn, I stand in a cloud of shower steam, the former night's conviction to quit solid, though it's daunting to face unmedicated whatever's beyond the plastic curtain I'm scared to draw aside.

By afternoon I can't abide Mr. Rogers asking me to be my neighbor without a cocktail.

20

My Concept of Commitment

My concept of commitment was
to take all you could give.
  —CHRIS SMITHER, *NO LOVE TODAY*

In the sunlit study of a couples' counselor, huge potted plants are thriving—ficus and mother-in-law tongue and wandering Jew with shoots sending out small explosions of streaky green. Across from us, the therapist smiles from a moon-shaped face. In the next room, one of her bespectacled kids saws through violin scales. This doctor—in her loose muslin dress and Birkenstock sandals, her long wavy hair dragged into a bun with a pen stuck through it—appears to have cobbled together what I want: a happy family. I tell her about snapping at Dev and making him cry—the reason we're here.

  She tries to reassure me that Dev's childhood, however shadowed by our scratching at each other, doesn't mirror my own. You're both very worried about Dev's feelings, she says, but he's in no way neglected. (In some ways, true enough. But having your parents circle each other—I still contend—splits a child in two.)

Warren's just a better parent, I say.

Is that true? she asks him.

His long legs in khakis bend and unbend, mantislike. He says, Mary's very loving, very good about seeing he plays with other kids all the time . . .

He trails off, and she says, But?

She gets very overwhelmed and snappish, he finishes.

He's perfectly patient with Dev, I say.

Well, probably, she tells me with that smile, if Warren was up all night like you, he might be less perfect.

I doubt that, I say. She asks me to say more, and I outline Warren's steadiness. How his devotion to poetry has inspired me to strive for a higher bar in my work. I praise his integrity and self-discipline, saying, I wanted a solid family. That's part of why I married him, for the stability he offered.

She leads me on, but now the stabilization feels . . .

Stultifying, I say.

She eventually turns to Warren. Why'd you marry Mary?

It seemed like time, he says. We'd been together three years. We loved each other—health insurance and so forth. She very much wanted a family.

I stare at him, awaiting some of his former warmth for me to squeeze through the stone, but he ticks off what might be qualities in a personals ad—attractive, athletic, smart. She's much more social than I, he adds, very loyal, a very devoted mother . . .

Whoever you married would have those qualities, she says.

I think he married me—I interrupt—to rebuke his up-bringing. Now he resents my absorption with the baby or that his father chips in my rent! (These pet theories conveniently skim over my own—at this point—innately repellent disposition.)

That's so damned unfair, he says.

It's Warren's turn, the therapist says levelly. Toward the end, when she asks how much I'm drinking, I halve it. Still she suggests I try out an evening support group for people trying to give up booze.

She turns to Warren, Do you think she's an alcoholic?

How insulting, I think, and brace myself for Warren's assessment, already dredging up a defense: I've never been five minutes late to pick up Dev. I'm a room parent, for God's sake. I lead toddlers around the aquarium on a rope.

No, he says.

(How my love for him doth bloom, the drinking mind thinks.) She likes a drink. (Or nine, the scolding, sober part of me thinks.) But who doesn't? he concludes. (Those WASPs down so much sauce—the sober mind observes—that Warren wouldn't know a dipsomaniac if one hit him with a polo mallet.) That's the kind of courtroom convened in my skull, prosecution and defense.

Back home the next morning, while Dev blanks out at the TV, I sneak around, reaching under beds and into the hamper, gathering ratholed beer cans and wine bottles. Once Warren's home, I drive around to unload them from the hatchback like body parts into dumpsters all over town. I also rotate liquor stores, telling each indifferent proprietor that I'm having a spectacular party—myself the honored guest.

One morning before New Year's, I'm trying to jam Dev into his coat, and he's slipping around in my hands like a greased pig. I get one arm in, and he collapses laughing on the floor.

I've been pondering the doctor's suggestion as I say to Warren, Let's quit drinking.

Sure, Warren says, why not. He crimps the top of his lunch sack. He, by the way, doesn't need to quit drinking, and being full-time at both work and grad school—and being I'm a sneaky bitch—he's missing the gallons I drink.

From my hands, Dev breaks free and dashes into the living room while I say, It's not like we're going to a party.

Going after Dev, Warren tells me not to start, for I gripe nonstop about our lack of social life. He returns with our maniacally snickering son tucked under one arm like a baguette. Warren asks me to toss Dev's coat upside down on the floor.

Okay, dip and flip, sweetie, Warren says, setting Dev so he stands with his feet at his coat's hood. Dev bends over, dips his hands in his coat sleeves, then upends the coat over his head.

Good man, I say as Warren starts to clip a mitten to a sleeve.

I ask him where—with his own patriarch's testy disposition—he mastered parenting.

He's hitching the second mitten on as Dev lurches to smooch my cheek. Hoisting him up, Warren says, I imagine what my father would've done with me, then do the opposite.

I tug at Warren's sleeve so he curves his tall form down, seeming to tolerate my peck on his lips. (Is this true or only my faulty interpretation?) The familiar masculine odor of him sends down my spine a surge of ardor as if stirred from a muddy aquarium bottom. I step back till my knees hit the chair edge and I just fold myself shut as he disappears out the door.

By this time one of us is perennially on the way out the

door, pausing to hand our boy off like a football. More and more often, he's our sole point of contact. Otherwise, we exist as a pair of profiles gliding past each other. If a laser had sliced each of us cartoonlike down the middle—half of each falling away—we may not have noticed the missing half for days. While I tell myself this is the normal way of careworn parents with handfuls of jobs between them, the distance feels like powerful magnets, once kissing, now turned to their opposing poles. It's not just that we don't eat out, don't take vacations at all—together or apart, expense being cited—we barely speak beyond necessity. Only in bed do we sometimes fall on each other like starved beasts.

Quitting drinking will reunite us. On New Year's, we down our last champagne, and two days later, a wicked flu fells me like a chain-sawed oak. The sole cure for which ailment—it strikes me—is whiskey toddies with lemon and honey. Purely medicinal, of course. Don't you want a drink? I say to Warren as I itchily shift around in bed. I can't concentrate on grading.

Not really, he says. The literary magazine he'd cofounded before keeps him editing manuscripts even nights he's home.

My limbs ache like I've run ten miles, and I'm clammy. In the past, quitting drinking was a breeze. I'd done it a thousand times—binge as a reward, say, or down it all one weekend then swear off on Monday. I whine to him that sleep'll elude me.

He yawns, hefting his folder to the floor with a thunk, saying (as a joke), I wish I couldn't sleep.

I sullenly kick back the covers on my side of the bed, pissed at how he'll twist off the light, and block out my insomniac pouting.

Downstairs, I stand before the brass thermostat swathed

in layers of sweatclothes and woolens, for this is how I bundle to sleep at the igloo temperature Warren insists on—again, expense being cited. I scrub my chafed red hands together like a fly then I twist the wheel right. Before it reaches eighty, I hear—from the bowels of the house—the furnace go *whomp*. I even rise early to dial it back low before Warren—soaked in sweat—comes down in the morning, wondering why the thermometer's red line holds at eighty, as I look mystified.

Since there's no liquor in the house, I concoct for myself a backache, filching a few of the blue valiums Warren rarely takes for his—truly bad—back. They're for sleep, I tell myself. (My creative skill reaches its zenith at prescription interpretation, i.e., the codeine cough syrup bottle seems to read: *Take one or two swigs when you feel like it.* I take three.)

In February I decide I'm under too much stress to quit booze cold turkey. Full sobriety as a concept recedes with the holidays. I'll cut down, I think. But all the control schemes that reined me in during past years are now unfathomably failing. Only drink beer. Only drink wine. Only drink weekends. Only drink after five. At home. With others.

When I only drink with meals, I cobble together increasingly baroque dinners, always uncorking some medium-shitty vintage at about three in the afternoon while Dev plays on the kitchen floor. The occasional swig is culinary duty, right? Some nights I'm into my second bottle before Warren comes in with frost on his glasses and a book bag a mule should've toted. Maybe he doesn't notice, since I'm a champion at holding my liquor. Nonetheless, by the end of March, I have to unbutton my waistbands.

Only drinking socially leads to a flurry of long afternoon lunches we can't afford with people I barely know, so—for thrift's sake—I often just split a bottle of wine while my lunch partner eats. In academia, meticulously split checks are the norm.

At the poetry readings Warren hosts for his job every few weeks, I swill plastic cups of vinegary white wine and yammer like somebody pulled a string on my neck till the library lights get turned off.

After one such event, Warren drives home with his jawline flexing.

What? What's the matter? I ask.

Do you have to stay till the last drop is drunk? he says. His sole mention of my drinking, as I recall.

Which pierces me. How hard I've tried not to drink. I call him the fun police and unleash the litany of chores that tip me out of bed every day at five a.m. That this was a dead echo of Mother's speechifying on Warren's not being enough of a party boy eludes me. The more I drink, the more weekends I split off, leaving Warren to care for Dev solo while I take naps. Also, evenings Warren comes home early enough, I hide in my study drinking as he and Dev play at making the bed, which involves Dev bouncing as Warren floats the sheet over his head, occasionally wrestling the little ghost form down.

Through the wall, I can't make out words, only Dev's staccato whoops and giggles, followed by Warren's deepthroated purr, which sounds like *hubbidee hubadub hubbadee . . . hum sally hum bum.* The timbre's barely tolerable, for when Warren speaks to me, the airspace is sandpapered and abraded, spiked as a bondage collar. I can't look at him without hearing some muffled verdict pounded out by my own heartbeat—*guilty guilty guilty.*

Across the months, I start to find myself first one place, then another, arriving in situations as if tipped out of a bucket.

I find myself in a restaurant before noon ordering a pricey Bloody Mary, telling myself the tomato juice makes it a vegetable serving.

I find myself cornered by a drunk writer of substantial reputation at a party. His expectant leer scares me out the door. At the car, I have keys in my hand but no purse. Where's my purse?

I find myself squatting in the bedroom closet with two incongruent bottles, whiskey and Listerine—the latter with accompanying spit bowl. Despite the dark, it feels safe in here, leaning against the back wall with clothes before my face.

On one of Warren's school nights, friends I once taught with ring my doorbell holding a twelve-pack, the ambush making me giddy as a prom queen. They pore over my shoe box of Dev's baby pictures while regaling me with their new projects—a play at Yale, a book of short stories. But even as I giggle and suck down beers, I know Warren's headlights are gonna swipe the house silent again. Sure enough, he comes in the back door and stops in the living room to shake hands before excusing himself. About eleven, he calls from upstairs, and I find him on the landing, shirtless in boxers.

He whispers, I can't sleep from the noise. If you don't ask them to leave, I'll have to.

I hiss at him, You're such a control freak.

He says, You knew I was like this when you married me.

The righteous cry of married men everywhere, for it's a cliché that every woman signs up thinking her husband will change, while every husband signs up believing his wife won't: both dead wrong.

So I send them home, then stay up nearly all night drinking and staring past the edges of the yard like a rabbit through chicken wire. What happened to those great poems I was going to set the world weeping with? Tomorrow!

How sweet its prospects for a drunkard the night before. There is no better word. Before the earth hurls itself into sunshine, nothing is not possible. Tomorrow, I will rise at three a.m. and log two hours writing before Dev stumps out. I'll take a five-mile jog, start a cheap but nutritious stew, submit a query letter to *The American Scholar* for an essay. If only I could be left alone for a few days to drink like I want to, I could get my papers graded.

Every mom trails undone chores—dishes in the sink, laundry going wrinkly in the dryer. I lug from room to office to playground reams of ungraded essays. With one hand, I use a fork to fiddle with chicken in a skillet. With the other, my red pen marks comma blunders on the counter. The papers I hand back sport grease stains and grass stains and smudges of homemade applesauce.

One night I get gussied up for a book party Warren would rather have been shot than attend, and sunk in the cavern of a leather armchair, I hold my liquor enough to hear—from the mouths of poets—work I'm itching to read, books I can vanish down into from my grind. The night is a burst of sea spray washed across my face, tangible evidence of a fresh existence only slightly out of reach.

Driving home in the spring rain, I imagine straddling my muscular husband in his desk chair and planting a soft kiss on his mouth.

But coming through the back door, I enter the household's tentative air, drawing back from the idea like a starfish to an underside touch. I find him typing a paper with the baby monitor on his desk. He glances over. How was it?

Great, I say, and I burble out a summary. When Warren announces Dev's been up feverish twice, the news stops me. However I long for a night off, taking one scalds me in guilt.

Did you give him the antibiotic in his lunch box? I say. If he'd forgot I'd be up a point.

You left his lunch box at school, I think—

Shit, I say. It's another black mark for me.

—but it's pretty much run out. His fever was over a hundred after Tylenol.

We stare at each other to stave off the inevitable spat over who misses work. Warren's down to his last few vacation days; I'd have to reschedule forty student conferences. But enough of the night sparkles through me that I say I'll handle it, then I add, It's good for me to get out every now and then.

I hope so, he says.

A few heartbeats keep me there in silence till I say, Was that sarcastic?

He meets my eyes again, saying, Of course not.

I start up the stairs and stop. I feel another urge to slide my arms around his strong middle and have him hold me, but if he withdrew, peeled my arms off—the refusal would've scorched me like a nuclear blast. I lean tentatively on the door jamb.

Don't you think I need to go out?

You believe so, he says.

Some rage burbles up, and from nowhere, I say—calmly but with force—That's a shit thing to say.

He shakes his head and says, You've had your night. Why jump on me now?

Excuse me for having a life, I say. That's the most fun I've had in months.

It's not all about fun, Mare.

Just fuck you, I say, and bolt up the stairs. Storming into my study, I flip the side switch on the massive IBM computer, which starts to growl and grind. The monitor begins to blink awake.

Inching through Warren's edits on the book review I owe his journal, I seize up like the screen's stalled cursor. I sit there ping-ponging back and forth between righteous fury and guilty shame.

There had been a time when the wide world was sunlit, every grass blade shining, but the sun's spotlight has shrunk smaller and smaller. Now Warren is squeezed out. He's a shade, an outline. I can't see him anymore.

(You could say I needed God then, which notion would've gagged me like a maggot. But if you're a nonbeliever, replace the word *God* with *truth* or *mercy*. To kill truth to defend my fear was—in one way—to kill God. Oedipus wound up murdering his father because he ignored the divine warning that he would. When he learned the truth, his guilt so ruined him, he stabbed out his own eyes. Without truth, I was blind, worshipping my own fear-driven thoughts, and the ground beneath me never stopped heaving.)

The next morning I find myself riding in circles around my dining room astride a truck, wanting to shriek with boredom, for that's what I think mothering is—doing whatever my son does, himself not yet literate.

That afternoon I bring Dev in solo to the warm-eyed psychologist, who tells me I don't have to play with him nonstop. She has on a bulky green sweater and heavy boots that ground her to the floorboards as she points to him happily moving cars around on the rug.

In tribal cultures, she says, mothers work in the fields, and kids—once they've learned not to fall in the cooking fires—run around in a gaggle like geese. Only in the 1950s did the bloated economy permit women to stay home concocting the current parenting fantasy.

Till then, I'd believed my job was to impersonate a preschooler every second I was with Dev. In some ill-considered way, I hadn't wanted him to feel so bad about being so short, so ill spoken and incontinent.

Dr. G. looks at me, her forehead bending into a little tilde of concern as she says, You can cook or fold clothes or relax.

But if I fold clothes, I say, he starts throwing them over his head.

Tell him to stop, she says.

I don't want to yell at him.

Dev looks up and—holding up his arms with open palms bent back to demonstrate the obviousness of her argument—says, then don't yell at me.

You don't have to yell at him, she says. In fact, if you yell at him, what happens?

He'll yell back? I say.

Worse. He'll stop listening.

Dev picks up two drumsticks and pounds out a one-two till he's caught a fast trill.

See, he's an extremely talented noisemaker, I say.

I am! he says, grinning with those black-lashed blue eyes of his as he bangs on.

I tell him, I'm ratting you out for the yeller you are.

Just worry less that you should be doing something for him every second, Dr. G. says. She tells me to call her in the afternoons if I'm reaching my wits' end.

After another trip to the grocery store, where Dev grabs all the candy bars off the shelf, the doctor teaches me how to put him in a time-out—a minute for every year of his life—which I initially hate to do, for it feels like punishment. So I wait till he's pulled stuff off the supermarket shelf six times rather than doing it right off. Which means by the time I get to it, I'm rattled, and he knows he's got me.

I sit moldering at midnight on the back porch, holding what's become a tumbler of whiskey sans ice and floating cherry—my ten thousandth last drink. The doctor has agreed to squeeze me in for an emergency appointment at dawn. Our couples sessions have become me alone in Parenting 101.

She explains that if I wait till I'm mad to put Dev in time-out, then anger becomes the only limit he'll recognize, and he'll wait till I'm screaming to stop. The time-out isn't punishment, it's a circuit breaker you throw.

Sleep. I crave sleep. That night his coughing keeps us up all night. I'm filled with wet sand. The doctor tells me that Dev has to learn to settle. I should only go in at increasing intervals, adding a minute each time. You can't engage him, she says, otherwise, it's reinforcing the waking.

Even if he looks like in *The Exorcist*?

Even if he's possessed by Satan, she says. He'll cry himself to sleep.

As I'm gathering my stuff up, she lowers the pen to ask again, What about your drinking?

For an instant, the plant-filled room inches over a little. I lie to her, saying, I've cut way down.

Not long after, on a warm afternoon while Dev's in the tub, Warren and I step across the hall to the bedroom to jack up our sniping. You *always* this, and you *never* that. We unzip our mild parental personas, shedding them, rising up like four-legged beasts reared back. The room is swirling with our invectives when—in the doorway—there stands Dev in his three-year-old body. He's naked and gap-mouthed. All the raging that swirls around us arrests into violent stasis. The fury in the room dispels itself like smoke siphoned up with a hose.

Coming from the tub, Dev's pale body shines with water, ringlets damp alongside his blazing cheeks. He's dragged behind him a brown and soaking towel like the hide of some slaughtered animal. (Almost twenty years later, he told me that this crisply drawn memory was the worst of his life.) I've never been on the receiving end of such a plaintive stare. Standing in a sniper's crosshairs would feel safer.

Later, as we draw the quilt up over him and his stout polar bear—named, prosaically enough, Mr. Bear—we practically sing our lame guarantees. Over his horizontal body, our shadows cross same as ever. We swear to him that the lady we're talking to helps us play nicer.

Like Martin Luther King? he says.

What does Martin Luther King teach, sweetie? Warren says.

Dev's twiddling a blond ringlet around his finger as he says, Take turns. Share toys.

You know Grandma Charlie marched with Dr. King in Selma, Alabama.

He wrinkles his nose, saying, No, she didn't.

So I tell the story. How she climbed in a van with a bunch of college students, and they rolled through the swamps and bayous to a city encircled by scary men with guns and blind batons that swung down even on bodies huddled in surrender. How with my daddy and sister eating our upended pot pies off TV trays, we saw fire hoses pinning people against chain link.

That was brave, Dev says.

You're brave, I say.

He nods as if considering. I am, he says.

But as Warren and I stand in his doorway with arms around each other's waists, swearing we won't fight anymore, Dev wears the wearied expression of someone who knows he's being lied to.

At the bottom of the stairway, the sob that comes through me nearly breaks me in half, and Warren unbends me to draw me to him. His white shirt smells of laundry bluing, and he strokes my hair in the old way and says, We can't do that in front of him again.

21

The Grinning Skull

The grinning skull begins to take on skin—
—WISLAWA SZYMBORSKA, "AN OLD STORY"
(TRANS. STANISLAV BARANCZAK)

The next night, still hungover, I sullenly drag in to the therapy group for people trying to quit. Maybe they know ways to cut back that won't make me too itchy. It's a Cambridge church basement—a musty yellow room whose ancient carpet smells of wet gym socks. Hung from the walls are giant posters like you'd expect at a high school pep rally, splattered with cornball slogans. There are rows of aluminum folding chairs, baby-shit brown in color.

I warp my mouth into a stiff rictus and begin trying to impersonate a good and sober person who's only wandered in through curiosity and happenstance. Here the coffee costs a dime, and you can read the styrofoam cup's manufacturer embossed backward on the bottom.

Standing at the urn, I hear a tweedy classics professor say to a big black marine with patches from Khe Sanh on his bulging arms: It's hard to be an articulate ghost. Illogically, as I hear this, some frozen inner aspect thaws enough that a small surge of pity swells through me. I heap my watery coffee with powdered cream and stop thinking about myself long enough to come alive a little. I notice in the professor's baggy face his red-rimmed eyes, and the care in the marine's gaze starts to plug me in to something invisible that rivers among these strangers. It's like running from my cardiac area, I've been dragging a long extension cord unplugged from all compassion, and it's suddenly found a socket. The room comes breathing to life.

I'm standing by a book cart loaded with navy blue hymnals, and through the tall windows, I can see dusk falling. The leaves of the oaks are dabbed with orange paint. A woman in a snug yellow sweater is polishing her tortoiseshell glasses with a red silk square.

We're asleep most of the time, I once heard the writer George Saunders say, but we can wake up. In that instant, for no reason I can discern, I wake up. Faces cease to be blurs and grow distinct features. Coming toward me from the door is a buff musician whose CDs I own. He's carrying a plate covered in foil, talking to a handsome, mustachioed friend whose leather jacket must've cost more than our rusting vehicle. I stand aside as he lowers the plate to the table and peels off the foil—homemade chocolate chip cookies melting into each other. People from around the room come up, and I snatch one and head to my seat, sinking my teeth into the buttery dough and warm chocolate.

Pleasure, I feel—mouth to spine to head. A small uprush of pleasure. This, I think, is why other people aren't screaming. I've briefly forgotten to feel sorry for myself, to worry, to generate any kind of report on my own performance.

The marine says to the professor, Days three to ten suck the worst. You can do it this time. Just drink a lot of water. And call me. Build a wall around the day and don't look over it. . . .

The chair I fold myself into chills my ass. That tiny discomfort unplugs me again, and I fidget and rifle my purse for hand lotion. Why don't I carry mints? There are people in the world who carry mints. But given a tin of mints, I'll eat every single one straight off. As novelist Harry Crews once wrote, I'm the kind of person who—if he can't have too much of something—doesn't want any of it.

In the front of the room, a lady asks for a moment of silence, and people on either side of me bow their heads. Are they serious? I look over at the buff musician and his friend— heads down, plus the tweedy classics professor. Lord, I think, this is some fake Christian cult I've wandered into. Then a guy at the front reads some kind of warm-up, saying they're not a sect or church, reiterating how nobody's the boss of anybody—we're all the same—the lie of equality that teachers tried peddling in high school, where, in fact, the reigning hierarchy would've tied stones to the feet of druggy teens like me and dropped us off bridges.

Then a laminated list of suggestions starts circling the room, with people reading a line at a time. It sounds to me like *Be good and you won't get in trouble* and *Stop having fun and grow up* and *Tell everybody how you're bad and face the firing squad.*

A woman stands at the front, saying her higher power helped her through a family wedding without drinking, though her soused-up relatives tried to force all variety of cocktail down her gullet, and it's all I can do not to bolt out the door. *Higher power, my rosy red ass,* I can hear my daddy saying, and *Church is a trick on poor people.* I look over at the classics prof, now giving the thumbs-up sign like she's scored a touchdown, and I think, What fun-house land have I crossed into, where the rich seek the counsel of the poor? Any minute, some snake-handling preacher might well get up and start stomp-dancing while his underage wife passes a hat. I slather on more hand lotion and sit perched on the edge of my seat like a bird on a wire.

The guy at the front calls on a lady in a bouclé Chanel suit, complete with gold buttons and long chains hanging down. She might've stepped from the pages of *Town & Country* magazine. She relates how she used to tuck her vodka bottle inside a turkey carcass stashed in the basement freezer. While cooking dinner, she'd run down and yank it out and guzzle a bit. And her family, who'd done two interventions, kept rifling laundry hampers and closets, looking to no avail for her stash. Then one night, she tells us in a demure voice, the frost had built up so deep she couldn't midwife the bottle out, so she just upended the whole bird, guzzling out of it.

She says, And that was my moment of clarity, thinking, Other people just don't drink like this.

Rather than scorn her like schoolmarms for the sin, the room roars—myself among them—while she gives a startled smile. And because I've never drained vodka from an icy bird, I think I'm nowhere near as bad as that crazy bitch.

Another guy talks about burying bottles all over his mother's yard before being dragged into rehab. Fresh out, he needed only to secret inside his Speedo bathing suit a plastic straw. Then he'd grab a towel and some tanning oil and step outside, saying he wanted to catch some rays. His mother would study him all day through the sliding door, totally flummoxed when he came crab-walking in—drunk and beet-red—at sundown. More laughter, and I hear myself join in since the company is more raucously alive than most dance clubs.

Was it this same meeting where a man told the story of trying to hang himself? The rope was too green, and at dusk, his wife tilted open the garage door to find him twisting drunk, on tiptoes, half conscious. She cut him down, called him a bastard, and packed her bags. He then went into the kitchen and blew out the pilot light and stuffed towels around the edges of the room. He emptied a bottle of sleeping pills into his mouth and finished the last of the whiskey.

Three days later, he woke with a crushing headache, and his first thought was, Boy do I need a cigarette. So he patted around on the front of his shirt and pulled out a stogie. Then he drew the Bic lighter from his pants pocket and rubbed up a single flame.

He didn't hear the explosion as the walls of the room were blown out. In his next conscious instant, he was smoldering in his neighbor's yard with his brows singed off.

When have I laughed so hard in company at the specter of human frailty? Not since the last great poetry reading I'd sat through, when some outcast put a fresh name on the unnamable. I don't know what I expected here—a bunch of guys who crawled out from alleys or under bridges looking for hot coffee and a bowl of soup. But the folks around me look mostly present and clear-eyed.

Among the academics and guys in suits sit working people—chamber maid, garage mechanic, diner waitress. I recognize the Latino guy who pours my coffee at the local donut shop. When they *share*—a word that right off makes me want to spit—about how hard it is to make the rent or whether the exhaust system wired together by a coat hanger will hold, I realize how far I've moved from the people I grew up around.

The next instant a gray-haired lady in pearls smiles at me, and I turn away, thinking, *I'm not like you, lady.* . . .

Nonetheless, I raise my hand a few inches, but when I don't get called on, I yank it down and start sitting on it again. How far I've fallen from the hand-flapping freshman, how saturated in shame.

That flip-flop keeps going on inside, as if opposing inner judo masters take turns body-slamming each other. One minute I'm thinking, *They're not all that strange.* The next, their laughter bounces off me like bullets from a cartoon Kevlar vest. I go outside to smoke.

In the common across from me, the bare trees are twisted into agonized forms. The bronze cannons seem aimed straight at my sternum. I look back at the lighted windows and hear a woman's unintelligible voice.

The door opens a crack, and in the spilled, triangular glow, a tall kid wearing a red bandana over his streaming brown hair slips out. He stops six feet away and bends slightly forward—almost a butler's bow—saying, Excuse me, Miss Karr. Mind if I join you?

Who is he? With his formal demeanor and gold granny glasses, he could be a student—some Ivy League suck-up.

Join away, I say, adding as I flash my wedding ring, I'm a miz.

My goodness gracious, ma'am, he says, those are some seriously blinding stones you're flaunting. We met before . . .

And we had. David was a Harvard Ph.D. candidate in philosophy I'd once been introduced to at the back of a reading by mutual pals. Some kind of genius, David's meant to be, though his red bandana is the flag of gangster or biker, ditto the unlaced Timberland work boots.

I ask him how long he's been coming, and he says not hardly any time, and I say it's my first go, and he asks if I get it, and I say if I got it, I wouldn't be out here smoking. He says same with him, adding while he drank a lot, he mostly did marijuana, which can't be so bad because it's natural.

I say—cleverly, I think—Strychnine's natural.

He concedes that's true but also points out how, since the average pot smoker doesn't tend to steal your TV, people don't frown on it like they do, say, smoking crack, then plowing over the crossing guard.

We stare at the cannons facing us, both agreeing we really have better places to be as we grind our cigarettes with our boot heels. Climbing the steps back to the lighted doorway, he holds the door, bowing as he says from his scruffily bearded face (this is the pre-scruff U.S.A.), After you, Miz Karr.

It brings me up short—his outlaw wardrobe paired with the obsequious *ma'am* thing—and I say testily, Are you fucking with me?

No ma'am, he says, his hands flying to his T-shirted chest.

Then it strikes me that he's just a shy kid from the Midwest raised to say *ma'am* like I do to every waitress and dry cleaner. We scuttle inside like a pair of field mice from our inept exchange.

Back in my chair, the filter of my head notices how people keep talking about being grateful, as in *I'm so happy to be thankful to be grateful to sit here with you nice sober folks.* I look around and think, Your lives must suck worse even than mine if this constitutes fun for you.

Eventually, I raise my hand high enough to get called on. I announce that I doubt I'm an alcoholic, since I never drink in the mornings, and nothing particularly bad has ever happened to me—not bankruptcy, car wreck, nor even the standard mugging. While I expect some indictment, everyone smiles that sugary smile I mistrust and nods, and the lady next to me whispers, Keep coming.

At the end, when everybody grabs hands to pray, it's like some dreary ring-around-the-rosy, and I refuse to mouth the words, instead gaping around at who's dopey enough to go along. The musician and his friend do, and the professor. Perfectly smart people, talking to air with grave expressions. Go figure.

On the way out, I pass bandana'ed David talking with great speed and animation to the musician. David's actually holding up his finger in some Confucian posture, saying, It's a logical fallacy that they're telling me I have a disease whose defining symptom is believing you don't have a disease, since this a priori implies that any citizen who denies they have this ailment is no doubt infected . . .

Like me, he's obviously here to educate them to their cult's fallacious thinking.

On the sidewalk, the night is cool and wet, and a few passing women hand me their phone numbers, saying call anytime, even to say hello, which feels slightly pitiful on their parts. What do they want?

One says, For me, a car wreck was a *yet*. I mean, it just hadn't gotten around to happening. Another says she'd wondered just like I had whether she really needed to quit drinking, but that underperforming or having a bleak inner life is a severe consequence of drinking even without an external loss like job or child.

The comment stuns me in a way. Inside I say to myself,

How dare you suppose I have a bleak inner life! Driving home, I check my puffy eyes in the rearview and tell myself that I look as cheerful as the next lady . . . don't I?

I know that I don't, and while I sit in the driveway smoking, I can catch—almost feel zip through me—a streak of the kindness I'd witnessed at the coffee urn. Just to be on the receiving end of a warm baked item while living so fenced off from husband and community brings me up short. Maybe, I think, I do belong among that peculiar company. . . . Well, maybe not those sad ladies who give their phone numbers out to strangers. What losers. I stuff the slips of paper in the car ashtray.

Inside, with my small family abed, I pour my tumbler of whiskey and drink it on the back porch. Before staggering upstairs to pass out, I fix a second, since I'll invariably wake around two or three, unable to cork off again without a few swallows.

The next morning I take the half-empty tumbler of whiskey before grabbing Dev to piggyback downstairs. There, standing over the sink, I look at the watery drink and say to myself—as I do every morning—Seems wrong to pour it out. So I swill down those dregs. Only this time I hear my own voice from the night before, righteously claiming I never took a morning drink. It's the first lie I caught myself in. In fact, I never *poured* the drink. Just drank it.

It's a snippet of a revelation, Dev's solid weight on my hip the only force cementing me to earth. I feel flying through me like a hard-hit ball David's phrase; *I have a disease whose defining symptom is believing you don't have a disease* . . . but I'm not ready to stop listening to the screwed-up inner voice that's been ordering me around for a lifetime. My head thinks it can kill me—as one lady at the meeting said—and go on living without me.

22

Mass Eye

Each spectral port,
each human eye

is shot through with a hole, and everything we know
goes in there, where it feeds a blaze. In a flash

the baby's old . . .
   —HEATHER MCHUGH, "THE SIZE OF SPOKANE"

Down in Texas, a botched cataract surgery has nearly blinded
Mother, and I suggest she have the corneal transplant to re-
pair it in Boston. Since Mr. Whitbread serves on New York
Hospital's board and likes to flex that helping muscle, Warren urges me to write him to find a doctor. I suspect (is this
true?) Warren really fancies Mother's presence will let him
vanish further into work and daddyhood. Still, I'm grateful

when Mr. Whitbread right off cops for Mother an appointment with the pope's own eye surgeon, who bumps Mother way up on the transplant list. That spring she comes to live in our dining room, waiting on a tissue match.

I'll help with my grandson, she says. I'll look after him while you grade or write in your study.

You're blind, Mother.

Not entirely. I mean, too blind to drive, but I can keep him away from sharp stuff.

The first day she does babysit, but the second, Dev scampers into my study with Mother right behind, and do I want to go to the park? By the third day, Mother makes the most infuriating announcement: I don't do kids.

I sputter, You had four of them, Mother.

Nobody helped me with mine.

Bullshit. Daddy took me everywhere.

She rolls her milky eyes toward the light fixture, saying, Here you go with that *my sainted daddy* shit. Your sister and I both wonder why he got a big pass for doing nothing whatsoever.

Daddy never left us at the movies and didn't pick us up.

He never did anything whatsoever.

He paid every bill.

We lived in absolute squalor.

He worked at an oil refinery, Mother. Did you fail to notice that?

Ragging on Daddy is Mother's de facto response to any complaint about our upbringing. She deftly pawns off her own failings on the desolation of her marriage.

So she bitches that Daddy had been offered promotions but wouldn't leave the union. And I counter that she'd been a Marxist when they married, and we dwindle into those niggling definitions until my fury boils over, and I lunge with the biggest weapon in my verbal sheath. I remind her that Daddy had never stood over me with a butcher knife.

I say it with a forceful little puff of air so the fact lands in her like a curare dart. All talk exits the room. We face each other in this vacuumed-out bubble, and part of me knows it's a pathetic fact that not trying to murder me was all he had to do to win the better-parent prize.

Mother sucks her teeth and sits down on the low-lying futon we moved into the dining room for her. But she doesn't collapse in operatic weeping like she's done in the past. Which is strange. She seems very still as she pats the side of the futon. She says, Sit down next to me.

I'm not in the mood to cuddle and say so.

Her eyes are cloudy as an ancient oracle's. She says, I've made amends to you, Mary. Best I could.

And that's it? You're sober now. I zero out your account.

You want to get mad at me, she says, knock yourself out.

I don't *want* to get mad, Mother, I say. I *am* fucking mad.

Well, get it off your chest, she says.

So I do, pacing up and down, ranting like a Pentecostal preacher while she sits in a Buddha-esque pose studying me. Finally, I float into place next to her like a soggy balloon. She stubs out the end of her smoke and looks at me with her misted eyes.

She actually shrugs. What will you have me do? she asks.

There's nothing she can do. I say so. After getting sober, you're supposed to make up to people you'd plowed over. Mother's sorry occupies two sentences: You know all that stuff that happened when you were little? I'm sorry about that.

She doesn't risk a joke, but I see mischief in her, some be-musement. It's disarming about Mother, her ability to laugh at the wrong instant.

Just stay sober, I say. Plus keep your grandson for one fucking hour without it being a federal case.

It interferes with my serenity, she says.

Lecia had gone through a similar fight where she'd told Mother, You don't cook. You don't clean. You haven't had a job in forty years. What exactly do you bring to the party? The way Lecia told it, Mother had looked puzzled. She'd actually cocked her head like she was trying to remember her purpose on the planet and had finally, confidently, popped out with: I'm a lot of fun to be with.

I remind her of that, saying, So what do I get? *You're a lot of fun to be with?*

Basically, she says. Or look at it this way: Maybe I left you a lot of good stories to write about. Maybe you'll make your fortune on me.

Or my misfortune. Poets don't make fortunes.

Don't be so sure, kid. I've been praying about it for you.

I won't inhale and hold it, I say.

You know what I pray'll happen for you?

It better involve money.

That you'll get this program.

For God's sake, Mother, stop proselytizing for one day. I'm not gonna be your cliché-spouting recovery acolyte.

Some kind of spiritual discipline might free you from some of this anger. . . .

I stomp upstairs, slamming the bathroom door behind me. Mother preaching to me about discipline is more than I can abide.

But over the weeks she's with us, I can't refute how calm she seems; funny, too—an equanimity I've never seen— patience, even. Feeling her way around my kitchen, she manages to mold little balls of corn bread into patties she fries up for us, and by day, she takes calls from her program friends and knits for me by feel alone a sweater the color of daffodils with the three-D pattern of a tree blooming up the front.

The day before the transplant, in a packed doctors' office, we waltz to the front of the line to see the doctor, as Mr. Whitbread arranged, everybody watching us pass like we were majorettes. Though I'd expected to feel radically glad—for once having the leg up that the rich always have—my throat sours as I look behind us, for we pass up all manner of near-blind children, including one knobby-kneed broomstick of a boy with a black eye patch; plus an entire family from Pakistan who've waited—their son explained—eighteen months and spent their savings journeying to get their father's eye cancer seen to. They aren't waiting for transplants, necessarily, but just getting to the doctor before them feels like cheating.

After the surgery, Mother lies with her head wrapped, wanly joking that she feels like playing pin the tail on the donkey. She listens to cassettes of *The Cloud of Unknowing*, Buddhist sutras, *Centering Prayer*, the writings of mystic Simone Weil—all brought from the hometown library.

Afternoons, young Dev likes to lead her around the yard, joyfully stranding her in front of the azalea bush. Or he dons a plastic knight's helmet and hands her a stick, batting at it with his plastic sword till she's holding a stub.

One evening I'm in the kitchen cleaning up dishes when he rushes in, claiming Mother stole the last cookie from him and threatened to slap him. She comes behind holding the cookie to her chest. Her story is they were doing watercolors together, and when she idly reached for the last cookie on the plate, he snatched it up and scampered to the other side of the table.

Give him the cookie, Mother.

But he had three. I had one broken one.

He's the baby, Mother. He gets the cookie.

She gives me a pitiful stare and announces it was the last one. I promise to fetch another package after the dishes, and she hands it over to Dev, who nyah-nyahs her a few times, then leaves the room doing a victory dance.

You can't slap him, Mother.

She stares at me with two different eyes—one blue, one green. The green one has a brown nick in it, like a fault in ice.

I didn't want to smack him, she tells me. It would've just been instinctual.

Batching your pants is instinctual, Mother. We don't batch our pants. We don't beat babies. That's what civilization is all about—reining in those pesky instincts. Dev's never been slapped.

She huffs, Maybe that's what's wrong with him.

Rising up through me with primordial force is the urge to grab her by the shoulders and shake her till her head pops off like a broken Barbie. The urge shoots through me like a barreling train, and I feel every single car flicker by before I say anything else. Breath comes in my body and leaves it.

I love you, Mother, I say with great measure, but if you lay one hand on him, I'll kick you till you're dead.

Okay, she says, exhaling slow. Okay, that sounds fair.

When I put Dev to bed that night, I ask him if Grandma scared him earlier.

He gives me a puzzled look. Why would she scare him?

About the cookie, I tell him.

He tells me, You'd never allow that to happen.

Which I repeat here as a boast, for that sentence might be the most gratifying endorsement I ever got.

23

Lather, Rinse, Repeat

First you wake in disbelief, then
in sadness and grief and when you wake
for the last time, the forest you've been
looking for will turn out to be
right in the middle of your chest.

—DEAN YOUNG, "SIDE EFFECTS"

One evening after I've dropped off some final files to the big-deal telecom consultant I once worked for, I lounge with him and his wife on their patio under a sprawling oak. In the spirit of farewell to my goofy career as a telecom marketer in business, he takes down a double album cover and begins to roll a joint.

We hardly do this—not since grad school—he says, but you deserve a send-off.

Ten days without a drink at this point, I say no. His wife

has a crystal wineglass in her hand and a winning grin. Sure you don't want some? she says. The sculpted garden spreads around us, neat as a plate of sushi. She has on a gauzy black dress, and as she takes the joint and tokes it, she drapes her long legs over the garden chair, saying, This is very different from drinking, right? I mean . . . She trails off into an exhale.

I think, It is different. Pot was never my problem—true enough—compared to the all-day bong-blowing, resin-scraping drug dealers I'd lived with—true enough. I view my hand reaching for the joint as if on a movie screen. The sober part of myself is vanished entire. The coal on the burning stick flares as I draw on it, then I hold the sweet smoke as it creeps up my spine to my brain stem, where a tight-closed lotus starts to flower open. Exhaling, I blow away all those creepy people from the church basement. The wind wafts them off into summer dust motes.

Later, my friends tuck me in a car, then stand, their arms waving side to side with the liquidy motion of seaweed while I ease off. I roll the window down so my hair streams along the side. The edges of the road have softened, the trees are giant scrambles of green fuzz. Just past the Star Market, right before the road splits to wrap around the local pond, my left blinker clicks on of its own volition, and my car tires cant to cut across the traffic. The vehicle surges into the liquor store parking lot. Ten days clean at this point, I tell myself I've straightened out, and a little wine with dinner won't hurt. . . .

Waking up with the outline of Warren's back—all I ever see of him—I feel soldered to the bed, with cobwebs yards long grown from head to floor. For an instant I convince myself the binge was an awful dream. Then the tinny taste in my gummed-up mouth floods me with self-loathing.

So I find myself in the shit-brown aluminum chair again. The guy at the front asking if anybody's had a drink since the last group, and though I wonder about raising my hand, it hangs in the air of its own accord. I tell them I'm no alcoholic, but I'd shared a passed joint with a former boss, not wanting to seem like an ingrate. I fail to mention the five-dollar bottle of wine I'd drained later.

Part of me expects to be handed some kind of hall pass that says the occasional joint—when part of a necessary business interaction—is okay. Another part of me thinks—hopes?—the group police will charge down the aisle, hoist me up by the shoulders, then show me the door.

But I haven't yet seen anybody get kicked out, even a hallucinating homeless dude and one individual with Tourette's syndrome who once hollered out, *I wanna suck your titties.*

Over the months, I keep going back to the bottle, though with each relapse, I come back one notch humbler, more willing to take a suggestion I've scorned.

Like, get phone numbers of ladies and pick one for a sobriety coach you can call every day till you can get a grip. So I pick a lady in an A-line denim skirt and penny loafers, and maybe because her society lockjaw accent has the cadence of my mother-in-law's, I never call before I pick up a drink—when she could talk me out of it—only after.

How does Warren miss all this? Maybe he conks out, or maybe I'm a sneaky bitch.

I wake one night on the back stair landing, choking on bile that's erupted from my throat while passed out. Feeling my way up the unlit stairwell, I see at the top my pajama'ed boy, his frayed polar bear tucked under his arm, and around him is glowing some pale blue corona from a source I can't name, and his eyes are acetylene torches. I hoist him in my arms and feel his soft arms around my neck, and he pats my cheek and says, Are you okay, Mommy?

I lie that I am, and after I've settled him in his brand new big-boy bed, he corkscrews his way back into a dream. Then I stay all night propped against the wall, watching the light sift over him as if grated from the moon. Get a fucking grip, you drunk bitch, the sober part of me says. The two halves seldom war anymore, because they're never in my head at the same time. They've worked out some system of shifts: the sober voice only gets in during periods I'm drowning in remorse; the drunk voice is otherwise resident as I hurtle toward a drink.

The next night I humbly return to the shit-brown chair, trying to read the Boy Scout aphorisms hung from the wall, and I promise myself the first woman who makes me laugh, I'll get her number and call her the second I get up tomorrow. Doing it alone is not working.

The speaker's named Joan—an elegant pageboyed social theorist at Harvard whose unlikely outlaw stint in Alaska involved going to the bar one night in subzero weather wearing a tutu under her arctic parka, just to stir things up. Since the night I woke up after puking, I've become semi-teachable, and I tell her that I'm ready to hear suggestions. She says, Do some volunteer work.

So I start scrubbing coffee urns with the black marine, who tells me that, yes, even if I consider dosing the coffee with cyanide, the act of making it still constitutes spiritual progress. Joan also urges me to start praying to some half-baked higher power whose existence I argue against.

No way, I say. Never happen, no offense.

But her voice—speaking daily to me on the phone—keeps me postponing the drink I often feel myself barreling

toward like a boulder rolling downhill. With her ministra-
tions, I do not—for two months—drink: a white-knuckled,
tooth-grinding effort that impresses no one outside the
church basement I go to a few nights per week.

The sun rises and sets. The moon makes two arcs over
the house I fail to sleep in. I remember no intersecting days
with Warren, aside from how he takes evening shifts with
Dev when I go to meetings. It's as if he doesn't even live there,
which can't be right.

I don't write. I can barely read enough to grade the bushels of essays I lug around. And when I long to drive off to
the liquor store to buy and suck down fiery elixirs, spiritual
directress Joan the Bone—a nickname picked solely for the
rhyme—tells me I can do it first thing I wake up: *even before
you brush your teeth*. And while I mock her one-day-at-a-time
ploy as a trick for the dim-witted, since it actually means no
day dawns in which drinking is a good idea, I have to admit
that—sixty days in—when she buys me a celebratory bagel
with my coffee, I feel fresher inside, albeit a bit scooped out,
like a gourd. Stick a candle in my mouth, and you could use
me for Halloween decor.

It's September fifteenth. We sit at a nameless coffee shop
I call Now Baking, for the neon sign in its window. It's before the age of bottled water, when ordering a cappuccino
gets you crap coffee dollopped with whipped cream, a zigzag
of grenadine syrup, and a cherry on top. So we drink that
day unadorned diner coffee, mine laced with fatty cream
and enough sugar to induce a diabetic coma, sugar craving
being the curse of the newly sober. (One newly sober pal stole
half-sweetened baking chocolate from the kitchen of a friend
he was visiting—the host later found the wrappers stashed
under the guest room mattress.)

Leaves aren't yet tumbling from the trees, but for me, all color is leaching from the landscape. I'm blunted, muted, starved, yet stubbornly refusing the one suggestion everyone sober for very long makes: prayer. I recoil from any talk of spiritual crap, though I can't fail to notice that the happier, less angry ex-drunks talk about such matters without any strapped-on, phony-sounding zeal. Joan the Bone claims some nonbelievers use the group as a higher power.

Here, she says, are a bunch of people. They outnumber you, outearn you, outweigh you. They are, ergo—in some simplistic calculation—a power greater than you. They certainly know more about staying sober than you. She sips her coffee. If you have a problem, bring it to the group.

You're asking me to put my life in the hands of strangers who give not one real shit for my true well being?

They probably care more than you do, Joan counters. She points out how many of my own bright ideas for solving life's travails involve buying a flamethrower. Her jet hair is salted with gray, though a smattering of freckles conjures some twelve-year-old Joan I might've climbed a tree with. In truth, she's written articulately about the most unpronounceable continental philosophers.

I'm very astute, I say.

Or paranoid, she says.

I complain that lots of people in the room are crazy. Real wing nuts. You're asking me to confide in crazy people. Fuck-ups, most of them. I chew my red coffee stirrer into a frightful state.

No offense. Joan sighs. The fact that you've continued to drink—given your history of depression and family trauma—borders on the moronic.

I sip coffee and blink.

You're not bringing a problem to one person, she adds. You're asking the group. The group is guided by principles that the individuals in it don't embody solo.

It's the *one day at a time* crap—

So you never sat over a drink, thinking, I'll quit tomorrow. . . .

Every night.

It's no more nuts saying *Just don't drink today* than saying *I'll quit tomorrow*. Put your mind where your body is. *One day at a time* forces you to reckon with the instant you actually occupy, rather than living in fantasy la-la that never arrives.

I quote something I'd heard at one of my first meetings: *If you've got one foot in yesterday and one foot in tomorrow, you're straddling today—pissing all over it rather than living in it.*

See, she says, you do listen.

I sit inwardly grumbling in the muddy mind-set of the reluctantly unmedicated. I do not feel redeemed. I feel fallen, a long way fallen. Not drinking has chipped off some armor I've hardened over my softest aspects, and now I sit in a coffee shop niggling with a woman who most days feels like the only roadblock between me and a truckload of flaming horseshit.

She says, You honestly think you're gonna sit here with me and figure out how to conduct every day of your life henceforth without a drink?

Why not?

Because nobody graduates. Each day you'll *feel* different. If you're numbed out, you act based on how you're *supposed* to feel rather than how you *actually* feel. You need a toolbox of sober alternatives. Get more women's numbers. If I'm not around, you'll have to call somebody else.

I hate everybody else.

For somebody who worries about being judged so much, you're a tough crowd.

I say, Maybe I should use Jake's line: *I tell people I have an allergy to liquor. When I drink it, I break out in handcuffs.*

See, you're starting to like the group.

The religious shit—

Spiritual shit, Joan corrects.

Whatever. It makes my skin crawl. Anyway, I don't get how it works.

Joan says, You don't know how electricity works, either, but you use light switches.

I suspect a trap, I say. Like those ladies at the meeting. They're always offering to take care of Dev if I need help.

This bothers you? Joan says. One of your big grumbles is how no one helps with your son.

Warren helps more and more, the more incompetent I get. I got more accomplished when I drank, actually.

At this point in your life, you don't know how not to drink yet. No alcoholic does. It takes training.

I watch the yellow leaves blow down the street and eventually say, Maybe those women want to kidnap Dev, even.

Joan shakes her head and grins. Now that I've begun to say aloud what I actually think, head-shaking is a common response. She says, You spend way too much time alone.

Cut off as I felt from Warren before I quit drinking, it's worse sober. Now everything he does just irritates the shit out of me. I say, The only time I connect with people is away from Warren. That can't be good.

You told me yourself, Joan says, how weighed down with school he is—plus work, plus your three-year-old. Give getting sober a chance. Try not to make any big moves. The only way I know to arrive at balance in my choices is through prayer.

Like I get on my knees and say to the air molecules, Do I get divorced—and some note with *yes* or *no* gets lowered down to eye level, suspended on a fishhook.

If you need God with skin on, go to your group and ask the first person you see.

You want me to go to this group of virtual strangers and ask whoever I see first whether to stay married or not, then do what they say?

If you get miserable enough, you'll start taking suggestions.

But I didn't share my difficulties, and I didn't pray, and a month later, I got drunk.

24

Affliction

Affliction makes God appear to be absent for a time, more absent than a dead man, more absent than light in the utter darkness of a cell. A kind of horror submerges the whole soul. During this absence, there is nothing to love.
—SIMONE WEIL, "THE LOVE OF GOD AND AFFLICTION"

I had not planned to get drunk. Ninety days without a drink, I was slated to read poems at Harvard College. This is—for a poet with a shiny new book being ignored for two years all over the planet—a big deal. Still, I inwardly shrink at the prospect of standing without numbing agent before an audience who would see through my thin skin to a rapidly agitating heart muscle. (Was Warren's not being there due to the perennial unaffordable babysitter? Or did I discourage it? Or did he have a paper to work on? So much between us is blotted out.)

The podium I approach sits in the middle of a student

lounge with chairs lined up like a tribunal of judges. In my hand, the sheaf of papers shivers. I lean on the podium. I feel my puppet's mouth open and shut, and I presume the words written down come out, though I say little between the poems.

At the end, I'm okay, not having pissed my pants or had a seizure from shame. Some of my students even show up, which touches me. When dinner's suggested, I'm steered to a restaurant not of my choosing, the first joint with a liquor license I've entered in months. Any trepidations I once had about a cocktail's proximity go poof the instant I cross the threshold, for the atmosphere is harmlessly convivial.

At the podium, I hadn't felt like a poet. But here—among the patrons in crisp-collared shirts and wools that look nub-bily expensive—I'm Gérard de Nerval in Paris, just in from walking his lobster down the street on a leash. Somebody takes my coat. Every glass I pass is glittering. The host squires us to the heavy linen tablecloth, the chatter weaving around me, and when the waiter bends at the waist above me, smiling conspiratorially, I hear my puppet mouth ask for a martini.

That inverted triangle of glass—with frost at its lip and a speared olive at its nexus—is the perfect accessory to the place. No lightning bolt splits the chandeliered ceiling to pin me where I perch. No one's expression alters one whisker, and I don't even consider canceling the order, since just placing it shifted some geological plates around my innards. It lends an almost sexual thrill to waiting for it. Delicious, crossing the threshold into abandon.

The martini must've come, and I must've drunk it, but the wine and cognac and whatnot that I took in that night cauterize the memory. I briefly wake, stumbling down wet streets, looking for my car. How had I been deposited in

Boston's fashionable South End? I turn around on a cobbled street. I have an image of sipping green chartreuse from thimbled glasses, feeling it go down like race-car fuel. Are those people I knew?

Then I'm driving on a flat tire that flaps and flaps in time with the wipers in the thunderstorm. The steering mechanism is pulling hard one way, and I struggle with it while the paltry defroster does little against the windshield's inner ice. With my cold bare hand—where'd I leave my gloves?—I claw at the frost, and in a flash, the road before me splits unexpectedly. I press the brake, and the car yields to a spin. Just as I master the turn, the car stops twirling like a top and slides sideways. I see a concrete road divider sailing toward my door. In slow motion, it comes, and I feel like a corpse flipped from a catapult, flying at a castle battlement. Rain has slicked the street into black metal, and I know in one soul-destroying eye blink that my son will wake without a mother, for I'm at last about to smash into something more solid than I am.

But I don't. In some flash of molecular inversion, my car and I become ghost forms. The car passes skidding sideways right through the concrete. I sit unhurt, facing the wrong way on the river drive. I climb out in driving sleet just as a truck whooshes by, blowing its horn. I climb over the fence that edges the river, and I bend over to puke my guts up. Then I wait for the police to come arrest me. But they do not come and do not come.

I move the car over onto the grass and start stumbling home. The pebbles in the wet asphalt look like scales on a snake's back, and the road has a nasty tendency to squirm away just before I set my foot down, so a few times I stumble over a curb and sit my ass in wet grass. A mile or so on, I turn back and find my car still sitting saggily, unmolested.

Next I know, I'm creaking into my suburban house as my husband pulls the door open from inside. He's been up all night.

You can get up with him and get him ready, he says.

I'm sober enough by this time and gushing apologies.

You should be sorry, he says. He heads up the stairs, turning back to add a sentence of a type and tone he never uses with me, and again I remember it so clearly because it was so out of character for him: You smell like a bum.

Which is my moment of clarity. Not blinding flash nor drunk-tank revelation, not drinking out of a turkey's innards, not setting myself afire, but the dull thunk of reality as my husband's muscled calves carry him upstairs.

A moment of deep self loathing makes not drinking seem your only conceivable option. But I know that day how swiftly such moments pass, how cunning, baffling, and powerful my own logic can be. My head is grinding inside like a peppermill, and by dawn, a hangover has landed a cold hatchet in the back of my skull.

After horking up my stomach contents in Radcliffe Yard, I drive to the home of poet Thomas Lux and his wife. On sultry summer days, Dev played with their toddler daughter while Tom and his wife barbecued for a ragtag gaggle of writers. Since his wife toils as tirelessly as Warren, Tom and I occasionally meet in a park or meander our strollers through a mall crawl.

In grad school, before he'd been domesticated, Tom outdrank every two-fisted sot who came through. His escapades were passed around with the cheap wine. A die-hard Red Sox fan, he'd once broken his toe kicking a hole in the wall after a grisly loss to Cincinnati. A girlfriend who caught him cheating dumped his clothes out the window onto a New York street.

Then in a Cambridge bookstore years later, he tipped up his sunglasses to show his clear eyes while announcing to me he'd stopped drinking. That morning after my weepy crash, I stand snot-nosed before Tom and his wife in their breakfast nook, waiting for both of them to deliver some healing whap in the head.

Great, Tom says instead. You'll get sober, and your poems will get better, and your kid will grow up with a happy mother.

25

Reprieve

God is the voice that says, "I am not here."
— DON DELILLO, *FALLING MAN*

After sitting through a local hospital talk on getting sober, I approach the thirty-year-old doctor who'd been at the mike the way a thirsty dog approaches a water dish, and she sits with me outside on the hospital steps under a mist-drenched moon. It looks like nothing so much as a dissolving aspirin, vague and bitter at its edges as I feel.

As I'd twitched in my seat, shaking and jonesing for a drink, her fresh-scrubbed face and sleek chignon had evoked some pampered childhood full of ballet recitals. But at age thirteen—long before med school—she'd been living on the street, giving blow jobs at the bus terminal for dope. Sober for fourteen years, she'd just finished her residency. And for that, she credits a god I can't believe in.

But I'm desperate enough that night not to struggle so much as before. I tell her how Mother's radical overhaul for years might be convincing me that sobriety can transform others, just not me. (Thank you, Mother, for saving yourself so conspicuously that it saved us both.)

On the moonlit step, the young intern addresses me as I used to speak to the Down syndrome women I taught, so slowly that I can see her tongue move, saying I have a disease. It's progressive and fatal.

I nod. For the first time, the disease idea isn't just metaphorical, though Joan the Bone had once said (regarding the patience with which she listened to me drone on): When I look at you, I see somebody swathed in bandages.

On those cold concrete steps, some black river is rushing through me down to my fingertips. If I close my eyes to ease the headache I get from even soft moonlight, I can feel the car spin and see the concrete divider hurling toward me.

Progressive means, the young doctor goes on, whatever jackpot you just hit last night, whatever blackout, whatever bottom you found—that's where you go down from. That's your highlight. The top of the curve.

My mouth forms an O and the noise comes out for it's dawning on me that liquor will never again salve my aches or loosen the knots that bind me so graciously, as it once did.

You've passed some line where it works, she says. I used to try to figure it out. Maybe it's how the pancreas handles sugar, or some enzyme we give off when we drink that sets up a craving. But whatever line it is, you've crossed it. Somebody who's crossed the line and craves liquor like you do and wants to keep drinking is like a pickle who wants to be a cucumber again. You can't. It's over.

And so it hits me: I have to kiss alcohol goodbye—no half

measures, no quibbling, no champagne at the wedding, no valium at the dentist, no codeine for the cough.

Ninety meetings in ninety days, she says.

I don't complain but must've pulled a face.

It's like you have cancer, she says, and coming here is really chemo. It's not a luxury. It's not a help. It's what stands between you and going insane or winding up in the boneyard.

Ninety meetings in ninety days, I say. Consider me the Navy SEAL of sobriety. All *yes ma'ams*.

You have to start giving the higher-power thing a try— it's the one suggestion you skirted. You didn't pray.

Jenny doesn't pray, I say, and she's been sober twenty years. (Jenny is one of the sober ladies I'm getting to know.)

And Jenny's disposition?

Mean as a snake, I confirm.

You might find sober people who don't pray, but all the happy ones have some kind of regular meditative or spiritual practice.

There are humungous dark trees in the hospital yard, and I gaze into the torn-out spaces between them at a few sequiny stars.

I've never felt anything even faintly mystical in my life and tell her so.

Faith is not a feeling, she says. It's a set of actions. By taking the actions, you demonstrate more faith than somebody who actually has experienced the rewards of prayer and so feels hope. Fake it till you make it. Didn't you fake half your life drinking?

Wouldn't any god be pissed that I only show up now, with machine-gun fire on my ass?

First off—can't you see this?—you have a concept of God already. It's one who's pissed at you.

Which is oddly true, given my godless upbringing. Where had that come from? She must see the slack look on my face, for she goes on, Let's say your kid falls down and bloodies himself, or he picks up a butcher knife and hurts himself with it. Are you mad at him?

Course not.

Well, drinking is like the butcher knife. You have to put it down before you can let God in. It's like you have to break up with the guy who's beating the crap out of you before you can scan the room and find the nice guy who's got a crush on you.

I'm trying to start hearing the word *God* without some reflexive flinch that coughs out the word *idiot*. Maybe, as somebody suggested, I'd have to practice internally repeating God-specific sentences to hear them in my own voice.

She tucks a few wisps of dark hair into her chignon. An ambulance screams by.

After a while, she says, You should be dead tonight. We both should be.

My mouth's dry. I nod. It's a striking concept. Mostly I've thought of life as my right and death as an unfair aberration, but inverting the formula is no less valid. Life is a blessed aberration, a gift, and death isn't my business yet. I wonder aloud how many hours I've squandered fearing death.

You were saved for something, she says. Don't die before you find out what. What's your dream for your life?

The very concept makes me sag. I tap a smoke on the hard pack and light it.

Why's that such a foreign question? she wants to know. Poets are dreamers, right?

I exhale a highway of smoke and stare down it, then say, Each day has just been about survival, just getting through, standing it.

Don't you see how savage that sounds? Like, that's the way men in prison yards think. You live in a rich suburb and teach literature.

Composition mostly, I say (Lord, was I dead then to my blessings, a self-pitying wretch if ever one was). We're the poorest in the neighborhood. . . .

From what you tell me about how you grew up, the husband, baby, book, job *were* your dreams.

Staying sober, I say. I'd really like to patch things up with Warren, make a good home for my son. If I could write again, whether anybody liked it or not, I'd feel like I was reentering a conversation with the gods I worshipped all my life.

She looks at me and says, Nothing else? That's it?

My innards are roiling. The smoke in my mouth tastes like creosote, so I flick its small sparks away. Money, I say. I'd like some more money. It sounds shallow, but hell. I kind of have an idea about a book I'd like to write, about when I was a kid and my mom went crazy and my family came apart. But when I sit down with my notebook, my head goes blank. My mind's just fried. Still, we need some fucking money.

How much money would seem like a gift from God?

Having only made nine grand that year, I tell her twelve would be nice. That'd be fair, I say. I'd like a tenure-track job with health insurance, but Warren has medical, so I don't really need it.

Then pray for it. Just pray every day for ninety days and see if your life gets better. Call it a scientific experiment. You might not get the money, but you might find relief from anxiety about money. What do you have to lose?

It's like you're showing me a tree stump and telling me to talk to it.

You can make up your own concept of what to revere. Like nature . . .

I hate nature, I say. I don't mean to, I just never felt much about mountains and trees and shit. I have a genetic memory of pulling a plow or tilling the soil that repels me from dirt and green growing things.

Then think of the good parts in people—some Great Spirit, like the Native Americans have. Talk to it. Practice reverence at it. Attend it the way you've been attending these fears of yours.

That night in the living room, with Dev and Warren in bed, I take a small cushion down and get on my knees for the first time in my life—prayer number one.

Higher power, I say snidely. Where the fuck have you been?

The silence envelops me. There's something scary there, some blanket of dread around me that feels like God's perennial absence, his abandonment, if he does exist. (Now I'd call it my deliberately practiced refusal of his presence.) It's hard to sit in. A few seconds later, I say: Thanks for keeping me sober today. Then I get up.

Wait, the sober mind says—that's trying? You could've died last night.

I flop back on my knees. And help me. Help. Me. Help me to feel better so I can believe in you, you subtle bastard.

Such is my first prayer—a peevish start, tight-lipped, mean of spirit, but a prayer nonetheless. I vow to make it regular, this half-baked prayer. I won't get on my knees usually. But I will silently say, every morning, *Keep me sober.* At night, it's *Thanks.* That's all I can stand.

I pace around downstairs for a while with skin twisting around my flesh. Had I gotten drunk the night before in front of my students? How much would it cost to get the wheel I'd driven on fixed?

Finally, I slip into bed, and Warren stirs as he rarely does. His voice comes up in the dark. Have you been at your group?

I've been downstairs, I say. I promise, I'm not gonna drink anymore.

And he rolls over in silence, which is what I've earned.

26

The Reluctantly Baptized

He kicked off his loafers and threw his long ugly body out across the water.
        —GEORGE SAUNDERS, "THE FALLS"

Two days into my new sobriety, I'm spotting Dev on the monkey bars when a rise in my gorge announces the arrival of projectile dyspepsia. I yank him off the bars and sprint the block home with his jaw jaggling against my shoulder. Dropping him in the foyer, I scramble up to the bathroom just in time to pitch the contents of my stomach into the toilet.

Mommy? Dev cries as he climbs up.

Ts' okay, I holler.

I sit back on my knees as he hits the doorway.

What's wrong?

I'm okay, my little peach pie.

I yank a towel off the shower rod and wipe my sour

mouth. Then I pitch forward again with dry heaves till I'm coughing like a cat with a furball.

I feel his small hand on my back as he says, Did you get a bad food?

Maybe that's it, I say. I crane under the faucet and drink the warm metallic water straight from the spigot.

Then I fall to my knees again, and what I just swallowed reemerges into the toilet's blue water.

When Warren comes home, Dev is staring into the silver hole of the TV, and I'm locked in the bathroom, evacuating my innards every way I can.

I open the door to Warren's concerned face and say, I guess this is detoxing.

That night at Joan's urging, I check in to the Harvard infirmary, where I log my first nights away from Dev since he's been on the planet. When the internist asks how much I've been drinking, I can't exactly say—a lot. In my narrow bed, I get IV fluids and B vitamins and packaged sandwiches for the weekend till I level out, which the doctor swears will happen in a few days.

Joan shows up with a quart of orange juice and a list of women's phone numbers, but I'd have to use the hall pay phone, so I'm stranded with my own head. Which (unfairly, it now seems) curses Warren's hide for not being there to hold my hand. Why hasn't his love filled the black hole I've been pouring booze into?

Four days sober, I leave the infirmary feeling very shaky, on an Indian summer day. At home, I'm meant to be fixing dinner for the three of us, but I cut myself peeling a carrot, which leads me to some burst of undefended incompetence as wife and mother. So I swipe all the unwashed vegetables off the drain board and into the sink and throw myself into a chair.

Poor Mommy, Dev says. He puts his hand on my leg. You need to relax!

You shouldn't have to take care of me. I'm supposed to take care of you.

My mouth's so parched, and—seeing Warren's seldom used bottle of valium above the sink—I instinctively grab it. Before I can open it, I do have the sense to phone Joan the Bone, who's on her way to the theater and can't talk.

This, she tells me, is a test of your new willingness. You've gotta keep calling till you reach somebody.

I hang up and stare again at the medicine bottle. Raising it to eye level, I study the small blue pills, now glowing ethereally.

Are you sick? Dev wants to know. He's holding a matchbox car, studying me with the intensity I no doubt brought to my own mother, whose invisible engines of misery could—at the slightest spark—ignite and blast her off into the stratosphere. That level stare of his guides my hand to put the valium back above the sink, where the bottle pulses and throbs. That night I ask Warren to hide it from me.

I phone Lux, who's barbecuing for his family. They have us over. It's a freakishly warm day, so they've gotten the wading pool out. He pokes at meat splayed on the grill while Dev splashes around the water. I ask Lux, Do you actually pray? I couldn't imagine it—Lux, that dismal sucker.

Ever taciturn, Lux tells me: I say thanks for all kinds of things.

For what? I want to know, for I'm a habitually morbid bitch. Even my poetry is obsessed with our collective hurtle toward death—the prospect of my own death seeming specially tragic and unsung. For me, everything's too much and nothing's enough. I honestly can't think of anything to be grateful for. I tell Lux something like I'm glad I still have all my limbs. (Why—I now wonder—couldn't I register the priv-ilege of tossing my wriggling blond boy off the pool float?)

Lux stands in his baggy blue swim trunks at the bar-becue, turning sausages and chicken with one of those diabolical-looking forks. In the considerable smoke, he looks like a bronzed Satan at the devil's cauldron.

Say thanks for the sky, Lux says, say it to the floorboards. This isn't hard, Mare. What're you so miserable about?

In truth, I dread Warren coming home that night, how we skirt each other's paths, how he still looks at me with suspi-cion after my short sobriety. *I really mean it this time.* I fear I've sculpted for Dev a childhood tortured and lonely as mine was.

But to confess these realities to Lux would reveal too much of my chewing insides. Instead, I babble on about my long-held grudges against the god I don't believe in, saying, What kind of god would permit the holocaust?

To which Lux says, You're not in the holocaust.

In other words, what is the holocaust my business? When my own life is falling apart, he wants to know, why am I taking as evidence of my own prospects the worst carnage of history?

The smoke coils around him as he says, Try getting on your effing knees tonight. Just find ten things you're grate-ful for.

Your effing knees! Dev hollers, kicking his feet to motor-boat the raft around.

That night after he's tucked in, I do try to stretch out my standard two-sentence prayer habit a little longer by dredg-ing up a list of stuff to be grateful for, though not on my knees—no way am I gonna grovel like a reptile. Sitting in a red leather chair, I notice the cherry furniture Warren's par-ents gave us. I close my eyes a second, saying, Thanks for the furniture. And the rent. Thanks Warren hasn't left me and taken our boy.

The exercise seems so self-helpy and puerile, but a few more things come to mind inadvertently. Thanks Dev doesn't have a fever. Mother's sober. Lecia's business is going great, and her new boyfriend's a prince. Thanks for Joan the Bone and Lux. Also the infirmary this weekend . . .

Enumerating these small things actually pierces me with a sliver of feeling fortunate. Then from that one moonlit meeting, the young doctor's face rises up in me, and I think of what she'd said about asking for my dream, so I add, While we're at it, I'd like some money. Not a handout. I'm willing to work for it.

It takes me a full five minutes to shut up begging, and it sounds crazy to say it, but for the first time in about a week, I don't want a drink at all. It's an odd sensation, since the craving's shadowed my every waking instant for the past few years. But I abruptly stop feeling my skin like a too-tight sausage casing.

(This an unbeliever might call self-hypnosis; a believer might say it's the presence of God. Let's call it a draw and concede that the process of listing my good fortune stopped my scrambling fear, and in relinquishing that, some solid platform slid under me.)

I know people needier and way more deserving have prayed far harder for stuff they needed more: to feed starving children, say, to get a negative biopsy result. Nonetheless, it's a stone fact that—within a week or so of my starting to pray—a man I don't know calls me from the Whiting Foundation to give me a thirty-five-thousand-dollar prize I hadn't applied for. Some anonymous angel had nominated me and sent in both my poems and a hunk of a crappy autobiograph-

ical novel about my kidhood—maybe pinched from the writing group I'd once been in.

But the call brings no celebration. If anything, I call Warren feeling awful I got the prize instead of him. Plus, the foundation insists on flying me to New York to pick up the check
at a ceremony flanked by two mandatory cocktail parties—a
small one before, a large one after. I know with clammy certainty that I won't last fifteen minutes at a cocktail party
without imbibing.

Later, I cackle like a madwoman when Joan suggests my
quote-unquote higher power orchestrated this.

Horse dookey, I say. Surely you don't believe that. The
foundation probably started considering me back when I was
drinking.

With neck tipped to keep the phone against my ear, I
scoop out Dev's second helping of mac and cheese—plop—
into his ABCbowl.

You going to the meeting tonight? she asks.

Warren's got school, I say.

Well, bring Dev. In fact, I'll meet you both in the park
across the street in fifteen minutes.

I start to argue, then remember my new Navy SEAL of
Sobriety pledge and say okay.

In the park, the wind is howling like around Dracula's
castle, the sky yellowing with dusk. Dev's never out this time
of day, and his face has the wonder of a scuba diver. He points
overhead to charcoal-colored clouds mounting. We find Joan
bundled in a navy peacoat and beret. She's taken a seat on
the merry-go-round, its candy-apple red barely visible in the
waning light.

Dev hops onto the sitting post opposite her, and I give the
wheel a spin. Preach to me, I say to Joan.

You have to consider prayer a factor in the grant.

Oh, horseshit, I say, adding, Those wheels must've started to turn when I was still drinking like a fish.

Joan and Dev rotate around one slow loop as she says, But the vote was taken the day before they called you, around the time you'd started praying your ass off.

Wheeling past me, she leans back and asks, You're certain you'd still have gotten the grant—prayer or no prayer?

Faster, Mom, Dev hollers.

Of course, I say. Feeling the cool metal post in my hands, I dig in to driving the merry-go-round, putting my back into it, sprinting a few steps.

Is it at least possible, Joan says, that something—some force you've never looked for—could've invisibly tugged the vote in your direction? I mean, you're a hundred percent positive?

I feel some fleet movement travel through my chest—a twinge, a hint. This faint yearning was not belief itself, but wanting to believe. Willingness, it was which for months Joan had been telling me I lacked. My inclination to refuse faith begins to lean a few degrees toward the numinous. And I let fall from my mouth my first inadvertent blip of hope: Maybe, I say.

So say thanks tonight, you ingrate.

While I haven't exactly surrendered to the practice of hope, I'll keep at this perfunctory gratitude the way a stout girl drinks diet sodas while stuffing her face with cheese fries.

The meeting's about to start, Joan says, dismounting from her post.

One more, Mommy, a really good one.

I run around a few times as Dev whirls through what's become full dark. The trees are whooshing overhead from wind.

To Joan, I say, Okay, okay. Maybe, yes. It's possible. I'll say thanks. I mean, I've never prayed before, and nobody's ever called me out of the blue to give me money before.

Dev gets off the merry-go-round to stagger dizzy a few steps like a drunk. Then he pulls his hat over his ears as if to steady himself from above. He sits down hard in the dirt, looking puzzled a second.

C'mon, angel puff, I say to him. He climbs up and staggers toward me. The three of us are walking toward the street when he says, Who made all this?

The park? Some nice liberals, I say.

No, this, he says, sweeping his upturned palm across the autumn landscape.

Joan says, I believe there's a magic force that made it.

Like God? Dev said.

Because it's Dev saying it, nothing in me resists the sweetness of Joan's saying, Like God.

He grabs her hand, and the three of us stop at a crosswalk down from the church.

Joan asks if I can fill in for her at Thursday night's charity event. Our group visits a distant group to put on a meeting, swap ideas, basically mix it up. Isn't Warren home then? she asks.

The green light flashes. Dev drags us across the street.

Hurry, he says.

I tell Joan I don't know the guy driving or anybody else in the car. The prospect of riding off with strangers sans Joan feels like being dragged to some hideous school dance without a date. But I'm either practicing a kind of surrender or following instructions my inner outlaw would never have gone for.

She hands me a slip of paper with directions, saying, You show up at the post office in Lexington. Be there by six.

James'll show up. He drives a silver Benz. He's a lawyer. David will be there—you know David?

Sounds like directives for a drug deal, I say.

We're coming up on the white church, light spilling down its steps, where a few down-jacketed humans stand in small groups.

About the Thursday meeting, Joan says. Anybody with at least nine months can speak. You just sit and look pretty. Try to identify with whoever's talking without comparing yourself. And confide in at least one person. Get some advice other than mine.

You promise none of these guys is an ax murderer?

I didn't say that.

Unsupervised, I could go to that distant group and spontaneously pull my dress over my head.

If you do, just yell out, *My higher power told me to do that.*

Climbing the stairs, Dev says, This is a church?

Once inside, he beelines for the cookies, and I follow with my bag of coloring books and toys. (In daycare, Dev'll introduce himself: *My name is Dev, and I'm an alcoholic . . .*)

We settle into two folding chairs close to the door. People are starting to end conversations and sit. A guy comes up and with extreme courtesy says, Excuse me. There are no children at this meeting.

For a minute I sag in my midsection. I don't have any child care.

Sorry, he says, next time get a sitter.

Being here is life or death for me, I say. (Is this the first time I believe that?)

Oh, well, he says.

And I think of Daddy as I pull Dev on my lap and say, Kiss my Texas ass, buddy.

27

The Untuned Instrument

Ever tried. Ever failed. No matter.
Try again. Fail again. Fail better.
— SAMUEL BECKETT

On the appointed Thursday, I sit in a parking lot in the pissy, indifferent rain you get in New England autumns, versus the open-firehose storms the Gulf had once dragged over us back home. After what seems an eternity, I feel a pair of high beams arc over my face like prison searchlights, then this big silver ship of a car lunges into place. I climb out, holding a newspaper over my head. A few knocks on the side window, and the heavy door swings open.

No sooner does the door slam shut than I inhale— through the cigarette smoke—the stinging juniper scent of gin. It brings me up short. Maybe somebody spilled gin in his car?

You must be Mary, James says, We're waiting for three other guys.

He has a bald, remarkably flat head, which he's combed a few russet strands across—plus a beaverish overbite. He asks how much time I have, and I confess it's taken me a year to put together my first two months.

Maybe not gin, I think, but shaving lotion. Or I have gin on the brain.

Big accomplishment, he says, those first few months. Mind if I smoke?

The automatic windows hum down an inch, and he pats around his pockets for a cigarette. His overbite makes him look very eager for it.

That coming in and out of sobriety? Hard. He depresses the lighter in its socket. You detox over and over. You never get to the good part.

I'm ready for the good part.

The lighter pops, and he presses it to the end of his smoke.

I have to admit, I say, I do feel better since I started taking Joan's suggestions.

As James goes to replug the cigarette lighter in the hole, you can see how—from his perspective—the hole keeps edging side to side to thwart him. His head sways a little as he jabs at the dashboard three or four times. Despite the lighter's having gone cold, he presses it again to the end of his burning stogie, sending sparks all over his lap. Finally, he just drops the lighter in the ashtray like it belongs there.

This, I think, is as drunk a motherfucker as I've ever seen, fixing to steer the car I'm in. As a kid, I was trained to give the shitfaced room. Small white droplets of rain tap on the windshield when a knock on the back car door makes me startle.

In climbs big-footed David, red bandana around his head, along with a guy from our group named Jack.

Jack of the red curly hair, skittery-eyed Jack, who—on being introduced to me first—explained that he had a little touch of the schizophrenia, as he held index finger one inch from thumb. Mostly he stays medicated enough to hold down a job at the box factory. But he once showed up to arrange chairs with tinfoil over his head molded into a knight's helmet with a kind of swan shape on top, convinced his girlfriend was beaming messages to him through the radio. It's a tribute to the radical equality of the room that I never overheard anybody ever challenge the reasoning.

We say our hellos, David inquiring after my son and Joan. Then everybody sits in unwieldy silence. I keep waiting for another passenger to ask where the hell the gin is, and when they don't, I convince myself I don't smell it. Paranoid—jeez. But then I look at the cigarette lighter lolling in the vast ashtray and wonder.

Jack says, I have a Tab I'd like to open, but I don't have enough to share around. We all tell him go ahead.

About that time, a whoosh of damp air sweeps in as another trench-coated lawyer, Gerry, swings open the back door. He squeezes Jack in the middle with his knees up, and he's holding the Tab like a bazooka he's about to fire off. I strap on my seat belt.

At intervals, streetlights flash across James, who squints at the road like a pilot trying to feel his plane toward a fogged runway, and to his credit, he drives slow enough. Ultimately, we halt alongside a whitewashed church. Stepping out, I see enough tilted motorcycles to ferry a whole clubhouse full of Hells Angels. The crowd out front is mostly ponytailed guys in leather jackets and vests and black chaps. Chains hang off their belt loops, and each foot is shod in a storm trooper's boot. I spy nary a female.

James heads for the bathroom, and I grab Gerry's elbow to tell him—a total stranger, nicely as I can—his pal James is shitfaced.

The rain's stopped, and a few shy stars are trying to blink.

You're mistaken, Gerry says. I know him. We've made coffee together in Lexington for four years.

Trust me. A drunk man. Extremely.

If that's true, Gerry says a little wearily, he can't speak. I'll take his keys away. But where is he, anyway?

Through the church full of assembling bikers, I follow Gerry back to check the men's room. We're outside looking around in the few seconds before Gerry's meant to start speaking when a guy with frizzled muttonchop sideburns says, You looking for the trench-coat dude? He's under that big low-growing Christmas tree over yonder.

Sure enough, James had crawled under the giant evergreen, curling around the trunk like a cut worm to pass out.

We figured he was too clean for homeless, a guy with a shaved head edges up to say.

James! Gerry hisses. He's squatted down to peer under the branches. James!

Y'all want us to pull him out? the guy with muttonchops asks. A nod from Gerry, and two fellows wiggle under the tree and drag James toward us.

One of his wing tips is missing. He sits on the ground with his head hung down. His hair has come unpasted, the stiff strands flipping up like a car hood popped open. A few stray pine needles stick to one cheek.

Looks like you been to a party tonight, brotha, the shaved-head guy says.

I'm sorry, James is saying at random intervals. His hands cover his face as he busts out in backbreaking sobs.

The bald guy pats his back, saying, That's all right, honey, we all been there.

A guy with a tear tattoo says, You're in the right place, buddy.

After a while, tear-tattoo asks me what James does for a living, and when I say *lawyer*, he says, Maybe I should get his card.

Gerry fishes around in James's coat pocket to drag out his car keys. Then the two bikers sling him up and shoulder him, spread-armed as if for crucifixion. They transport him up the church steps with the unwieldy shuffle of good bouncers. The bald guy asks if this is where we want him. When I say sure, they deposit him, aslant, onto the back pew.

In corner chairs in the back kitchen, we find David and Jack bent over a can of pink cake frosting, each holding a tablespoon. David's spoonful of icing has twin teeth marks raked through it like Jeep tracks in mud.

Busted, David says.

This was extra from the cupcakes, Jack explains.

Gerry tells them about James's fall off the wagon. Jack sits folded in half, hugging his knees as his forehead creases. With the toe of his shoe, he outlines the same linoleum tile over and over.

David strokes his beard, saying, That is genuinely terrifying. Why'd he go out drinking?

Gerry shakes his head, saying, Mood and happenstance don't drive us to drink. Turning to Jack, he says, Explain it to the newcomers.

He got drunk, Jack says, because he's an alcoholic. We are given a daily reprieve based on our spiritual condition. Without spiritual help, the lure of the drink is too much for most of us.

Is he quoting something? I ask David.

It's their book, he says. The once über-logical David tells me with aficionado's conviction that at the halfway house where he's a current resident—and Jack a former one—there's a hard-core book study every Sunday. I should go.

Riding back to Lexington in the backseat, I sit between passed-out, openmouthed James—his breath on the side window spreading and receding like a tide—and curly-headed Jack. I think with rue of Joan the Bone's injunction to ask the first person I saw about my marriage. I'm still angling to prove what crazy bullshit her much vaunted surrender-to-the-group concept is. Whatever Jack's brief spells of clarity, he rarely goes to a meeting without jabbering out something nutty.

So I start whispering my tale of marital woe to Jack, who sits in the hunched posture of somebody tensing against a blow. Occasionally, he'll tug a red curl over the crease in his forehead.

Eventually, I wind down and ask, what should I do? And I wait for the word salad of his scrambled cortex to spew forth. Instead, his eyes meet mine evenly, and he says—as it seems everybody says—You should pray about it.

But what if I don't believe in God? It's like they've sat me in front of a mannequin and said, Fall in love with him. You can't will feeling.

What Jack says issues from some still, true place that could not be extinguished by all the schizophrenia his genetic code could muster. It sounds something like this:

Get on your knees and find some quiet space inside yourself, a little sunshine right about here. Jack holds his hands in a ball shape about midchest, saying, Let go. *Surrender, Doro-thy*, the witch wrote in the sky. *Surrender, Mary.*

I want to surrender but have no idea what that means.

He goes on with a level gaze and a steady tone: Yield up what scares you. Yield up what makes you want to scream and cry. Enter into that quiet. It's a cathedral. It's an empty football stadium with all the lights on. And pray to be an instrument of peace. Where there is hatred, let me sow love; where there is conflict, pardon; where there is doubt, faith; where there is despair, hope . . .

What if I get no answer there?

If God hasn't spoken, do nothing. Fulfill the contract you entered into at the box factory, amen. Make the containers you promised to tape and staple. Go quietly and shine. Wait. Those not impelled to act must remain in the cathedral. Don't be lonely. I get so lonely sometimes, I could put a box on my head and mail myself to a stranger. But I have to go to a meeting and make the chairs circle perfect.

He kisses his index finger and plants it in the middle of my forehead, and I swear it burns like it had eucalyptus on it. Like a coal from the archangel onto the mouth of Isaiah.

The night sky edges across our windows, and I'm carried inside this tank of a car. James wanting to get drunk makes sense to me, and I like how nobody rebuked him after. But there were also no-bullshit acts like not letting him speak— crazily he'd wanted to testify about his sobriety. But Gerry took his car keys, and made him sit through the meeting.

It's my life outside these oddballs that scares me.

David? I say, leaning forward.

Yes, ma'am. He turns down the radio.

Any chance you cadged that frosting?

Gross, Gerry says. You're not gonna eat that.

David unzips his backpack, flips off the frosting lid, and hands it back, saying, I feel like I should wipe the edge on my T-shirt. You know, sanitize it.

Taking the can, I dig in and run my finger around the edge, then stick it in my mouth just as Gerry's hand reaches back, hovering for the handoff.

28

Halfway Home

. . . Everyone I met
Wore part of my destiny like a carnival mask.
"I'm Bartleby the Scrivener," I told the Italian waiter.
"Me, too," he replied.
        —CHARLES SIMIC, "ST. THOMAS AQUINAS"

Rather than rejoice about the grant, I start to steel myself against the ceremony now rushing toward me like a jail on wheels. David and Jack convince me to join their Sunday study group at a shambling halfway house. The place sits on hospital grounds across from a methadone dispensary. A favorite joke of the residents is to use magic markers to manufacture a *closed* sign on the clinic, so eventually the panicked methadone addicts holler and pound the door.

Walking into the house, I expect to find tattooed thugs and strippers and former felons, which I do. But most are

working stiffs, plus a professor. There's even a disbarred lawyer who'd once passed out in a snow bank and woke in a hospital with neither hand nor foot—the blackened appendages
having been amputated—a fairly common injury among the
homeless, it turns out.

On my first afternoon there, David bends over a former
hooker's study guide for her high school equivalency exam,
and I see the hooker later help a Boston banker handle his
own toddler during a visit—the same unlikely, democratic
exchange of skills as my Cambridge meeting.

The house director is a woman I hate on sight: a stork-
thin blonde with manners that strike me as prissy, like she's
instituting a no-cussing rule for the house, for one: say a bad
word, you chip in a buck to the party fund. Save for a slightly
spastic right hand, she looks like a runway model, being
nearly six feet tall with long hair the color of sunflowers. In
the recovery community, she's legendary. Mother Teresa with
altitude, I overhear one resident say. She did biochemical research for NASA before her career in chemical dependency.
The white Mustang convertible she drives has a high-test engine, and I once heard a felon remark she looks like a dentist's
wife, i.e., never done a day's work in her life and somebody
always taking care of her teeth.

Her name is Deb, and when I whine about how hard it
is not to drink on afternoons alone with Dev, she invites the
two of us to stop by the house for a snack. I can bring a video
for him. She'll even personally counsel me if she has time.

Fat chance, I think at first, but the lure of a sober hang-
out proves too great to stay away. The writers I once passed
flasks of vodka back and forth with have been scarce since I
pledged off.

On Dev's first visit to the house, he passes two residents

exhaling plumes of cigarette smoke, transfixed by a Thai kickboxing movie. I tuck Dev's head under my coat, and he says, What're they watching?

Grown-up show, I say.

In the director's office, Deb stands to greet us, and her shaggy dog licks Dev's face, almost knocking him over. She holds out her slightly drawn-up hand for him, and he wastes no time in asking what's wrong with it.

She bends to fix her brown eyes level with his blue ones to explain that she got drunk and overdosed on a nasty drug called cocaine.

I try to steer Dev off the subject, but Deb says, It's normal to be curious. Anybody with a disability needs to be comfortable with answering questions about it. She holds out her arm, saying to Dev, You can touch it if you want to.

He pinches it like a melon, then grabs her wrist and pulls it away from her body, as if to straighten it through his own grunting will, saying, Does that hurt?

Deb says, No, it just feels tight.

You were drinking cocaine, and your arm just spronged up that way? Dev wants to know.

Oh, no, she says. The stuff kind of poisoned my head, and I fell down and hit it. I woke up and I couldn't move at all. Paralyzed. Couldn't talk, either, not even yes or no.

Which dramatic bottoming out is hard to assign to one so put together as Deb. You can believe that she was married to an Oxford biochemist, that she modeled, that she ran a lab—all true. But that she drank like me and couldn't quit? Impossible to picture.

I was four or five years in and out of rehab, she tells us. On the night of my head injury, a cabdriver—actually an Indian guy I'd met in one detox—found me passed out in a pool of blood on the kitchen floor. He'd driven by the house and seen my car parked sideways in the driveway, gotten worried, and broken in.

Dev says, What did you think when you woke up and couldn't move?

I'll tell you exactly what it was, she says. *Boy, do I need a drink.*

Dev giggles at this. Part of me thinks, Maybe if I'd heard this at his age, I wouldn't have wound up such a sot.

It took me a long time to learn how to talk again, she says. I could show you how to eat with a spoon, but I couldn't say the word *spoon*.

Over months and months in long-term rehab, she learned to speak again, then read, then write with her left hand.

Let me see you walk, Dev says.

She rises, and the dog rises. She walks across the room, doing a kind of swaying swagger to heft the less mobile right leg forward apace. She does it with a rock star's prance, adding a runway spin at the end.

Dev says, You walk pretty good. That leg goes a little crooked, but you go fast.

She looks at me and says, Do you need to have a grown-up talk?

It pains me how visible my shakiness is, but it touches me also. (Such small kindnesses—so commonplace in my life now—dismantled me then.) I've spent so long hiding how I really feel; now that my brassy attitude's stripped off, I feel naked as a frog.

She tells Dev to put in the video we've just picked up. I tell her the guys in the front room are in the middle of kick-boxing, and Deb says, They won't mind. From her doorway, she announces to the two guys on the sofa that the afternoon

movie is a cartoon of a Rudyard Kipling story from India
about a mongoose who has to fight a cobra.

Picture the blond tyke on the couch with a paper plate
holding potato chips in his lap. He's flanked by two muscled
and tattooed guys named Sam and Joe. (I'll later learn that
black-haired, wasp-waisted Sam was a former Mob hench-
man who once trafficked in pallets of stolen government
cheese.)

At a nearby table, I ask Deb how she came back from
the head injury. Looking at her, I figure rich parents bailed
her out.

Both my parents had just passed, she says, about a year
apart, and I was an only child. Then my doctor husband divorced me the second I woke up.

Told she'd never walk again, by month three, she wowed
the once skeptical staff by using a brace and a cane to peram-
bulate around.

And when I came to this house . . .

As a resident? You were checked in here?

Yeah, she says, from a public detox, because all my insurance had run out. I got here still not quite mobile, and
my counselor told me I had one day to feel sorry for myself,
then I had to get to work. I started praying all the time, took
a clerical job at a bookstore. Soon as I had enough money, I
bought a broken-down Mustang convertible, hiring guys in
the house to rebuild it in bits and pieces. The doctors had told
me I'd never use my right hand again, and I knew the stick
shift would loosen my arm up.

I'm staring at her as if for the first time, for it would never
occur to me that somebody as well turned out as Deb had
suffered trials that dwarf my own.

Part of me clings to the idea that *I* am the most disadvantaged person trying to get sober—a joke, given that I'm thin

and white and employed, HIV-negative, with insurance and reasonably straight teeth. Before I judge somebody or indulge a groundless fear, Joan says I'm supposed to ask myself: *What is your source of information?* If the answer is—as it usually is—*I thought it up*, I should dismiss the idea.

Deb sips her coffee as I say, A head injury and a divorce—what an excuse to drink.

The head injury convinced me I had to get sober or die, she says. I was on the surgical table twenty-four hours. If the cabdriver from rehab hadn't come by, I'd have died for sure—a lot of coincidences went into getting me here. Plus, they said I'd never walk again. Those things were gifts.

A gift? I say, blinking with disbelief, for this is the kind of shit people said that makes me nuts.

Without my brain injury, Deb says, I'd never have quit drinking. It saved my life. It was a higher-power thing.

I don't get that stuff, I say.

You're not praying yet? Deb wants to know.

I am . . . well, barely. I figured out that asking for relief from the craving every morning seemed to make it go away. I figure it's like I mesmerize myself. But God? No way. I'm an agnostic.

A spike-haired blonde passing by with a cup of coffee says, Another intellectual? Lucky you.

Janice, this is Mary.

Janice slides next to me, saying, Like the Blessed Mother, huh? She gives off the kind of outlaw ethos that appeals to me.

Deb says, Mary's reluctant to get down on her knees because she doesn't believe in God.

I add, What kind of God wants me to get on my knees and supplicate myself like a coolie?

Janice busts out with a cackling laugh, You don't do it for God! You do it for yourself. All this is for you . . . the prayer, the meditation, even the service work. I do it for myself, too. I'm not that benevolent.

How does getting on your knees do anything for you? I say.

Janice says, It makes you the right size. You do it to teach yourself something. When my disease has ahold of me, it tells me my suffering is special or unique, but it's the same as everybody's. I kneel to put my body in that place, because otherwise, my mind can't grasp it.

Out of the kitchen holding a crockery mug comes a lady with cropped dark hair and eyes the color of fresh-dug earth. Liz has the frank, inquisitive gaze of a trained scientist, but softer in its aspect. The clubhouse/college-dorm feel of this place suggests a camaraderie lacking with my writer pals.

Can we help her not drink? Deb asks Liz. And it appears a sincere question.

Absolutely, Liz says, pulling up a chair. We're all about the not-drinking thing.

From the TV in the living room, the mongoose is announcing his name in a chittering falsetto: Rikki-Tikki-Tavi!

Deb explains that Liz had run a lab at MIT, adding, She had a hard time with the higher-power thing, too.

I stayed sober a year, but I was white-knuckling it, Liz says. It was hell, and I drank again. Second time around, I started the prayer stuff. You get miserable enough, you'll take suggestions.

Liz envisions her higher power as a sober part of herself— some saner, more adult aspect of her own psyche. She says, It's not so different than Freud's superego—or healthy ego.

I tell her maybe I could pray easier if it was a positive-thinking exercise.

From the next room, Sam says, The smart money's on the cobra. Wanna make a gentleman's wager?

Two'll get you four for the mongoose, Joe says.

Dumb money, Sam says, but I'll take it.

I'm thinking, This doesn't seem like a cult or a trick, there's something—I don't know—*realistic* about these women. They don't seem misty-eyed or drippy. So I tell them how shaky I am inside, afraid my marriage is a mistake, and how I can't even read anymore.

Liz says, Try lying in bed, picturing yourself held by two giant hands.

Giant hands?

Liz says, I know what you're thinking. *That's idiotic.*

For some reason, my eyes well up, and I find myself saying to women I just met, I'm afraid I'm not a good mom.

Dev runs up to me, announcing the victory of Rikki-Tikki-Tavi.

While Sam is fishing bet money from his jeans, Joe says, Never mess with a mongoose.

Sam drops quarters into Joe's open palm next to a wadded-up dollar, adding—genially, it seems—Eff you, brother.

Deb shoots him a look. Joe pockets the change, then pulls it back out. He offers to buy Dev a soda.

Can I, Mom? Dev says, for soda is contraband in our house, and I say sure, and later in his life, Dev will remember the chesty rumble of the soda machine in the basement of that place, the faded tattoos on the bulging biceps of Joe and Sam. He'll also remember the claim of Philosophy David (who's working a security job while trying to start a novel) that a doctor made him keep the bandana on his head else it might explode. Several afternoons a week we spend with this company.

Let go, they urge me. Let go. I have no idea what this letting go means beyond surrounding myself with sober women—I mostly talk to women—and grouchily taking their suggestions.

But each sober day seems to widen the chasm between Warren and me. The halfway house is another hiding place from our troubles. With our therapist, I sit across the room and rail. Rather than scrutinize my own absence—first via booze, now via recovery—I devote each session to old griev-ances. How Warren went running during Daddy's funeral, took his paternity leave when Dev and I were still in the hospital, left every single late-night feeding for me to han-dle alone. Not that these complaints don't have weight, but I nurse my grudges like foundlings.

For his part, he succinctly itemizes the shrewish railings I've unleashed on him. Eventually, he says, I can't undo the past, Mare. What about now?

Surely you're not gonna be one of those women, the doc-tor says, who gets her husband's attention and then bails out just when there's a chance to get a marriage she wants?

But I am. I say, I just don't trust that he cares for me the way I want.

What you want, nobody can give you, he says.

Intimacy exercises that involve backrubs and kissing, I flatly refuse to do. There's a door slammed shut in me that I've barred. And Warren says—on the topic of our nonexis-tent sex life—*One day you're gonna reach for me, and I won't be there.* (From today's vantage, my withdrawal and coldness seem so corrosive and mean, I want to shake my young self.)

Prayer isn't patching up the marriage yet, though applied to small problems from time to time, it sometimes yields up a feasible idea.

Stranded without child care once, I figure out after a prayer—it comes to me—that I could slip Chris, an ex-hooker from the house, a few bucks to hang out in the quad with Dev for a spell, which seems safe enough for an hour or so.

After, I snap Dev in his car seat and drive Chris home. She's nineteen, six months clean, with lush dark hair and the pink cheeks of a cheerleader. In the car, she talks about heroin as a devious lover. Her voice is smoky as a lounge singer's, a real Billie Holiday rasp.

I look in the rearview. She ran Dev around so hard in the quad earlier, he's slumped over in his car seat. So I ask Chris how sobriety's treating her. This is the cusp of my starting to ask after other people—a change from pouting alone on the porch before.

I'm starting to feel all clean inside, she says.

How does that happen? I want to know, for I keep having dreams that I'm getting sneakily drunk and trying to hide it from people in my group.

I'm making amends to people I've screwed over, she says. Like I shoplifted a bunch of stuff from this deli, and so I brought the guy thirty bucks. Korean guy. He was really nice about it.

The snowy roads make us fishtail now and then, and traffic has started to drag.

See, I resent this shit, I say, pressing on the horn, adding, Even the fucking traffic feels orchestrated to fuck me up. Dev needs to eat. You need to get home before dinner curfew or you're grounded.

It's funny, she says, how everybody else is traffic, huh?

I laugh, saying, Making amends to other people isn't high on my list right now. I'm still too pissed at everybody.

Think of all the ways you've let yourself down, resentments against yourself, she says, and she looks at me from down her turned-up nose.

I say, I'm too much of an asshole even to contemplate looking at that carnage.

Listen to how you let your own mind talk to you, she says. You'd fight anybody to the ground who said that shit to you.

Just as traffic starts to ease up, the car's engine light goes on. A mile or so later, steam starts pouring from the hood. I steer to the far lane, cars whooshing past in snow. Dev wakes up blinking and crimson-cheeked in his down jacket, really hungry.

Stepping out of the car, I land ankle-deep in slush and start swearing under my breath.

But no sooner do I pop the hood than a vehicle pulls alongside. Joe and Sam happen to be driving a borrowed tow truck that has—another stroke of fortune—jugs of blue engine coolant. From a paper bag on the dash, Joe's massive mitt draws out a glazed donut for Dev. He says, Here you go, tough guy.

We all stand on the side of the road in the blue dusk, Dev snug in big Joe's arm and gnawing the pastry as Sam doctors the radiator. For an instant, I can feel the gratitude seep up from my damp footsoles—one of my first pure instances of it. Back in the car, I announce it to Chris.

Say thanks, then, she says.

I just did. Joe wouldn't even let me pay for the antifreeze.

I meant, she says, say thanks to your higher power.

I look at her round girlish face. She still has a few snowflakes in her dark lashes.

Thanks, H.P., I say, but it actually shames me, for some reason, to say such a dumb thing.

(A year later, Chris would flee the house to stick up a bank with a machine gun. She'd cop heroin and overdose in a park. I last saw her in a public hospital, where she was blind, HIV-positive, and pregnant with a baby who died—I believe—around the time Chris did. She didn't make it to twenty-one. Thanks, Chris T., for hauling my ass into the light that day, and still.)

A week before the Whiting ceremony, Lux and I take our kids to the park, settling them in to swing through their low-slung arcs. It's near dusk when I ask if he has any truck with a supreme intelligence.

C'mon, he says. There's a force that fuses the greeney flower. Look at these damn kids. There's an energy that threads through us that deserves your reverence. It's not all serial killers and Hitlers.

Of course it is, I say.

Ever notice, Tom says, your mind immediately leaps to the most extreme position—like, if you turn to God, He's gonna nail you to a tree.

I'm scared I'll drink at the Whiting ceremony. A week away. A year ago I'd have killed to get to go to double-barrel cocktail parties.

Lux looks at me sideways and asks, Want me to go with you?

Though I'm a champion whiner, inclined to blame people for failing to help, I almost never outright solicit a favor. The offer stuns me. I'm teaching in New York that day anyway, Lux says. I could make it to the second party—the big public one.

On the appointed day, I stand before the Park Avenue hotel they booked for me, wondering why it looks so familiar. As I stare up at the facade, it hits me that—at some point in the 1970s, I scored cocaine in this very building.

At the elevator, the numbers glow down to me while I stifle an animal impulse to bolt.

Help me, blind power, I think, get through. (Prayers of

real desperation like this—however sparse—are starting to come unbidden. Sometimes one even leaves a sense of peace—or at least hope that peace is coming.)

I fling my hanging bag on the bed and instinctively draw the drapes against light. Looking at myself in the bathroom mirror, I decide that the black dress I zipped on thinking it made me look employable as a professor in fact has shoulders padded like a linebacker's.

I flop on the bed and click the TV on to channel-surf when I notice that, just under the screen, sits a minibar. I can picture the frosty air it holds, its tidy array of bottles. Eyeing it like I would a crocodile sloe-eyed on the bank, I back out of the room and take the elevator downstairs again.

The desk clerk says housekeeping can take it out eventually, but they're overloaded. So I sit in the lobby, hands twisting in my lap, until it's time for the drinks I can't have.

29

Ceremony (Nonbelievers, Read at Your Own Risk: Prayer and God Ahead)

YOU ARE HERE.

— A MALL DIRECTORY

I don't enter the Morgan Library for the second reception thinking, Wow, I've arrived, my life will change now. I edge in sweating like a sow, shaking like a dope fiend, and heavy with dread. I feel the paste pearls around my neck and the cardboard soles of my cheap shoes.

The party spreads out inside a book-lined cathedral— forty-foot ceilings lined with volumes. Glass cases around its perimeter glint in the low light. One holds a Bible printed by Gutenberg, another a Shakespeare folio, another etchings by poet William Blake. Standing there, I study a knot of people at the room's center with no idea how to elbow my way in. Then with some jostling, the crowd parts, and there stands Toby Wolff, looking immensely hearty dead center of that vaulted room. He wears a blue blazer and has a beer in his hand. Hardly anybody reads memoirs much, but I check them out by the armload, including that year Toby's *This Boy's Life*, his own hair-raising account of battles with a bullying redneck stepfather.

The fact that Toby's origins are almost as scabby and unfortunate as my own partly make him approachable. Plus he taught me in grad school before he was a big deal. I'd even written him for advice on how to rework the discombobulated novel I'd cobbled together into nonfiction. (The concocted protagonist had served as a correction to the real me—beautiful and noble; she'd volunteered at the local nursing home and did differential calculus in sixth grade.) The letter Toby sent back got taped over my desk. It said:

> *Don't approach your history as something to be shaken for its cautionary fruit . . . Tell your stories, and your story will be revealed . . . Don't be afraid of appearing angry, small-minded, obtuse, mean, immoral, amoral, calculating, or anything else. Take no care for your dignity. Those were hard things for me to come by, and I offer them to you for what they may be worth.*

For the unbeliever I am, Toby's wave in my direction is incalculable shithouse luck. (I'd later call it grace.)

He gives me an avuncular hug and claps my padded shoulder. He's mustachioed and fit, with a military bearing earned in Vietnam. Good for us, huh, Mare?

I'm trying not to drink, I tell him, a confession he barely registers.

Stand next to me, then, he says, adding, I'll drink for you.

Toby doesn't drink for me, of course. But he feels like a pillar propping me up. I woodenly shake hands with men in suits and ladies in cocktail clothes. Who they are, I have no clue, beyond knowing they outearn me. In the midst of this, Lux shows up, and between him and Toby, I manage not to accept a single glass of the nonstop champagne flutes foisted on me from various silver trays.

Later, I'm called onto the stage, where I'm supposed to stand immobile while they read my résumé—skimpy compared to every other. Then I'm meant to shake hands with one paw while I take the check with the other. Instead, I've fallen into such a flop sweat that a pause in the speech causes me to grab the check, thus failing to strike for the photographers the pose of humble gratitude I'd practiced for weeks in front of a mirror.

At the party, Toby introduces me to his agent, a whippet-thin blonde with silver bangles up her muscled arm. She wears a raw-silk size-zero pencil skirt and is almost exactly my sister's height in pricey heels. She lets Lux and me tag along to the expensive dinner for Toby.

At the table, I feel conspicuous not ordering a drink, and—since water glasses haven't shown up—as everybody else hoists a glass at Toby, I feebly hold an invisible glass in the air, as my head says, *Do you think they are convinced by the nonexistent drink you are faux-lifting?* I look at Toby, and the fact that his eyes don't meet mine makes me wonder if he actually asked the agent whether Lux and I could come, or are we crashing? Am I supposed to pay for this meal? Next I know, Toby holds his glass aloft again, saying, And to my old pal Mary.

A few minutes after everybody's gone back to their conversations, I blurt out to nobody special, *Thanks for having us.* I say it loud enough that neighboring diners look over, but nobody says anything back. Lux keeps talking to the woman on his left. About that time, a passing waiter stops beside me to lift my napkin and lower it into my lap.

I keep sweatily waiting for somebody to ask me why I'm not drinking so I can fire off one of the salvos Joan and I came up with, for to an alcoholic, not drinking is conspicuously freakish. (Now I realize nobody would notice except another sot.) Maybe I'll just say *Fuck you* or *On second thought, maybe I will . . . Waiter!*

I look at my watch. Fewer than ten minutes have elapsed since we sat down, and the night yawns before me. I slip off to the pay phone to call Joan the Bone—no answer. Ditto Deb. Coming back to face a full wineglass, I see Lux isn't in his seat. I stare around at Toby, his agent, his editor—their faces are at the pinched end of a telescope. At one point, I think, *What if somebody says something to me?* The next instant, *What if somebody doesn't?*

In the bathroom, I splash some water on my neck and study how pasty I've gone. Plus, my nose has grown gargantuan pores—I never exfoliated! And boy am I shiny. I shift the pins at the back of my head around, but a tendril keeps springing loose on one side. I try slicking it down with a few flecks of water. The hair spray in it enlivens it to jut out.

Eventually, I latch myself into a stall, heart thumping, dizzy. It occurs to me I actually need to brace my hands on either side of the walls. My insides are ricocheting around when the old advice burbles up.

Pray. Get on your knees and get still.

So I kneel down, my bony knees in a puddle of Lord

knows what. None of the promised quiet comes to me. *Breathe,* Joan tells me all the time. *If you don't believe in God, you know there's scientific evidence about the psychological benefits of meditation, even among nonbelievers. Breathe deeply to calm yourself. Then count your breaths to ten, over and over.*

But when I start counting breaths—slow, deep inhalations—I almost hyperventilate. Correcting for it, I speed up my breathing till I'm panting like a pooch. After a lifetime of effortless breathing, I've forgotten how. For a few minutes, it feels like gasping underwater.

I try to detach from the scattered thoughts that float up in me, and they start to drift away from the small damp spot I'm kneeling in. Silently, I say one of the few prayers I know, the serenity prayer—maybe my second or third truly desperate prayer.

I clasp my hands together before my chest, and where my head has been jabbering, I find unusual space. *Please keep me away from a drink. I know I haven't been really asking, but I really need it. Please please please.* Starting to get up, I kneel again. *And keep me from feeling like such an asshole.*

Those of you who've never prayed before will cackle like crows and scoff at the change I claim has overtaken me. But the focus of my attention has been yanked from the pinballing in my head to south of my neck, where some solidity holds me together. I feel like a calmer human than the one who'd knelt a few minutes before. The primal chattering in my skull has dissipated as if some wizard conjured it away.

I walk back to the table with a pearl balanced in my middle. And Lord am I hungry.

Lux is in place, and my wineglass has been swept away, replaced by ice water. I ask for the bread basket and tear off a piece of the rough Tuscan bread and dunk it in the peppery green olive oil—never has bread tasted so good. I gobble up three pieces before the salad comes.

For most of the meal, I sit dumb as a stump, honestly listening to other people's tales with little thought for where I can wedge in a comment to justify all the chow I'm wolfing down.

As the dessert plates are being cleared away, Toby nudges me to ask after Mother, whose travails I regaled him with as a student. Since I've just been in Texas to clear out her ex-boyfriend's belongings that summer, her latest romantic misadventure is fresh in my head.

Toby says, This was your mother's new boyfriend? What happened to the nurse?

She got sober. He didn't, the nurse. That's the hell of it. She picked this subsequent guy sober.

At first Mother described the new guy as a boarder. Ben Barker, his name was. I expected some homely local Joe, but in the picture she sent, Ben towered over Mother with the lean frame of a basketballer. He had steely razor-cut hair and deep blue eyes. A health nut, Ben occupied a room in a house whose curtains were saturated with menthol smoke. He introduced to Mother's kitchen the Cadillac of vegetable juicers along with a flat of wheatgrass for squeezing all the chlorophyll out of.

It's supposed to clean your liver, Mother told me. It's filthy stuff to drink.

How can you tell your liver's dirty? I said.

That's what I wanted to know, Mother said.

Tell me he's got a job at least, I said.

He's retired, she said.

I thought he was, like, fifty.

(Which, by the way, was way younger than Mother.)

She told me Ben had done well farming all over the Midwest, but the crop prices kept dropping and he'd sold out.

He kept his truck parked in the garage but mostly tooled around the county on a racing bike worthy of the Tour de France. He also had a fancy fiberglass kayak he took out in the bayous at dawn among the alligators and morning glories.

He got Mother taking pricey vitamins by the fistful. He wanted her to flush out her nose with salt water snorted from the spout of a porcelain Indian neti pot, but she eschewed that and kept burning cigarillos, though she did sip infusions of Chinese herbs he bought at the Buddhist temple run by Vietnamese monks.

One morning Mother called me to ask a question I found strange.

Did you ever meet somebody you thought wasn't who they said they were?

I hadn't. I'd met all manner of strange individuals. But other than a tripped-out guitar player who'd told everybody he was Moses, I'd never met anybody whose stated identity I questioned. How, I asked Mother, had she come to this?

Well, she said, he'll be telling a story, and he'll say, "The guy said to me, 'Bill . . . '" And I'll say, "But your name's not Bill; it's Ben."

At that time the sheriff in our town was a guy I used to steal watermelons with named Stooge. On the phone, Stooge didn't sound overexercised. Ben Barker's truck was registered legal in the name he'd given Mother. Stooge doubted the guy was some lost gangster.

Lecia told me the guy seemed too well spoken, too well read, to be outright dangerous. (Which, I now think, fails to take Ted Bundy into account.)

Another morning the phone rang early, and Mother

whispered that Bill was in the shower, but she'd gotten his license out and his name wasn't, in fact, Ben Barker. It was Wilbur Fred Bailey, she said. And his ID was from—let's say—Kentucky.

At this point Toby interrupts to comment on the poetic perfection of the guy's actual name. Wilbur Fred Bailey, Toby repeats. It has a Faulkneresque ring.

I notice the rest of the table has gone quiet. The agent has her hand on a glass of water. Toby's editor is leaning forward.

Fred's the ideal middle name for the guy, Lux says, who's heard the story before. *Fred* has that foreshortened, temporary feel to it. A real trailer-park name.

So what'd your mother do? Toby asks.

I briefly stall like an arid engine, for it's different telling the story sober—and to these people. But Lux gives my elbow the slightest tap, and, since the current of the story has me in its grip, I start right up.

The morning Mother found the license, I told her to run to the library and xerox it, then drop it by Stooge's office. She did copy it but changed her mind about the sheriff, because—it turned out—Wilbur Fred was paying all her bills.

Which pissed me off, since I was paying her gas bill and grocery bill. As was, it turned out, my sister. I made Lecia go down there and call me with Mother on the line, so we could confront this bookkeeping inconsistency.

Mother elided it by saying, Oh, Ben doesn't pay those. He helps me out all kinds of ways.

Helps you out how? I wanted to know.

How? Lecia said.

Well, he cuts the grass, Mother said.

I pay Sweet to cut the grass, I said, referring to an old pal of my dead daddy's.

I pay Sweet to cut the grass! Lecia said.

The agent said, Hilarious. Triple-dipping. What a woman.

Lecia said, Let's you and me talk after this.

Mother said, If Sweet lets the grass get too long, Ben cuts it. Plus he edges the walk real straight. He takes the tops off jars. He hooked up my VCR. He takes me out for Mexican food. . . .

You could be in danger here, Mother, Lecia said.

He's good company, Mother said. Besides, I'd hate to be a dime-dropper.

A what? Lecia said.

A snitch, Mother said. A tattletale.

But drop the dime Mother did, after Ben, aka Wilbur Fred, took out the trash one day, failing—as she'd told him to do a zillion times—to reline the can with a plastic bag afterward. She later said it had been the straw that broke the camel's back. The very morning of the unlined garbage can, she called Stooge, who called the feds, who descended on my childhood home with dope-sniffing dogs.

What're you looking for? Mother asked the agent who checked her in to the Holiday Inn, courtesy of the government.

Guns, drugs, and money, he said.

They found none.

Four days after Wilbur Fred vanished back into the penal system from which he'd escaped, Mother got a call from a young woman from Detroit. She was mother to Wilbur Fred's kids and alleged that he'd left her—hidden in Mother's house—some much-needed cash.

Sure enough, in Mother's old magazine rack under a batch of New Yorkers, Mother found a paper sack containing ten thousand dollars cash—money Mother decided was hers.

The woman threatened to come down there armed with some of Wilbur Fred's posse, and Mother told her, Come on, I'm locked and loaded for bear down here.

Where, Toby finally asks, did she meet this guy?

Church, I say. At which everybody laughs.

You should write a memoir, the agent says, and across the table, she hands me her creamy card, which I resist pinning to my dress like a merit badge. No way is the card a ticket to ride. It is a chance, though. For years I've circled Boston agents like a horsefly on the off chance they might drop a card.

On the way back to the hotel, Toby says, Don't be disappointed if my agent doesn't sign you. She's never taken anybody I've recommended.

That worries me not at all, since I'm so unable to get a pen to traverse a white sheet, I doubt I'll ever have a single page of anything to send her.

But a small part of me wonders if prayer wrought that whole series of wonders. Joan tells me without it that I'd never have gotten (a) sober, (b) the grant, and (c) the invitation to the table where the agent solicited me and not the other way round. Nor would I have (d) dared tell Mother's goofball story without Toby drawing it out of me, for I'd have been too busy trying to pass for an East Coast swell with an Ivy League hookup instead of the cracker I was.

That may be so, I tell Joan. But I've also prayed to write as well as Wallace Stevens, prayed to be five-ten, and not had those prayers answered. As Emile Zola once noted: The road to Lourdes is littered with crutches, but not one wooden leg.

30

Hour of Lead

This is the Hour of Lead—
Remembered, if outlived,
As freezing persons recollect the Snow—
First—Chill—then Stupor—then the letting go—
        —EMILY DICKINSON, "AFTER GREAT PAIN"

Only an alcoholic can so discombobulate her insides that she might weigh in her hands two choices—(a) get drunk and drive into stuff with more molecular density than she has, and (b) be a present and loving mother to her son—and, on picking the latter, plunge into despair.

Which explains why I don't deplane in Boston, saying, *Lucky me, freed from paycheck work. Let's settle down and raise a book.* Instead, I come back feeling alternately mite-sized and unworthy, panicked as a felon facing the electric chair thanks to that fat grant. The time I'd bitched for years about not having now falls in abundance. But each day becomes a gray tundra I wade across.

Notebooks from that time contain increasingly ornate doodles, designs and lines like (I kid you not) *I am sad, the end, by Mary Karr.* In the past, I've been able to learn poems or whole paragraphs by heart. Now lines pour through me like water.

Guilt shadows every underemployed breath. Maybe I steer clear of Warren so much because while I do less, he slaves like a field hand—a forty-hour work week, classes three nights a week, with massive course work and a book-length master's thesis on Robert Lowell to finish, plus Dev in the evenings and the magazine. Any night he's home by six, I saunter out to a meeting. Our couples therapy has trailed off. The trips to his parents' big house, I virtually stop going along on—Christmas being an exception—arguing that the abundant booze makes me nuts.

The more Warren does, the more lardassed I get, wallowing in my dusty psychic moonscape. I complete not one sit-up, squat-press no weight, trot not a block. Thrown into a pool, I'd have sunk to the bottom and drowned before flapping a stroke. My daddy's phrases for the lazy sometimes flurry through me—*Wouldn't say sooey if the hogs were eating her . . . Wouldn't hit a lick at a snake reared back . . .* Standing in the shower, I feel something on the back of my leg that turns out to be my ass.

One day I might splay across the sofa staring at infomercials with the sound off, wondering whether the Abdominizer is the answer, or the Pocket Fisherman, or that glittering altar of knives.

My mental function drags. I walk out leaving the refrigerator open, lock keys in the car more than once. Warren and I sleep together on separate sides, and while for years my revved-up libido has amused me in private, now even that has puttered to a halt. At the halfway house, I develop an aficionado's taste for Thai kickboxing. Or I languish on their porch among the disabled, pondering the design on a pack of smokes. Or I sit alone in a donut shop drinking coffee with shaking hands till it's time to get Dev from daycare.

Still depressed, my shrink tells me, and she gives me pills that send color flushing back into the tips of leaves at least for a week or two, but I don't know how to write about color. My only vocabulary belongs to feeling dark and dead. I go days without obsessing about a drink, then—pushing Dev's stroller past the sour fumes of a beer joint's door—have to restrain myself from running in and downing the first Bud I can get my mitts on. These powerful urges are close to complete madness, the old drunk self so fully occupying my body, it's like being possessed.

Joan praises my prayer regimen—however minimalist— the one or two sentences morning and night. But she wonders why don't I apply prayer to my other woes: floundering marriage, the work, insomnia?

Oh, please, I say on the phone. For me, *god* is a lowercase noun. God with skin on, as you said. You women keep me sober.

You haven't let go yet.

People keep saying that. What's it mean?

It's like there's some hook in your head. You're still fueling your fears by intellectualizing them, thinking this way and that.

Everybody needs a hobby.

Unless it's gonna lead them back to the bottle. You're not even kneeling yet.

Sometimes I am.

Yeah, like twice, she says.

Why don't I feel better? I say. I've doubled my Prozac.

You do feel better, she says.

The fuck you say, I shoot back.

You were sobbing uncontrollably the first day we talked. You had to check in to the infirmary. Now look at you.

The more I stall, the more Dev cranks up. In the park one day, he takes his best friend's front tooth out with a stick. Another afternoon I'm collapsed on the sofa, and he pulls on my hands, trying to drag me upright. Get up, he says. The most cutting memory isn't his fury as I recede from him, but his playing quietly, studying me with squiggles of worry around his mouth. I think our therapist has gone to France, or have we stopped seeing her after over a year of spinning our wheels? My focus is sobriety, not therapy.

Maybe that time is so blurry to me—more even than my drinking time—because we remember through a filter of self, and of self I had little, having been flattened like a cartoon coyote by an inner anvil. With no self, experience streams past. Time lags until it's sponged up. What I've forgotten from those sober months astonishes me.

I can't even dredge up how Warren and I decide to separate for the summer. I pushed for it, I think, or did I only find the sublet? The marriage is an airless box. Outside it, I'll spring into being—so I believe.

I do recall confessing the decision to Joan. I've dreaded telling her because I think she might stop taking my calls. On the phone, I blurt out, Warren and I got the separate apartment. We're gonna try it for a few months this summer. Dev will stay at home. We'll go back and forth.

I don't recommend—

—I know, that I make any changes before I've been sober awhile.

At least a year, Joan says. Before you make any major decision, take a year for a cold look at all *you've* done wrong in it. Just chronicle the resentments that are really chewing you up. Get it down on paper.

I've been looking at myself in therapy off and on since age nineteen, I say.

A lot of therapy is looking through a child's eyes, she says. This is looking through an adult's. You have some nutty ongoing resentments about loads of people.

Like about my writing group? I say, for I'd told her at some point I feared my writing group looked at me like I was stupid.

Any chance that's from your head alone? Joan asks.

Maybe, I say, but it's terrifying to think I might not be able to trust my instincts.

Joan sighs over the receiver. I can relieve your mind right now: You *can't* trust your instincts. What makes you think they think you're dumb?

Just how they look at me.

Aren't these, like, the smartest people—in literary terms—on the planet?

They are. Doctors of this and that, translators from many languages.

Joan says, Let's just assume, then, that you're the dumbest person in the room—

Ouch, I inwardly say, for her sentence sang with truth, reverberating like the bronze of a bell.

—all things considered, that's not so dumb. I mean, in terms of the general population.

Which is true. I actually feel relief at that.

If you live in the dark a long time and the sun comes out, you do not cross into it whistling. There's an initial uprush of relief at first, then—for me, anyway—a profound dislocation. My old assumptions about how the world works are buried, yet my new ones aren't yet operational. There's been a death of sorts, but without a few days in hell, no resurrection is possible. You don't have to be Christian for the metaphor to make sense, psychologically speaking.

My weight drops back to the double digits. I'll be walking down a street, and I suddenly feel panicked, as if the earth beneath me has caved in and I'm free-falling. My head buzzes constantly, as if an electric shaver's running over it, some tugging metal teeth traveling over my scalp. I can hardly sit still.

Crazy. What I've always feared the most—that I'd go cuckoo, like my mother—seems to be happening. I don't hallucinate. I lack any grandiose Napoleonic fantasy. But every aspect of my existence has canted me deeper in a dark space. The mind I thought would save me from the trailer-park existence I was born to is not—as I've been led to believe—my central advantage.

When does the idea of suicide become a secret relief, a pocketed worry stone I can rub a slight dip into?

It's an old specter. As a kid, I watched Mother disappear into the occasional locked bathroom with a gun, and I'd alternately banged my fists on the door, begging her to come out, then stood back and hollered she should go ahead, I was sick of her shit. My best friend from high school, Meredith of the leonine hair, tried after law school to cut her own plump throat and nearly bled to death—the first of ten or twelve attempts over ten years. I'd flown her to stay with me a few times, checked her in to the hospital a few times, more than

once gone to a shrink with her. (She'd die of liver cancer fifteen years later after a brief but brilliant legal career, medicated into a stupor, weighing near—no exaggeration—four
hundred pounds, which size kept her off the transplant list.)

Before I was twenty-two, I knew a spate of successful (is
that the parlance?) suicides. On my childhood block, three fathers took the wrong end of a gun into their mouths. Of my six
California roommates, I buried two as drug casualties. Quinn
the Eskimo shot himself with the gun he'd brought to California to defend his old man's honor.

But Forsythe went most crazy of us all. On the beach,
he'd picked up and brought home a girl with a baby, and after
the girl passed out in his room; he dumped a bag of pot all
over the infant in its portable bassinet. Forsythe's roommates
found the walls scrawled with toothpaste, the baby wallowing in marijuana, and an album going on the turntable with
a framed photo of Forsythe's father propped up and circling.
Within the year, Forsythe died in the family garage of carbon
monoxide poisoning.

Suicide as an idea seeps into your lungs like nerve gas.
No precipitating event prompts my fixation on dying, just
the dull racket of my head's own Chihuahua-like bark—*death
death death*. It becomes the one rabbit hole that will hide me:
I can just cease to be. Picking up a drink would betray everybody who's poured effort into my sobriety—like my suicide
wouldn't? But death—now, there's a one-stop-shopping idea.
Over the months, I start to convince myself that Dev'll be
better off without me (a grotesquely self-indulgent notion no
parent can afford).

One Saturday morning, after sitting up all night re-
writing a suicide note whose maudlin, pathetic details are
thankfully lost to time, I take a call from Deb in the halfway

house. She offers to buy me lunch. I can interrupt my death for lunch, right? Writing the suicide note made me feel good enough to have lunch.

At some point, I confess that I have a garden hose and duct tape in my car trunk.

She signals for the bill and stands, saying, C'mon, I'm checking you in to the bin right now.

But I begin to backpedal and prevaricate. I'm joking, I say. She presses, and I press back. Warren could get custody of Dev if I go into the hospital. We may divorce, and he has all these lawyers in his family, and he'll get custody. . . .

Promise, she says, promise you'll call or go to the hospital if you need to.

The next day, after a sleepless night when the dead space inside me spread like spilled ink, I drive off under the cobalt blue summer sky with the garden hose in the back of my car. But with every small click of the odometer, my doubt grows, for starting to glow inside my shadowy rib cage like a relentless sun is Dev's face. I can't leave him the legacy of suicide, I think. I just can't. He'll find out somehow. Flying past me are objects I might swerve into instead—telephone pole, tree, a ramp I could sail off the edge of into oblivion. I unclick my seat belt and try to imagine my face shattering the glass into exploding stars. But I'm a coward, and I also suspect it's just my luck that I'll only crush my body to live on wired up to a breathing machine.

Finally, I pull off the road into a gas station, where I bend my head to the steering wheel, sobbing, and suddenly flying through me comes a new image of Dev charging around my study with his red cape behind him. He's coming for me, I think, like a superhero. He's flying me out of myself.

A teenage girl taps the far side of my windshield to ask,

Are you okay, lady? And I nod and wipe my eyes. I reattach the seat belt and edge up to the road with my blinker on to turn around. Heading to the halfway house, I drive for the first time in my life under the speed limit, obeying every arcane law, slowing to let grandmothers cut in front of me. It's a relief to place myself before the staff person on duty, asking him to call my doctor, because I'm fixing to off myself.

PART IV

Being Who You Are Is Not a Disorder

Being who you are is not a disorder.

Being unloved is not a psychiatric disorder.

I can't find being born in the diagnostic manual.

I can't find being born to a mother incapable of touching you.

I can't find being born on the shock treatment table.

Being offered affection unqualified safety and respect when and only when you score pot for your father is not a diagnosis.

Putting your head down and crying your way through elementary school is not a mental illness . . .

—FRANZ WRIGHT, "PEDIATRIC SUICIDE"

31

A Short History of My Stupidity

The history of my stupidity would fill many volumes.
—CZESLAW MILOSZ, "ACCOUNT"

Remembering the day of my suicide, I see myself at the hospital's intake desk, holding in my nail-bitten hand a red and white health insurance card embossed with the seal of Harvard University. *Veritas*, it promises: Truth. Weighing in the low triple digits, I'm sheathed in a black knit minidress with a boat neck (*Vogue* headline: SUICIDE DRESSING: THE FINAL CHALLENGE).

In sobriety, I haven't so much gone insane as awakened to the depth and breadth of my preexisting insanity, a bone-deep sadness or a sense of having been a mistake. Maybe because I feel I am not now who I was then, I have to stare askance at that time, squint to see past clotted and curdled thunderheads to the initial instant of what then seemed like my last crash—a time I now call my nervous breakthrough.

The woman who takes my insurance card has tangerine-colored nails and a soft Caribbean accent. She hands me a fistful of pink tissues and asks do I want some herb tea. She keeps some in her drawer. It's Sunday, and the office is empty but for her and a guy in golf clothes in the corner.

I want the tea but say no thank you, for that's how I believe the human economy works—on some perverse system in which people who offer to do nice things for me are furtively pissed off by acceptance. So it's better to refuse most kindnesses I come across, an interpretive model of human behavior that—it's clear enough now—fosters the crappiest of conceivable attitudes in me.

It's no bother, she says. I'm getting some tea for myself.

The warmth beaming from her face can't reach me. I'm too bent over some rotted core, as if to protect it from her. She stands, and a glance from the golf-clothes guy makes me want to crawl under her desk.

God how pale I look in the hospital. Crying through my globbed-up mascara has pinched my lashes into clownlike points, and the swollen eyes give me a lizard look. And rivers of snot I keep honking into wads of pink tissue. How long have I been crying? Days, in some ways, years.

(If I could tap my own shoulder, I'd say, *Of course you're crying, honey. You're fucking starving. Drive through a burger joint. Hell, supersize it, spring for a shake. Then go home and take a bath with some dish detergent. Tell your son you've gone to Tahiti for an hour. Take the longest bath in the world.*)

I'm so watery at my edges, so permeable, so easy to hurt, and my inner monologue—what you would hear more or less constantly, should we turn up the volume on it—went, *Oh shit, stupid bitch. What've you done now? Fuckup fuckup*

fuckup . . . The only way I know to twist the volume off is to choke it with exhaust.

Hence my need for custodial care at the place all Harvard spouses go. The diagnosis was underwhelming: severe depression, along with insomnia and unfettered sobbing. With the tagline—persistent suicidal ideation—came the inpatient recommendation of my therapist, whose house I'd been driven to by Granada House staff. My shrink had been on her way out of the country, and maybe I had the sense to go inpatient before she vanished.

The intake nurse brings me back a steaming mug of tea, taking from her drawer packets of honey and sugar and little red plastic stirring sticks, and the small civility of this makes me want to run out the door. I'm in a state of mind that can only be described as feral.

She settles back to typing the form, asking, You and your husband are at the same address?

We go back and forth, I say. We've been separated less than a month.

I've refused to call my husband so far, though my therapist rang him before she arranged for me to get admitted. The mere sound of Warren's voice would slam down on me a sledgehammer of guilt at leaving him to care for Dev solo.

If my four-year-old has a nightmare—a new trend since his dad and I split up—I pretend to unscrew his head and shake the scary parts out, and that's what I hope the hospital staff can do for me. (Ever notice, a lady in a meeting once said, that people only shoot themselves in the head?)

After the paperwork is done, two large but understated men show up to steer me to the ward.

Before I walk out, the Caribbean lady studies my face with a notch in her brow. (Where is she now? Maybe she told her husband about me that night, or maybe she just got on her chubby knees to pray for some peace in me, and maybe that's why I'm alive to type this. Dear Caribbean lady, last seen typing up my plastic wrist bracelet: You mattered.)

One guy offers to carry my purse, and I start to say no thanks when I realize I signed away my purse and who gets to carry it the instant my name flourished across the paper saying I was a danger to myself.

We cross the sloping green hills as evening comes across, me bookended between the two men. The high windows on the redbrick buildings with shades half drawn seem like lidded eyes looking down at my collapse. The grass level is straight as any crew cut. The grounds seem grander than my college.

Are you at Harvard? one guy says.

My husband works there, I say. I teach one class.

I feel so dead inside, as if the giant oaks are moving across us rather than us under them. I wonder aloud if I'll keep that teaching job after my stay.

No worries, the other guy says.

It's true that Warren's former teacher Robert Lowell wrote of himself among the blue-blooded "Mayflower screwballs" here in Bowditch Hall.

> I strut in my turtle-necked French sailor's jersey
> before the metal shaving mirrors,
> and see the shaky future grow familiar
> in the pinched indigenous faces
> of these thoroughbred mental cases . . .

We reach a metal door, gray as a slab, and one guy draws a heavy ring of keys from his belt. Without warning, I think of my son. The image comes unprompted and hits me like a linebacker's tackle, with the force of Old Testament thunder that all but knocks the wind out of me.

If I were right in the head, I'd at that instant be bathing him, gathering his slippery body from the suds, rubbing his head hard with a towel. I could pause to bury my face in his buttery neck.

I could ponder Warren making the bed as Dev bounced naked on it, his sturdy body flying under the flapping mainsail of our king-size sheets. How Warren would bundle him up like a ghost and wrestle him down and let him escape—the pure loving ritual of all that I've walked away from.

The attendant slides the key into first one heavy metal door, then another. Each man holds one open for me, and it's all I can do to keep from buckling in half, folding up like a lawn chair.

But my legs obediently carry me into the metal stairwell. I hear the deadbolts twist behind, and a clawed panic starts scrabbling through me.

We face a final door whose long glass window is embedded with chicken wire. Through it, I see people move as in slow motion. The door swings open, and their heads turn curiously to stare at me, and stepping onto the ward, I smell piss.

Piss is the territorial marking of the predatory animal. It also signals the uncontrolled release of fear in terrorized prey. I know people pissing in hospital corridors is frowned on and must be quickly mopped up. But the smell persists anyway, and as I enter that urinous climate, the kernel of fear I'd kept buried in my center cracks through its shellac casing. Terror begins to sprout its black ivy up my spine and down along the insides of my arms. I become very small then, telescoping down in some inner tunnel as the world shrinks and gets far away.

And pumping through me like methamphetamine is the screaming message that I've *lost Dev, lost Dev, lost Dev* . . .

I sit woodenly before the next intake nurse, water coursing down my mask face.

She has an open face—Italian, maybe—round as a skillet. And she's tiny. She could be in fourth grade, except for being pregnant enough to use her belly as an armrest.

By the time she asks, *Did you have a plan?*, I've already told so many strangers, I forget to be embarrassed. I was gonna spirit away our rusting car to a town called, metaphorically enough, Marblehead—the very name seemed apt—like I have a big, swirly marble on my shoulders where a human face should sit. There I'd suck off a garden hose purchased for that purpose.

We can take care of the insomnia starting tonight, she says.

I don't want any barbiturates, I say. Nothing addictive. No valium. No ambien.

I'm almost crying again. It's as if some paper-thin membrane in my head holds back this flood, and any discomfort tears through, cranking the sob machine to full bore.

The nurse looks up from her notes to describe some old antidepressant I can take as a sleeping pill—only if I need to. Not addictive at all. No side effects other than dry mouth in the morning. She sets down her pen, saying people who are sober take it all the time. (She pronounces it *sobah*, in the manner of the inner-city Bostonians at the halfway house.)

Do you mind if I talk to somebody about it? I mean even tonight—on the phone. Before I take it.

She fixes me with her almond eyes, and the calm she gives off reaches me. Maybe it's some pregnancy hormone juju, for her skin is dewy in the manner of the seriously knocked up. But just

sitting there, I sense a warm light the color of faded violets settling around us.

She asks, Are you in some kind of recovery?

Nine months, I say, digging into my purse side pocket
for the little medallion I'd gotten. I suddenly notice that the
hand holding the medallion has a plastic wrist bracelet. I tell
her I'm not exactly a poster child for the sober.

You're laughing at yourself, she says. That's good. Were
you depressed before you quit drinking?

A thousand times worse then. That's the nutty part. I'm
actually better now, but look where I am.

She'd twisted her black hair up the back of her head, but
it's that frazzly kind of hair that could tear loose any instant.
She asks, Do you have a higher power yet?—pronouncing it
hi-yah powah in a way that loosens the knots in my shoulders.

Telling her about the few sentences of prayer I march
through morning and night, I notice around her neck a small
gold cross. She says, So nothing changed with the praying?

It sounds so fake to say it, but only after I started praying
was I able to put sober days together.

The nurse is looking at me with a steady gaze. You know
what's amazing? she says. Even planning a suicide, you didn't
pick up drugs or alcohol.

I knew they didn't work anymore, or I would have.

Which is both miraculous and true. I tell her how many
people helped me, how drinking or doping would feel like letting them down.

When I ask what I should call her, she tells me her name
is the same as mine.

On the narrow bed, I lie in the sweaty certainty that I've
saved my own life but lost my son. Surely Warren will divorce
me now and take him from me—that's part of the fear that

has kept me in the marriage, his family redolent with law-yers. Every fifteen minutes, a flashlight shines on my face to be sure I haven't hanged myself, and—so I'm not unnerved by the light—the person whispers *check*, which process I intend to speak to them about tomorrow. If you're not suicidal when you get here, these intervals could drive you to it. *Check*.

My roommate looked at me with glassy eyes when I came in. She didn't budge then, but now, every time they shine the light and say *Check*, she shifts around under her sheet.

I think back to the morning when I'd worked on the sui-cide note feeling already dead. It's a thousand years ago, the writing of that note.

Six a.m. I'd been in the old house alone with Dev, get-ting ready to leave for a few solo days in the sublet. I stared into the small screen of the big honking computer, typing onto its moss green surface, which was free of any welcoming iconography, a blinking letter C is the cursor. The C had a greater-than sign after it: C>.

C for *cunt*, I thought, for that's what I am, a worthless cunt of a mother who can't take care of her own kid without ingesting enough alcohol to stun an ox.

To my left, the light shifted, and there was the red-cheeked Dev in his Superman costume, half the cape listing in back. To his blue shoulder, he'd attached one side with Vel-cro and kept reaching behind himself and twisting in a val-iant attempt to find the other piece of Velcro on the opposite shoulder so he could fly right.

I captured one arm and dragged him to me. I sank my face into the doughy flesh of his neck. His shoulder rose to squeeze my face out. For a few minutes, he airplaned around the small office.

He stopped abruptly to lay a pudgy arm along the chair

rest. He picked up the photo of Mother sketching when she was about my age.

Is this you drawing? he wanted to know.

It's Grandma Charlie, I said. Dev fingered his grandmother's profile with curiosity. She has your face, he said. Now she was alive and newly sober, and her demon had entered me, her face submerged my own.

He'd inherited her artist's eye and the keen intelligence that found subtle likeness. As a room parent at his daycare, I'd recently planned an activity that involved making faces to show different feelings. But I'd discovered that most three-year-olds have only *sad* and *mad* and *glad*. Dev had *surprised*—eyes wide, mouth a perfect O, eyebrows lifted. He had *hungry*—a leering look at imagined cookies. He had *worried*—a subtle look in which the twin trajectories of his royal-blue eyes dragged themselves inward. He had *guilty*, which was *sad* with the inwardness of *worried*.

I have a monkey face, I said, adding, Your nose honks when I pinch it. I pinched his nose and made the squeaky clown-nose noise—*ee-oo, ee-oo.*

The note I would leave for Warren told him how, within weeks of scattering my ashes, he'd find some cheerful, barrette-wearing Elizabeth of a girl, a blonde from Smith or Barnard or Wellesley. Her Fair Isle sweater would fit better into her in-laws' Christmas photo than my black schmattas. She would give Dev blond siblings. I'd get scissored from his memory like some grubby nanny from a distant past. He needed to be rid of me if he was to thrive.

Looking into Dev's face, I could almost feel the darkness leave me, but something in me held on to it.

(*Where is God in this scene?* my current spiritual advisor would ask. Now I'd say, He's right there. In full power in the body of the boy, whose light I had to defend my misery from.)

Dev said, No more work.

I said, No more work, just play.

Which in some lackluster fashion, I did until his father came to keep him for the weekend, while I disappeared into my sublet. Before Warren got there, Dev was Superman, and I was a distinctly unwondrous Wonder Woman.

Check.

In the hospital dark, lying there, crying for my son, I realize that one of the last big suggestions I'd failed to take regularly was praying on my knees.

Janice's voice comes back: *You don't do it for God.*

In the hospital, I have this urge to kneel, yet to do so in public—in front of my sighing, unsettled roommate—seems, well, obscene somehow.

I tiptoe to the bathroom and bend onto the cold tiles. *Thanks, whoever the fuck you are,* I say, *for keeping me sober.*

I feel small, kneeling there. Small and needy and inadequate. Pathetic, even. Like somebody who can't handle things.

Which is fairly accurate, after all, for the average inmate.

If you're God, I say, you know I feel small and needy and inadequate. And tonight I want a drink.

The silence fails to say anything back. I glare at it. It feels like judgment, the silence. And at that silence I give off rage; I start a ranting prayer in my head that goes something like this: Fuck you for making me an alcoholic. For making my baby sick all the time when he was so tiny. You're a fucking amateur, torturing a baby like that, you fuck. And my daddy withering into that form. What pleasure do you get from . . . from smiting people?

I feel something stir in me, a small wisp of something in

my chest, frail as smoke. It is—strangely—the sweetness of my love for my daddy and my son. It blesses me an instant like incense.

My eyes sting, and I blurt out, Thanks for them.

I feel the stillness around me widen a notch.

Thanks that my son is sleeping safe at home without fever or coughing; and my husband, who may yet take me back.

The boundaries of my skin grow thin as I kneel there squinting my eyes shut. For a nanosecond, I am lucent.

Inside it: an idea, the thread of a different perspective than any I've ever had. It's a thought so counterintuitive, so unlike how I think, it feels as if it originates from outside me. The voice—the idea—comes in solid quiet in the midst of psychic chaos, and it says, *If Dev hadn't been sick so much, you'd have kept drinking. . . .*

Which is wholly true. If Dev had been one of those blank-eyed, anesthetized little blobs who slept infancy away, I could've sotted up his early years. Staying up with him—what with the trips to the hospital, which I'd thought were my punishment or ruin—I'd found a strange kind of rescue.

(Vis-à-vis God speaking to me, I don't mean the voice of Charlton Heston playing Moses booming from on high, but reversals of attitude so contrary to my typical thoughts—so solidly true—as to seem divinely external. And quiet these thoughts are, strong and quiet. View it as some sane self or healthy ego taking charge, if you like. By checking in to the hospital, I've said in some deep way *uncle*, or—as they said in my old neighborhood—*calf rope*, referring to an animal hog-tied in a rodeo arena. I've stopped figuring so hard and begun to wait, sometimes with increasing hope, to be shown.)

Then it hits me. I'm actually kneeling before a toilet. The throne, as other drunks call it. How many drunken nights

and slungover mornings did I worship at this altar, empty-
ing myself of poison. And yet to pray to something above me,
something invisible, had—before now—seemed degrading.

And I start to laugh, kneeling there in a striped industrial robe—a barking laugh that devolves into a skittery madwoman's giggle, so I have to cover my mouth before somebody
comes in thinking I've gone off.

32

The Nervous Hospital

What fresh hell is this?
                    —DOROTHY PARKER

After fourteen hours sacked out in the bin, I wake to find my mouth glued together. Beside my bed are a pair of green foam slippers embossed with smiley faces, which design seems a grotesque mistake on somebody's part. I step right into them. I tie on the striped robe they'd given me, then stump out to accept whatever I've signed up for.

At the nurses' station, I'm handed a paper cup with another double dose of antidepressants to toss down.

In the dayroom, I find a game show blaring at two women. One's a large woman holding a teddy bear missing both eyes. The other's fortyish, with a flapper's curly bob and a small, muscular frame.

I'm Tina, she says, manic-depressive.

I'm Mary, I say, depressive-depressive.

On TV, the correct door has been chosen by a woman who bounces up and down and claps at a new bedroom set.

Tina's dressed in bike shorts and a lime-green striped athletic jersey with the Italian flag on the sleeve. She says to the other lady, Do you want to tell Mary your name?

I'm Dimples, she says in a little girl voice. She's white as parchment, with soft flesh that spills as if poured from her sleeves and shorts legs.

On TV, a horn honks. The audience sighs with disappointment.

Tell her your bear's name, too, Tina prompts. But Dimples just covers her face with the eyeless animal and falls quiet.

We're supposed to engage her, but she's no Dale Carnegie. Multiple personality disorder. Tina says, Do you work out?

This starts me crying.

For the first few weeks, I turn into a regular waterworks. In my family, we claim to cry at card tricks, but with no card tricks in sight, I sob my guts out. Anybody who'll listen to my sorrows gets an earful, and since each shift features a nurse ordained to hear me out—Mary, preeminently—at least twice a day, I boohoo my head off. Plus group therapy. Plus a shrink they assign me three times a week. Which makes those first days dissolve together into a kind of steam-room fog I sit red-faced in the middle of, blowing my nose.

I mostly cry about the pain I know I'm causing Dev by going inpatient. And I sob about his dad, whose tenderness for me has perhaps been killed off by my small black heart. And I wail in abject terror that—now I'm not only an alcoholic but also a lunatic—Warren will divorce me and take Dev.

When Warren comes in wearing khaki shorts and a kind, owlish expression to meet with the social worker and me, saying he wants to work on loving each other better, I blubber with hope at our prospects. I swear forever to love him till death, and while there's still a blank between us, I mean it.

(Here, I mistrust my memory, which holds no long talk between us of the type I'd have insisted on if our roles were reversed.)

He and Dev come every afternoon to eat dinner with me in a private room. I cry before they arrive, then weep when they stride out.

I cry for Mother to come. She's about to head off on a spiritual retreat in Mexico counseling other alcoholics. Ponder the likelihood of that one—Mother as sober guru. Landing here is final proof I can't outrun her, but neither can I get her to spring into action for me. Our phone call is brief.

I'm in the hospital, I say. I wanted to kill myself.

That's terrible, honey. Are you okay? Did you hurt yourself?

No, I was gonna use carbon monoxide, but I never did anything.

Why'd you pick that? She sounds curious, like somebody idly shopping for suicide attempts as she might a ball gown.

You don't make a mess. You leave a very livid corpse.

That's just awful. Does Warren have Dev?

Yeah. I get to see him every afternoon. Warren seems like he wants to really work on things, but we've been living like strangers for so long.

Y'all should work things out.

I know, Mother, I know. Since I was sixteen, you've wanted to pawn me off in matrimony to somebody.

I just want you to be taken care of. . . .

This marriage hasn't exactly brought comfort and succor, otherwise I might not have planned to cash in my chips.

He's just so sweet with Dev.

I don't suppose you want to come up and help out a few weeks. (Actually, Warren had said it'd be awkward, the two of them in the house alone. Despite that and despite a marrow-deep certainty that she'd never come, I want her to want to.)

She says, I just can't, honey. You know I've had this trip to Mexico planned for a while.

After she hangs up, I cry because part of me still wants to drag her behind my car. But the other part still wants to crawl into her lap.

On the phone, Lecia tells me to snap out of it.

That's a Republican thing to say, I say, sniveling.

She's a fixer, and her inability to fix my mood makes her crazy. Or afraid, or both.

I'm serious, she says. Tell me what you're so miserable about. Do you want me to come up there and kick somebody's ass? What?

I feel like I've turned into Mother, I tell her.

This draws an actual guffaw from her. You *are* crazy, she says. You're nothing at all like Mother.

I'm here in the Mental Marriott, like her.

Well, you pay your taxes, for one, she says. You never shot at anybody . . .

Wanted to, I say.

Who doesn't, she says. Then she adds, Also, unlike Mother, you have a job. Several jobs, if you count writing a book and raising a kid. Your second book!

Three years ago, I say, my book came out.

Whatever! You've got the yeah-buts, she says. If it's Dev who worries you, notice the ways he's Pete Karr's grandson.

He is, isn't he? I say. And it's true that I see Daddy's fire in Dev's limbs. His grit.

I'm hanging up, Lecia says. I gotta go make a living. I love you senselessly. Don't kill yourself till I give the go-ahead.

Checking into the hospital, I surrendered to a sobbing that I'd always held back, thinking if I started in on it it would never, ever, ever stop. Then it stops after a week or two, as if a lifetime's portion of grief has boiled out of me. The ferocious internal motion I've been praying would end finally—almost in a single nanosecond—stops. It's a pivot point around which my entire future will ultimately swivel. That first night, kneeling before the toilet, I let go, as they say. Or call it the moment my innately serotonin-challenged brain reached level X.

The change happens before my eyes, the muted colors of the room brightening from gray to a cool azure. Now when I begin obsessively to gnaw on my fears, I try to wrestle them loose from myself (who are these two halves?) the way you'd take a slipper from a Doberman. It's in my higher power's hands, I tell myself. They say *More will be revealed*, not *More will be figured out*.

I feel well enough one afternoon to ring Walt and give him the lowdown. (His wife was ill with cancer at the time, so the call was brief.) You're in the best place, he says. I wish I'd known you were having such a hard time.

That's the nature of it, though, I say—isolation.

But you're feeling better? You need me to fly out there and bring you a hot-fudge malted?

Hold that thought, I say.

That afternoon, when Warren and Dev show up, I feel a rush of delight just seeing them. Warren opens the stairwell door with one hand so Dev can slide past him, and the instant stays haloed in gold, for it's my first conscious memory of something solidly good. Though their afternoon visit is always the day's highlight, it routinely sends a volcano of guilt up my middle, since Dev always steps onto the ward with such hesitance, a posture almost soldierly in its wary vigilance. (Even now, from a distance of eighteen years, he remembers how scary the place was.)

Dev was born into a bold certainty of feeling. About nearly everything, he held convictions. As a newborn, he had the appetite of a jackal. As a toddler, once faced with a tea service at my in-laws', he'd stuck his fist in the sugar bowl and upended it, sugar spraying all over as Mrs. Whitbread hissed that no other child in that house had ever *interfered with a tea*. While other toddlers had winced at new food, he had a taste for sashimi, for steak tartare with raw onion and egg yolk. He approached stray dogs with his arms open, ran full speed into waves.

Yet he was all sensibility. (In a few years, I'd see Dev stand once for a long time before two Cubist paintings—one Braque and one Picasso—announcing, *I know I'm supposed to like the Picasso more, but this one's stronger.* And so it had been.) He was sturdily resolute in all his tastes.

That day in the hospital, Dev comes in dressed in a Hawaiian print shirt, looking like a miniature Miami dope dealer, and wary that way, as if expecting to find machine guns in the hands of rival gang members as he slides under Warren's arm.

But, instead of my usual stab of concern or guilt, I see this as a single instant in his life amid a zillion other instants with attendant feelings—love, curiosity, desire. His curls are damp around the edges from the heat. I heave him up and inhale an odor of wet earth in his hair, and he plants a dry kiss on my cheek. I let him down and greet Warren, balancing a coffee holder with two steaming cups and a crumpled pastry bag. His white shirt, rolled up at the wrists, shows the lineaments of his brown forearms. He holds the coffee to one side, bending so I can kiss him, and in his preoccupied expression is infinite gentleness. I place my lips on his square jaw and taste the living salt of him.

In the kitchen a few minutes later, the first creamy sip of strong coffee gives me a distinct flood of pleasure. I remember a few similar instants when I first quit drinking.

Nothing has changed, really. The uncertainty of my marriage is still there. But some equanimity exists, as if some level in my chest has ceased its endless teetering and found its balance point.

In my life, I sometimes knew pleasure or excitement but rarely joy. Now a wide sky-span of quiet holds us. My head's actually gone quiet. Some sluggishness is sloughed off. I am upright all of a sudden, inside a self I find quasi-acceptable, even as I'm incarcerated. Maybe this giant time-out has given me rest I sorely needed. Basically, some fist pounding on the center of my chest has unclasped itself. I've let go.

I don't know if Warren notices the difference, for—other than two sessions with a family social worker—we don't see each other except with Dev, which speaks volumes about the space between us. (Were we both waiting for me to come home? Why didn't this wall between us stay down, even when we both willed it? Because we didn't trust each other as much as we trusted the distances we'd grown up in?)

The morning after this sane visit, I lift my just-scrubbed face from the towel to meet my own gaze in the metal mirror, and I almost see a bold outline around myself, as if inked with magic marker. Alive, I am, a living, breathing Mary of myself.

Hello, stranger, I actually say out loud.

In occupational therapy, the other women in the ward—who've been vague holograms viewed through a scrim of tears when I checked in—have turned into full-fledged human units whose stories I begin to follow like daytime soaps.

We're supposed to be fashioning decorative wreaths, those circles of dried flowers and herbs that happy housewives hang in suburban kitchens from grosgrain ribbon. A grassy aroma rises around us as we work. I sit before a styrofoam ring, concentrating on the dumb task of wrapping florist's tape on a green wire.

Across the art table from me sits Pam, a strapping blond psychopath—a diagnosis she stays volubly pissed off about. Pam claims her broke-dick husband has slam-dunked her for partying with truckers at roadhouses, which is preferable to folding his effing socks and stuffing the faces of her five mouthy kids.

In group therapy that day, Pam got called out for wearing a *Please Kill Me* T-shirt. This message terrorized the only guy on the ward, a schizophrenic kid named Willy. Willy has scarlet acne emblazoning both cheeks, as if he's being continuously slapped from the inside.

He's at the next table hunched over watercolor paper, meticulously painting a Greek keyhole pattern using black ink and a brush made up of only a few hairs. Two seats down from him is beautiful Flora, whose raving red hair hangs a torch in any room she enters. Often screaming in psychosis, Flora spends a lot of time in a padded room, tied down by leather four-point restraints. Medicated into a stupor, Flora is that day, and a nurse helps her odd crafts projects of gluing together hunks of foam into a kind of arctic-looking city.

Pam says, You know what we should call this?

The Maniacs' Art Club? Tina says.

Crafts for Cunts, Pam says.

Please don't use that word, says skinny Betty. Lovely Betty

with the swan neck and the shiny black hair. St. Betty of the Perpetually Ducked Head. Age about thirty, looks sixty. As a child, Betty was consistently raped by her famous professor father, which kept her ever after starving herself almost to death. She's assembling a wreath of fragrant eucalyptus using shades of muted green with faded yellow roses.

You've gotten really good at this, Betty, I say, and it's true she's found a meticulous but subtly tinted order.

You should work in a florist's shop, Tina says. What do you do, anyway, I mean, for a living?

She shrugs. (I'd later find out she took care of the wheelchair-bound father who'd raped her.)

Do you find it morbid, Tina says, that we're making wreaths? What does that conjure for you?

Wreaths make me think of Christmas, skinny Betty says. That is my *least* favorite time of year.

I meant gravestones. You find them on gravestones, Tina says.

Maybe they want us all dead, Pam says. Well the feeling's mutual. I hate those bitches.

Which ones? I want to know.

All of them.

I say, What's not to like? They're nothing if not nice.

You're like those people who fall in love with their kidnappers, Pam says. Like what's-her-name. Who held up the bank. The rich bitch.

Betty says, Patty Hearst.

How many suicide attempts does everybody have? Tina blurts out. I have unlucky thirteen.

People go around with their various numbers.

I have only about half of one, I say.

You're bullshitting me, Tina says.

A beacon of mental health, the Virgin Mary here, Pam says. One half-assed attempt. Well, I can beat that weak-assed shit. I have zero. There are some other motherfuckers I'd seriously like to kill, though.

On the way back to the ward, Pam tugs my elbow, saying, I've got some contraband.

Tell me it's chocolate, I say, for that day's brownies had vanished from the ward kitchen.

Better than that, she says, and she draws from her sweat-shirt pocket a small black Bic lighter. Then she whispers, I've also got a lightbulb in my room.

What fun we're meant to wreak with these items, I can't figure out, but I'm feeling well enough to let the opaque op-portunity slide.

33

Waking in the Blue

We are all old timers.
Each of us holds a locked razor.
—ROBERT LOWELL, "WAKING IN THE BLUE"

Three weeks after the lamest stab in suicide's history, I sit typing in the sunlit hall of that asylum so famous one Ivy-League poet later suggests I include my time there on a résumé. In my blue-striped robe and vomit-green happy slippers, I'm finishing a poem about a particular circle of hell in which a sinner is fixed on endless video reruns of her every screwup. An eternity of reruns with eyelids held open by clothespins. Crucifixion by television.

Which is how the end of my drinking felt—the anesthesia of liquor had stopped working, and there was nothing much else to aspire to. It's a crappy poem based on an old idea, but I haven't written in nine months, so I type it with a jeweler's lapidary care, the goal being to get through without having to trek to the nurses' station to borrow white-out, which my shrink has banished.

How's it dangerous? I ask Mary after my next typo.

People find creative ways to hurt themselves, she says.

Do I look like I wanna hurt myself? I breathe frost on the window and inscribe my initials with a little heart.

You're not the only one on the ward, she says. It pleases me that she plays along with my breezy, confident subterfuge, when I was a sobbing wreck two weeks before.

I'd guard it from the other madwomen with my life, I say.

She looks around to be sure the other nurses are still doling out meds, then whispers, Your doctor is lobbying to read your poems, in case they're bad for your mental health.

She can't do that, I say. All kinds of poets wrote here—Anne Sexton, Robert Lowell.

She can, I'm afraid, Mary says, her lovely face wearing a look of concern that unsettles me.

I say, Don't you think I'm ready to go home next week? My husband starts school. He's working full-time. I've gotta start teaching.

I don't get to decide, she says.

C'mon, Mary.

Another nurse steps into the room with a piece of mail Warren had that morning dropped off for me. A delinquent bill, I figure. But the return address holds the scarlet shield of Radcliffe College—the Bunting Institute for women scholars.

They're probably writing to reiterate my rejection, I tell Mary, since the year before I'd applied—for the ninth time—for one of their fanciest postdoctoral fellowships. They gave you money and an office. Because my academic credentials were so stank, and my one book had proven ignorable. I'd never expected to get it.

But one poet had decided not to come, and I'm runner-up. It's maybe the first gift that I understand fully as such. Rather than feel the button-busting pride I've been chasing with a decade of arrogantly filled-out grant applications, I feel toadishly unworthy. Mary reads over the letter while I stand stumped in the shine of it.

They make you an officer of the university, she says. What's that mean?

You can charge drinks at the Faculty Club.

Drinks?

Club soda and coffee, I say. O.J. Iced tea.

She's still rubbing her belly with a pinched look on her face. She hands me the letter.

What? I say. What aren't you saying?

That says you have to go to a meeting this Monday, Mary says. Have to go. It's an all-day orientation.

I know, I know. I get keys to my office. I get to meet the other scholars. I can't wait.

She'll never let you go, she says, referring to my in-house shrink: Alice in Wonderland. That's what even the nurses call her behind her back, based on the platinum hair she wears past her knees, despite being on the far side of forty. It flaps behind her like a ship's wake, or she pushes it back using horrid headbands with bows big enough to stick on a birthday convertible. (My doc was on August holiday, or she might've vetoed Alice.)

She barely lets you go to the drunks' group in the detox on Tuesday. Escorted.

Won't I be out by then?

Mary shrugs, adding, Maybe not.

Alice in fucking Wonderland, I say.

A passing doctor hushes me and nods toward the mailroom, where the shrink in question—tiny, humorless, and ruthlessly well groomed—is reviewing charts.

It's such a cliché to hate your shrink when you're in the bin. (In truth, all of my other shrinks contributed heartily to saving my life.) Dr. Alice herself would claim I'm projecting a buried hatred of my own seductive, narcissistic mother. But even other doctors seem to stiffen at her presence in group, and her lack of humor is legend in these halls. No one ever sees her pancaked face risk the breach of smiling.

She beckons me now, and I summon the bravado to flounce behind her to an office. She slips behind her desk. She's wearing a peach-colored headband to match her Chanel suit. She's a buyer of name brands, this one, no thrift shops for her.

Sitting primly in the chair across from her, I try to dazzle her with modest confidence. She has a tendency to bring up penis envy every session, and I swear that this time, when she does, I'll confess to my intense longing for a dick of my own, for in most places that pretend to value honesty, I've usually found that sucking up is an underrated virtue given how well it works.

Reviewing my chart, she squirts a dollop of lotion into her hands and rubs them together with the untroubled air of a woman who's never picked up a check and never gone to sleep without flossing.

She says, You're still refusing the sleeping medication?

I'm sleeping so well, I say. I think all our talks are paying off.

What's your objection to the medication?

I'm worried about the side effects.

Your addiction? she says. She gives me a watery smile. She finds my addiction droll.

That and priapism, I say.

Since a raging hard-on is one side effect they'd mentioned from the sleeping pill, I'm throwing her a bone, so to speak, and her face goes all eager.

She says, Do you feel there's something missing from your body?

Funny you say that, I say. I do. Some absence. That's just how I'd describe it.

She waits for me to say more, but I can't think how to elaborate without bursting into lunatic laughter, so I try another tack.

The big problem when I came in was my head, I say. If there had been a transplant list, I'd have signed on.

Does this head of yours urge you to hurt yourself? she asks. (Is it paranoia that causes me to hear enthusiasm?)

I tell her no. I feel like an asshole about the whole thing. I want to get better. I want to work on my marriage and be a better mom. I want to stay sober.

Rubbing her hands together again, she asks, Not even any *fantasies* about suicide? Are you *cutting* yourself?

I never did that, I say.

Never? she says, adding, Most people who set out to hurt themselves rely on self-destructive acts for relief. She sounds disappointed.

My relief is that I didn't hurt myself, I say. My thinking was skewed by years of drinking—there's your destructive behavior. You're the one who told me alcohol's a depressant.

Any fantasies about hurting your child? Hurting your husband? she asks, probing like a dentist for a raw nerve.

I've already done that, I say.

You seem upset.

I'm in a mental institution.

Less than a month after a suicide attempt.

Suicidal gesture. (You pick up the distinct lingo your chart needs pretty fast in those hallways.)

How are you prepared to manage your life any better?

The antidepressants have obviously kicked in—

They should've kicked in before you arrived.

Well, then I'm rested for the first time in years. I ask people for help all the time. All I do is ask for help. I make, like, five calls a day to people in recovery to talk about how I feel. I talk to all the nurses.

Yet you think you don't belong here.

I belonged here when I came. Now I'm taking up somebody else's spot.

I wait till the end of the session to show her the Radcliffe letter (though with a shrink I trusted, I'd have gone bounding in like a puppy). She cocks a waxed eyebrow, saying that the treatment team will judge whether I'm able to go to the orientation. She's concerned that my regular therapist is still out of the country.

You've been in touch with her. She'll be back by Labor Day, I say, and I'm on the mend.

But you have me, she says.

How lucky is that? I say, and I mold my features into the unwilled smile of a store-bought doll.

As part of my program to look like a model inmate, I organize something I call Health and Beauty Day.

Joan has been called to the West Coast to nurse her father in hospice. But Deb and Liz bring in meditation tapes patients can listen to while lying on the dayroom floor in the morning. I also arrange for staff to take us on a long walk around the campus and to the gym, where we idly thwap around basketballs. Before dinner, we make facial masks from yogurt and honey and lie supine on mats in the kitchen with cucumber slices on our eyes and mayo slathered on our hair—homemade spa treatments I clipped from a magazine. Pam jokes that we should have a fashion show involving the papery nightgowns that show our flubbery asses.

After dinner, Betty invites me to her room so I can borrow some petal-pink polish for my toenails. She nicks into the bathroom to slip into her pajamas. Coming out, she pulls a daffodil-yellow sweatshirt from a drawer, and as it slips over her head, I catch a glimpse of burn marks up one arm above the elbow—a line of festering sores of varying depths. I grab her wrist, and she jerks away.

What did you do? I say.

Nothing, she says. It's none of your business.

How did you even do that? I ask.

Leave it alone. It's been there a long time.

Those were fresh. You've been here three months. How did you find a way to burn yourself?

You think you know about everything, Betty says in a hissed whisper.

Betty—

Miss High and Mighty. Miss Harvard Everything.

—you gotta tell your doctor about this.

All you've done since you got here is get fat! You're disgusting. And your son is fat! He's fat because you're mean to him. You're crazy! Your husband should take him to protect him from you. I'm gonna testify for him too if you mess with me. Get out of here. Get out of my room. You came in here to make a pass at me. You're sick! You're a fat, sick perverted lesbian!

She runs back into the bathroom and slams the door.

What's going on in here? says a nurse, sticking her head in.

Nothing, I say. Betty's worried about her complexion, I think.

In the dayroom the next day, Tina's sketching a design for her wreath as I whisper what I've found out.

She shrugs. You've gotta stay out of that.

Some of those sores look infected, I say.

She tilts her head to the door, and I follow her toward the phone booth. She sits on the wooden stool under the pay phone while I stand in the hall. She glances past me to be sure the coast is clear, then pulls up her ankle-length nightgown. On the very top of her thigh are a series of red slash marks, inflicted with surgical proficiency at varying depths.

How'd you do that? I say.

Pam sold me a lightbulb.

Sold it to you. . . .

For cigarettes. She sold Betty the lighter. We all do it, Mary. I've done it for years.

It's a messed-up thing to do.

You don't get it—we're not trying to kill ourselves. I even use betadyne to be sure it's clean.

But Betty could wind up getting shock therapy again. Y'all could wind up staying here a long damn time.

I like it here, she says. I find it restful.

She stands up and slides her finger into the change slot, checking for left coins, as she says, Do you fancy a bedtime yogurt? Dairy products encourage healthy sleep.

With me trailing behind, she starts toward the kitchen, adding, Or maybe a cup of that herb tea. Chamomile eases internal inflammation, also redness in the face.

You could wind up in the Monkey House, Tina, I say (That's what we call the more restrictive ward). Or medicated into oblivion like Flora.

In the kitchen, she flips on the fluorescent light—a blinking hum. She says, Everybody has to work out their own shit. Isn't that what your meetings tell you?

I don't know where I get the sentences to speak to her. Maybe honest care for her just infected me, but I say, Whenever you cut yourself, you're carving your mother's sick message into your flesh.

Digging through the freezer for ice, Tina says, How many shrinks does it take to screw in a lightbulb?

I'm serious, I say.

None, she says, emerging with a container of yogurt. She adds, The lightbulb has to want to change.

I mean it. It's like me with a drink. Every time I used a manhattan to take the edge off, I never got any better coping skills.

Like what?

Making a cup of tea. Going to the gym. Calling a pal to unload.

She's pouring tea over ice that crackles in its plastic glass. She turns to me and says, What if none of your pals are home? What if you don't have a single fucking pal? What if you're a boy trapped in a girl's body and the kids at your school call you Pussyeater and Butch and Muffdiver?

You tell yourself they're shitheels and find somebody lonelier than you to be nice to.

What if there's nobody lonelier than you? she says. She turns away to shield her face.

I'm standing in the chasm of her statement when she whirls around and throws the yogurt—with the force of a major league pitcher—into the trash can so it splatters up the sides. She stalks out, hitting the light switch on the way.

The next morning I wake early, hearing flame-haired Flora in the quiet room, howling in some unintelligible tongue. I step from my room into the faint odor of eucalyptus. The aroma builds up as I get close to the dayroom. A nurse brushes past me, her arms braceleted in red-ribboned Christmas wreaths.

Peering past her, I see dozens of wreaths of every kind. They fill the chairs where residents usually hang out. The nurses are stacking them on a dolly the custodians would (with bemused faces) wheel onto the service elevator.

Off to one side, Pam stands with an orange ping-pong paddle, occasionally bouncing the ball on it. She says, You missed the showdown.

It turns out Tina planted in Betty the hope that—with her extraordinary talent for floral arrangement and Tina's acumen—they could make millions selling wreaths. Betty could be free from her father's house, and Tina could leave public housing. So for weeks they've been ginning out an extra wreath here and there, squirreling them away in the art room.

But in the small and densely packed confines of Tina's skull, the plan's gotten larger and larger—visits on *The Oprah Winfrey Show* and *The Tonight Show with Johnny Carson* are involved.

After she stormed out on me the night before, she convinced Betty to break into the art room in the wee hours, even luring Flora and Willy to chip in, like stockholders. At dawn, the day nurses found wreaths by the stack. Even Willy made one out of doll's heads painted blue with tempera paint.

A nurse passes by with more wreaths. I ask Pam where everybody wound up.

Betty's modeling the latest in four-point restraints up in the Monkey House. Her insurance has run out anyway, so the minute she's stable, she's gone anyhow. Flora's in the safe room. Willy's medicated.

What about Tina? I say.

Mighty Tina. She executed some impressive kickboxing moves, Pam says.

On the nurses?

Just the orderlies. I actually don't think she made contact with anybody. I came out of my room and saw her do a flying side kick. Very Bruce Lee. Then later, she went bye-bye on the gurney.

We stand in silence outside the barren dayroom for a while. I'm conjuring their tormented faces—Tina's and Betty's, Flora's and Willy's—arrayed before me like plucked blossoms.

The prayer's automatic, and it comes like a burst of lightning—some version of *God help them*. Petitioning whatever light I'm starting to believe in to shine on them. Give Betty a bite to eat, and free Will's face of sores. Chase the demons from Flora, and lower Tina into a single pair of loving arms. Whether you believe prayers like this affect external affairs doesn't matter. They measure the overhaul in my psyche and character.

Time for meds, ladies, a passing nurse says.

Pam turns on her heel, but I hang there a long time in that eucalyptus odor, which conjures up so many sickrooms. Mine when I was a kid and I viewed the world through a scrim of fever, and my mother's white hands smoothed Vicks on my chest; Dev's those nights he choked for air in the vaporizer fog; Daddy's before he died.

It's unhip to fall to your knees, sentimental, stupid, even. But somehow I've started to do it unself-consciously.

Behind a door, my body bends, and the linoleum rises. I lay my face on my knees in a posture almost fetal. It is, skeptics may say, the move of a slave or brainless herd animal. But around me I feel gathering—let's concede I imagine it—spirit. Such vast quiet holds me, and the me I've been so lifelong worried about shoring up just dissolves like ash in water. Just isn't. In its place is this clean air.

There's a space at the bottom of an exhale, a little hitch between taking in and letting out that's a perfect zero you can go
into. There's a rest point between the heart muscle's close and
open—an instant of keenest living when you're momentarily
dead. You can rest there.

How long passes? Somebody knocks on the door for group.

I creak to my feet, feeling lucky—which I maybe haven't
felt since the early glory days with Warren—lucky for my nut-
burger family, and for the near-strangers who've carried me
the past nine months. Joan, before leaving town, and Deb and
Liz and Janice come every day. Most of my putative friends—
writers and academics and drinking buddies—not at all. Even
Joe, who's landed back in the joint on an old car-theft charge,
sends me daily missives using stamps he can ill afford.

Somebody has given me a copy of a prayer attributed to
St. Francis, and beginning that day, I set my dull mind to
memorizing it. The prayer—which Jack of the Tinfoil Helmet
first said that night going home from the meeting—now rivers through, sometimes dozens of times a day: Lord, make
me an instrument of your peace. Where there is hatred, let
me sow love . . . The first time I said it, I bridled against the
phrase "O Divine Master" and the last two lines about eternal
life, which I thought were horseshit.

O Divine Master, ask that I not so much seek
to be consoled as to console;
to be understood as to understand;
to be loved as to love.

For it is in giving that we receive.
It is in pardoning that we are pardoned,
and it is in dying to self that we are reborn
to eternal life.

As I slow down inside, the world's metronome seems to speed up, for without keen, self-centered focus on your own inward suffering, clock hands spin. Days get windstormed off the calendar. Rather than thinking about spiritual practices, arguing them out in my head, I almost automatically try them. That, I suppose, is surrender.

My final few days at the hospital whipped past, so I recount them here in rough outline. I prayed to get to go to my Radcliffe meeting, and—without being asked—Mary offered to escort me on her day off. On a steaming August day, I attended my first scholars' sherry hour wearing a plastic wrist bracelet I tried to hide under the sleeve of my gabardine jacket. Shortly after that, Warren ran into a friend of ours who was a shrink, and I called to ask if he could get me the fuck out of the bin, and he waved a wand that made Alice in Wonderland disappear like the ghost she was. I didn't even get to say goodbye.

Then I was stepping through the door of my own house. Then my son's smooth arms were around my neck.

34

The Sweet Hereafter

I am welcomed on a boat—it's a canoe hollowed from a dark tree. The canoe is incredibly wobbly, even when you sit on your heels. A balancing act. If you have the heart on the left side you have to lean a bit to the right, nothing in the pockets, no big arm movements, please, all rhetoric has to be left behind. Precisely: rhetoric is impossible here. The canoe glides out over the water.

—TOMAS TRANSTRÖMER, "STANDING UP"

(TRANS. ROBERT BLY)

In the loony bin, I surrendered—not full bore, the way saints do, once and for all, blowing away my ego in perfect service to God—not even close. But watching the world through chicken wire convinced me that my unguided thought process would no doubt swerve me into concrete. Before, I'd feared surrender would sand me down to nothing. Now I've started believing it can bloom me more solidly into myself.

So once home, I take suggestions I'd carped about before with a new zeal, albeit with the occasional snotty look on my face. I sit squirmy in prayer while conflicting thoughts zip through my skull like so many simultaneously slammed tennis balls. Before, prayer had involved bouncing on and off my knees so fast it resembled a break dance move.

Make a daily gratitude list, Joan said, using every letter of the alphabet to delineate what you're grateful for.

Like *J* for Joan the Bone.

Bingo, she says.

You're not serious. That's so puerile.

Childish things for stubborn children, she says.

I'm teaching again with some ease, and the writing started in the hospital plows forward.

Warren and I exist like kindly intentioned siblings, though he's putting forth more effort. On my birthday, he stuns me by gathering friends at a restaurant to holler *surprise*, but when he reaches for me the next morning, I roll away. The prospect scares me. Never, I think, could I kiss that handsome mouth. Whatever his reaction stays shut inside him. I follow the old advice of St. Jack of the Tinfoil, who'd counseled me to fulfill my contract unless otherwise guided.

Right before I hit a year sober, Joan suggests starting a women's group for gab of some spiritual variety—think quilting bee where we stitch on each other's souls, autopsy where the corpses take turns carving. In my office at Radcliffe on Sunday nights, we meet—about four or five sober women trying to stay that way.

Nobody operates from a formal religious construct, no church ladies or temple mavens. Joan rustles up a list of discussion topics she used in a similar group, and we start off talking about prayer. When Deb claims her regular prayer is for a joyous day filled with serenity, I say, You can ask for that?

Nights I put Dev to bed, the St. Francis prayer becomes part of our ritual, in the form of call and response. I say, *Where there is hatred, let me sow,* and he shouts out, *Love.* I say, *Where there is conflict,* and he hollers, *Pardon.* Afterward, if I have trouble sleeping, I lie in a hot bath with a washcloth over my face, saying prayers I hardly believe but take blind comfort from.

I'm still given to cussing any traditional notion of God.

What god would deny you children? I say to Deb, for she's enduring torturous in vitro hormones trying to conceive. Some afternoons at the house, I inflict the agonizing shots, the big needle stiff in her muscle, while in the next room, a house resident may have popped out a second or third addicted or HIV-positive baby. Deb's calm baffles me.

I've let go, she says.

If you've surrendered, I say (I get maniacal in these arguments), wouldn't you stop using the hormones and harvesting the ova?

Deb says, It may not be right for me to conceive. But to pursue them and not get them will somehow turn out in my favor in some way I can't foresee now. (Years later, Deb will divorce, and her ex will kill himself, and she'll tell me, *Now I see maybe why we could never get pregnant.*) I tell the other women that Deb doesn't even mark on her calendar when her period's due. Her doctor does that. She needs to relinquish all control.

Joan wonders if the rest of us could manage such faith, and we strike a deal that we'll all let go our own wills as openhandedly. In fact, until each of us has given up care of her life to some greater force for good, the group won't go on.

But I quibble so much about arcane definitions of *will* and *care* that the women wind up voting that I've surrendered already and am just being a bitch about it.

And to their will, I yield, which is a start.

With the group, I finally succumb to Joan's long-running nag that I list stuff I feel most crappy about—every single grudge and humiliation—a private exercise we all talk about over a month or so. I break mine into columns with the crappy thing on the left, the particular way it hurt me in the middle, my part in it on the right. In some cases—being sexually assaulted, say—my part has been burying or ignoring the awful event in a way that restabs the wound. Almost eighty pages, mine gets to be. Theirs are way shorter, since they've done this before.

Sitting in my posh office in low lamplight one Sunday, we unscrew Oreos and sip muddy coffee while privately rolling down our individual columns—we cherrypick what to share—and it floors me to see laid out how fear has governed pretty much my every moronic choice. I've never regarded myself as a fearful individual. I've hitchhiked in Mexico and blustered drunk into biker bars all mouthy. Those acts now strike me as more pitiful than brave—the sad bravado of a girl with little to lose.

We're supposed to go over the full grudge lists with another person, and Joan gives me a list of sober preachers and rabbis and priests who'll listen. In my shame, I half expect a religious guy to hurl lightning bolts down on my head.

A man with a thick Irish lilt answers one call. Come on over, he says. But would you mind bringing me a Coca-Cola? I crave the stuff and can't afford it.

I wind up in a room facing a guy in a monk's robe, a giant crucifix hanging from his belt like a scalp. Brother Francis (not his name) is over eighty and skeletally thin, with sunken cheeks and blue veins all over an age-spotted skull. The liter of Coke sits on the low table between us, alongside an ashtray. The instant I sit down, he pulls out a pack of rolling papers and constructs an immaculate ciggie while I light up. Both of us smoke like tar kilns the whole time as legal pads I flip through quickly pile in my lap—minor offenses. But when it comes to the wreckage of my romantic past, I stall, holding my styrofoam cup as I press my thumbnail around the rim in a series of half moons.

We seem to have reached an impasse, he says.

Well, Francis, there are some things I'm uncomfortable talking about with you.

His thin lips draw on his hand-rolled stogie. He says with an expression of terrifying hilarity, Are they things of a *sexual* nature?

I nod.

He exhales smoke and says, Maybe I can put you at ease, for I've had more experience in that area than my vows would suggest.

He tells me some pretty hair-raising stories about his life in South America, when he was still on the whiskey. How he wound up joining a twelve-step program for people whose sexual natures were—in his words—severely disordered. His tale doesn't involve pedophilia or some fetish for disemboweling kittens or anything gross. But my betrayals—cheating on a college beau, making out with my English boyfriend's Afghani squash-playing pal—pretty much pale alongside his. I sit and listen until dark comes, and the next morning I come back for most of the day.

At the end, jazzed to the gills on many plastic bottles of Coke, I sit drained over the overflowing ashtray, and Brother Francis blinks behind his smeary horn-rims, saying, Leave all that stuff here with me. God wants you to put this stuff down now. Go wear the world like a loose garment. And be of good cheer. If you let God in, He'll take this shame from you.

Descending the subway stairs, I no longer ooze the sweaty, reptilian stench I walked in with, but I can't say I feel like I've wholly shed my past. That night, though, I sleep like somebody clocked with a sledgehammer. The next morning in the bathroom mirror, there's more shine in my eyes. Throughout the day, when my head lurches for the old miseries to start gnawing on, I have a touchstone phrase— *That's done*—I blurt internally as often as need be. The mind, whirring for decades at thousands of rpm's per second, keeps trying to fill in new freefalls of quiet. For the first time in my life, I go to sleep every night soundly, without medication, sometimes nine hours a pop.

Don't get me wrong. The irritation that once drove me like a cat-o'-nine-tails can start flailing in an instant. But now the car door I slam or the snipe I let fly at Warren trails an apology. I blurt out *sorry* nonstop, since I never again want to nurse such bitterness as I'd stored up before.

Once, I'm laden with parcels and carrying Dev up slick stairs on my hip after he's hurt his ankle, and he calls me *poopy head* so many times that I'm ready to fling him down and swear. But a quick prayer—*Please let me be a loving mom*—leads me to bust out laughing instead.

When a guy honks and cuts me off and shrieks at me, calling me the c-word, my hand does not automatically flip him the bird—a small change, maybe, but for me profound. That spring-loaded trigger has eased off. The guy's comment just flows past as if I've been lacquered over. Every so often I find myself praying for citizens like him, though in the past I might have petitioned for a machine gun.

One morning at my desk, an essay I've had an idea about

starts to unreel itself like a satin ribbon. Six hours later, I look up and realize I've been writing with ease.

Some days, premenstrual self-loathing can transform me into a ring-tailed, horn-honking, door-slamming bitch. But those incidents now strike me as 100 percent my problem, regardless of provocation. And they bring me to my knees, for it's on their back end that I sometimes fantasize about a slender glass of innocent champagne with some berry-colored crème de cassis making a little sunset in the flute's bottom.

Therapy rescued me in my twenties by taking me inward, leaching off pockets of poison in my head left over from the past. But the spiritual lens—even just the nightly gratitude list and going over each day's actions—is starting to rewrite the story of my life in the present, and I begin to feel like somebody snatched out of the fire, salvaged, saved.

35

I Accept a Position

"I accept the universe" is reported to have been a favorite utterance of our New England transcendentalist, Margaret Fuller; and when someone repeated this phrase to Thomas Carlyle, his sardonic comment is said to have been: "Gad! she'd better!"

—WILLIAM JAMES, *THE VARIETIES OF RELIGIOUS EXPERIENCE*

Just when I've stopped craving a drink, a job offer from Syracuse floats down, with grad students and colleagues like Toby, plus a curriculum that'll let me scavenge the library like in the golden days of grad school. But I can't picture staying sober outside the circle I've conscribed—the women I hang out with, the house, coffee making for meetings, a meditation group. The further I get from that rainy night my car skidded sideways on my last drunk, the bleaker the outlook of toppling back into the tar I've just slithered out of. A beer has come to seem like a bullet in a gun's chamber. But the occasional urge for icy oblivion can still tear through me with brute longing.

So after some prayer, I turn down the first few Syracuse offers. It's not the money, I swear. There's just way more quiet in my head around staying than going, which Joan says is how a spiritually inspired idea might rival a will-driven or egocentric one. I'm trying to train myself to tune in to the quiet messages inside. (That's the kind of softheaded loon—I sometimes think—I'm dwindling into.) After each refusal, the chairman calls back with an offer of stuff tacked on—a parking place, teaching for Warren, a new computer, moving expenses, a foreshortened period of time before I come up for tenure.

The last time the phone rings, I'm shocked to hear the guy again, more so at how fetching the whole enterprise sounds all of a sudden. I get a solid little click in my chest, some new peace at the prospect of going. I try to buy a day, but he exhales impatience, giving me till five.

My first impulse in telling this is to claim that Warren had wanted to leave Cambridge worse than I did. That's how I remember it. His book was almost due out, and teaching appealed to him. We'd settled it with a phone call. Except that's horse dookey. So empty is my head when it comes to us, so seared of detail, I fell to rifling old notebooks, which held an opposing truth: Warren and I went back and forth when the offer came up.

Again, there's that mysterious dead-head space around the marriage's unraveling. This blanking out has the same flat quality surrounding my time with Daddy before leaving home. The Freudian implications aren't lost on me, of course. But what do these two radical disconnects mean in the story?

Maybe my forgetting is how I absolve myself for bailing out in both cases.

Ultimately, I ring the chairman back to accept. He says, You're the toughest negotiator I've ever dealt with. This was our final offer. I was calling the next candidate if you said no again.

How can I tell him that had I been negotiating, I'd have taken the first offer?

Right before decamping, I go with a few women from my group plus Dev for a weekend on Cape Cod. He splashes in the waves with the ladies, and at night we boil lobsters and stuff ourselves with mounds of herb-sticky pasta.

At dusk on Sunday, we all pat together an ornate sand castle with moats and levees and bridges. We mold bucket-shaped turrets. The courtyard's tiled with seashells. The scene blows back to me now with a high, clear oboe note of joy, a feeling then so unfamiliar, it no doubt accounts for my vivid recollections of that day—the sound of Dev's yellow shovel going *shush, shush* in wet sand. Behind us, winds in long grasses *hiss*. The sky is fading to purple with a fat sun red as a cough lozenge about to sink into the sea.

I lounge in a low deck chair, a glass of lemonade jammed in the sand beside me. Dev's hunched over, moving down our ranks, packing sand over each set of feet. Deb adds her own pebble toenails.

Why didn't I ever go on vacation before? I wonder.

You and Warren never went? Liz asks.

Just to his folks' houses. We were always so broke, trying to find time to write.

Deb says, Didn't you go to the Vineyard once?

That's right, I say. See, I still fail to remember the good stuff very much. (In my head, I can hear Joan—who wasn't there—say, *Work on that.*)

Warren and I fought on the ferry going over, I remember, because he didn't want our friends to come for the weekend. He wanted to write the whole time. So I pouted most of the week.

You figured he was being stubborn, Deb says.

But I was being—(I flounder for a word and hear Joan say *stubborn*)—stubborn.

You could've taken other holidays, though, Deb says.

Liz comes around with more lemonade and tops me off.

That's what our therapist says. Maybe we can swap houses with somebody in another city.

Dev, done with patting sand on my feet, informs me it's his garage; my feet are cars; I need to reverse them easy so the structure doesn't collapse. I gingerly slide them out, and he whoops, then runs down to get a bucket of water. The sandpipers clear him a path. We watch him lug his bucket sloshing back and set it next to me.

What's this for? I say.

To wash your feet off, he says. He dumps the cold water over my callused dogs.

Deb says, This is how he's gonna think women are—just lined up in front of him, cooing approval.

Now bury my feet, he says. Soon as he slides down in the deck chair, though, his body folds in on itself. His head drops. Every line of him loosens. The sun's low, the western sky burning. Smoke from somebody's grill drifts over us.

I sit cross-legged on a towel, and we talk about how the group has changed us. Deb says, You just don't seem so mad anymore.

Mother and I talk on the phone every morning—not about much, but the connection's clearer. She doesn't exactly know she's my mother—she's not housewifey Donna Reed but Madonna Reed. That's okay now.

The waves keep slapping the sand and withdrawing with that hushed hiss of gravel tumbling. A single gull hotfoots away from the water.

Deb asks us to guess at the shape of our lives five years down the pike. I say, I'm scared to speculate, since I have a habit of wanting the wrong thing.

Now that's real progress, Mare, Deb says.

Mostly, Liz says, I wish I'd found it easier to love myself without having to love you two.

After a second, I give Liz the finger, and she gives it back—it's our group handshake almost, so I snap a picture of Deb and Liz doing it from their deck chairs.

I'm scared to leave you guys. I don't even know if Warren and I are gonna make it.

You'll be okay, Deb says.

I pick up Dev's plump and sandy foot and weigh it in my wide hand, sensing from its heft the resolute slumber in him. Behind him, there's a see-through moon, like part of it's sanded off. The sky's going midnight blue, and it calls up in my mind the eyes of Chris—Dev's babysitter for a day—with snowflakes in her lashes. I quote her to the ladies: *Why is it that everybody else is traffic?* Deb and Liz saw her the week she died. She'd lost an eye and tried to get one of them to take the baby she didn't realize was dead. She couldn't comprehend she wasn't pregnant anymore.

Could've been us, Liz says.

The incredible fortune that it wasn't floods up as Deb lifts her lemonade, saying, To Chris. Nobody even says how corny it is. Our empty glasses gleam in the salt air.

36

Lake-Effect Humor

The smiles of the bathers fade as they leave the water,
And the lover feels sadness fall as it ends, as he leaves his love.
The scholar, closing his book as the midnight clocks strike, is
hollow and old;
The pilot's relief on landing is no release.
These perfect and private things, walling us in, have imperfect
and public endings . . .
—WELDON KEES, "THE SMILES OF THE BATHERS"

So we move to upstate New York, into a house on a leafy block with a skylit master bedroom off which is a balcony so buried in branches that it feels like a tree fort where you can smoke cigars and shoot off a pop gun. Is it Warren's August birthday or Christmas when I get him a golden retriever puppy from Deb's dog's new litter? Grace, we call her. There's a park two blocks away we go to every day and a pond with ducks and a trail in the woods. Dev walks to kindergarten in the frosted mornings with his backpack on. Warren and I keep differing orbits and finally start sleeping in separate rooms. I whipsaw back and forth on whether to stay or go, but no solid message shows up, as if the magic 8-ball's still saying, *Ask again later.*

Otherwise, the landscape seems less blunted and mono-chromatic. Stepping outside some mornings, it's like that instant in the optometrist's office when the right lens clicks over, the letters on the chart sharpening. There are individual leaves on trees where once was a lime smudge.

The writing has come back—with a polished quiet around it. Somehow I feel freer to fail. But the work mortifies me. Previously I'd seen the poems as adorable offspring, but they've become the most pathetic batch of little bow-legged, snaggle-toothed pinheads imaginable. Even the book I pub-lished with such pride a few years before—eager to foist it on anybody who'd read it—now seems egregiously dull, sopho-moric, phony. If the pages were big enough, I might well use them to wrap fish.

In the past, I strafe-bombed poetry editors with pages, the old insatiable-for-praise ego desperate to carve my name on any vacant surface. Now my instinct is to rathole.

Just before Christmas, the publisher I most admire—an aging patrician I've never met—writes me the only fan letter I ever got. James Laughlin from New Directions published and palled around with titans like Pound and Williams, plus Trap-pist monk Thomas Merton, whose spiritual books I've fallen for. Laughlin wonders do I have a second collection, adding cautiously they hardly ever take anybody on.

Usually, I'd have retyped everything with a watchmak-er's precision before mailing it off in a fancy binder. But so certain am I that the rejection letter's going to wing back like a homing pigeon, I just jam what I have in an envelope with an apology for how cobbled up it is.

Getting the poems off my desk frees me to label a folder MEMOIR, which stays pristinely empty for months, till I stuff a few scrawled notes in. Next summer maybe I can set off down that row.

That winter, snow falls without letup. From the eaves, the icicles grow jagged fangs big around as my thigh, past the windows. Living in the mouth of the winter witch, a friend calls this phenomenon. Also, we must've pissed off the snow-plow driver, who has a nasty habit of dropping his shovel loads in our driveway. Hours on end, Warren and I, faces chapped, hack away at mountains of ice while Dev frolics in his blue snowsuit.

The marriage has become nights on end of cordial agony. In the two years since I've gotten sober, Warren and I have alternately clung to or given room to each other till—over a tense series of months—we can no longer hold on.

An old sociological or Darwinian theory holds that when we're looking to gin out babies, we're biologically propelled toward the partner who'll color in dull spots in our own genetic code. So when opposites attract, they're bi-ologically combining to form the perfect offspring. Looking back, I can see how Warren's very essence looked like a cor-rective to who I was and didn't want to be, which is unfair to him. Nor does that theory account for the love we had and the long, pure, edifying conversation we shared. Still, it must be said that someone who doesn't like herself very much (i.e., me: age twenty-five), someone who views a man as an antidote to her very being, will find—over time—that antidote becomes an irritant. I don't want to rehash the times we wooed each other again and the times we withdrew, or the million fights we had. The truth is, as noted, we're inclined to gloss over our failures.

One spring morning my students come to help Warren lug his parents' cherry antiques with all their heft and curli-cued fittings from our small house. We unhitch our son's bunk bed into halves for his dual households, since we'll share custody. There's a schedule magnetically stuck to the fridge with a red mom's house and a blue dad's house and an iconic Dev who slides from one to the other. At the kindergarten graduation, while every other kid heartily sings and claps and stomps, Dev rocks from side to side, staring from one to the other of us and barely moving his lips. Stabs of guilt like flaming arrows fire into me at his blue-eyed puzzlement.

We're poor, all of us. You can't turn one home into two the same size. Since my salary comes closer to making the mortgage than Warren's, he takes a town house in a ghetto complex near a graveyard. With the Whitbread furniture gone, Dev can skateboard in the living room. Even after I rent out my attic to a grad student—a motorcycle-driving lesbyterian who sets my Republican neighbors' tongues wagging—I can't make ends meet. At first Warren and I plan to sell the house to give back Mr. Whitbread's small down payment, till Warren figures out my engagement ring could buy the whole place outright, so I fork that over instead.

That's the kind of stuff we bicker about. Maybe he feels, as I do, that he's given too much up—in furniture and car (on my part), house (on his part), or time with our son (on both parts). But when two different lawyers urge us separately to chase payouts we both know don't exist, we fire them. With a mediator, we hammer out a deal neither of us can imagine surviving on, then we sign it.

The Whitbread family tree sports nary a divorce, and it

shames Warren to break the news. Once he does, the chan-
nels between the family and me snap so totally shut, I don't
hear the fallout. While my clan views the split as a done deal,
Mother can't feature me without Warren's solidity. The boat
I row (financially speaking) is fully loaded and taking water,
but so's Warren's.

Warren loans me our sole vehicle pretty much on de-
mand, but it galls me to ask him. Facing walls of ice at my
drive's end, I try to tell myself that not having a car to shovel
out is a bonus, but climbing over slippery, filthy edifices to
reach a bus stop, Dev's mittened hand in mine, I curse the
oyster-gray sky and the fat flakes that Dev never tires of
catching on his tongue. The bus to Dev's after-school takes
a full hour each way, and pulling him in a red wagon to and
from the grocery store leaves me feeling stranded as a polar
explorer. (People who've never seen a credit-union employee
roll her eyes when you request a two-thousand-dollar car
note will say, *Just borrow.*)

In Syracuse, I find another circle of identical shit-brown
chairs occupied by sober strangers, and I call Joan the Bone to
complain about the mildewy carpet and the chilblains I get
wearing wet boots in the unheated room. She says, Uh-huh.
Are they sober?

While Joan's never more than a phone call away, she
can't be my polestar at such a remove. Before I moved, we'd
agreed I'd have to find a local contender. You're irreplace-
able, I tell her on the phone.

I am, aren't I? she says, nudging me by phone to court
Patti—a former English teacher who helps run an outpatient
rehab—a petite woman with a blond bob and the energy of a
fire truck. She has enough outlaw in her to start, at one point,
dating a biker in our acquaintance, and while I see her heart-

shaped face at public lectures and bookstores, I also catch sight of her at a stoplight on the back of a Harley-Davidson, staring from the helmet's visor like a road warrior.

Over coffee, she worries that she doesn't have the time to counsel me, what with her hellacious job and raising two kids alone while caring for an aged mother. But she takes my calls and listens to me whine. (Still does, seventeen years later.) When Dev has bronchitis and his codeine cough syrup looks tasty one night, it's Patti who squirrels the bottle away in her glove box and drives by after work every evening to dispense his single teaspoon.

But—shameful confession in this land of relentless, capped-tooth cheer—I'm lonely. Within weeks, Warren's taken up with a smart blonde I call my girlfriend-in-law, which act stings a little, however long our dissolution has been in coming. Seeing them hold hands at school events shines a spotlight—in my mind—on me in my solo chair. Part of me is glad for him, glad for the note he writes calling our match a poor one. It's the hand of friendship. (Ever after, we've shared parenting with conviction if not always ease, which is more than the divorced usually get—joint birthdays and graduations; phone conversations about school.)

Not long after, I'm sleeping on a pallet on the floor when I hear a glass-blasting crash downstairs. I grab Dev's aluminum bat and edge down all bug-eyed, reaching bottom in time to see our black cat devouring Dev's pet frog, the flippered feet disappearing between the tom's thin black lips. So determined had the cat been to eat the frog—he'd been studying it through the glass for weeks—that he must've gotten behind the aquarium with his shoulder and body-blocked it off the table.

With my insides thumping from the adrenaline, I sit on

the glass-spattered floor stroking the sleek tom a long while, figuring that's the closest I'll get to male company.

The next day in a bookstore with Patti, I tell her woman does not live by bread alone. I have a sexual nature, I tell her.

Who doesn't? she says. But right now you'll glom on to anybody who makes you happy in the sack. That's how I wound up remarried to the coke addict. Just date for a while.

I never really dated.

Then you need to learn how. Try different kinds of guys.

I thought I wasn't schtuppable yet. If I start kissing a guy, he'll start to look like Elvis.

So we come up with a plan dubbed date-o-rama, whereby pals fix me up with a long string of guys, regardless of age or education level, income or looks. It's neither boyfriend nor sport-fuck I'm after. In advance, I offer to pay my own way and warn all comers that I don't so much as kiss. This is my way of demystifying the whole gender, plus giving myself wardrobe opportunities—an excuse for witchy shoes and lip gloss.

There comes a string of good eggs who never make boyfriends, all ages and shapes. If it moves, I'll date it. At a faculty party, I agree to dinner with a surgeon who turns out—how?—to be in his mid-twenties. (Our sole point of commonality is that I'd babysat one of his undergrad frat brothers.) I date a local mogul twice that age and stay friends with his family for years. A comedian and a fireman, a legendary undercover narc, the occasional prof or publishing dude, an arbitrager. None of these do I so much as press lips to.

Only one straitlaced captain of industry even tempts me. Fit and well traveled, he shows up in a snazzy convertible, and it thrills me that he doesn't drink. On our second phone call, though, he confesses a sex addiction that involves—among other shockers—*hospitalization for masturbation injuries.*

Meanwhile, I'm broke enough to be filching toilet paper from the school bathroom. It's Patti who suggests I put God in charge of my financial woes, which sounds nuts unless you've spent a few years during which prayer keeps you from driving into stuff.

God's just gonna tell me to have another tag sale, I say, I'd sold every silver pie server and cake plate we got for our wedding.

So you know what God thinks now? (*What is your source of information?*)

I confess I don't much know what God thinks.

Patti proposes that I pray to accept whatever reality I'm in, staying alert for practical solutions rather than issuing orders in prayer. It takes discipline to stop beseeching the heavens for wheelbarrows of gold ingots to roll to my door. I manage it for three or four nights max. Then—when Dev and I pick through trash piles for furniture—I find myself upending dresser drawers and (once) even pawing through an old golf bag in case somebody accidentally threw out any bearer bonds. After the mortgage, I have a few hundred bucks each month for every bill, morsel of food, and tube sock. During a sweaty night praying over a stack of unpaid bills, I literally kneel before them (in some ways worshipping my fear, it strikes me now).

Because I signed up to take my whole salary over the nine-month academic year, all money clicks off in June. Even with summer jobs, I face missing mortgage payments. If I had a few years to cobble up a book, maybe some publisher with sufficiently low standards would pony up enough to pay off my maxed-out credit cards so I could qualify for a rust-bucket car loan. But that'll take years. How to start while teaching, raising a kid, and working in some local restaurant? It's a bone I pin between my paws at night and work with my jaw teeth.

I once read some science article claiming that 90 percent of what our brains gin out involves jockeying for position. *Will I get that subway seat? That job? Does he like me as much as I like him?* This mind-set works in a pack of lions inclined to tear deer meat out of your chops. But in my case, it pits me against others, keeps me inwardly growling. Cut off, it leaves me. Maybe this is the brain's natural instinct, but so is my urge to boink the UPS dude, who—as I get lonelier—starts to look like Sean Connery, which is why the phrase *Think twice about that* proves useful.

37

The Death of Date-o-Rama or the Romance of the Prose

Every lover is a soldier.

—OVID

Ill advised though it is, I start trolling for a beau—forget the semaphores Patti flaps in warning before my face. Reading St. Augustine's memoir, I come across his seminal line: *Give me chastity, Lord. But not yet.*

Which is my battle cry by the time David of halfway-house fame shows up. He leaves Boston to rent a boxy monk's cell spitting distance from my house. Ponytailed David with his gangster Timberland boots and red bandana holding his head together. Not yet thirty, with the habit of referring to his less than bright local bed partners in meetings as the Bimbo Brigade, David must've seen me—a single mom in academia—as some final doorway toward a cleaned-up act.

He'd looked like an old friend when he'd first rolled in that summer with a pal. Both were shopping for a cheap place to hole up while finishing freelance writing projects they'd taken advances for. (A prodigy like David did Harvard philosophy as a mere detour.) Over cheap Chinese, we all sat for hours reordering green tea and bowls of deep-fried whatnot till fortune-cookie slips confettied the linoleum booth top.

Back in Boston, we'd always talked books—nobody had read more than David. When I'd whined in early meetings about not writing, from across the room, he'd shoot a conspiratorial grimace. He edited Joan's dissertation before it was published, and a year later, he and I even swapped and slashed up each other's first, sober work. But he'd seemed like a stray and forlorn undergrad on Easter when Warren and I had invited him over.

In Syracuse, I must bat my eyes at him or fluff my hair like some cartoon seductress (*What a ma-yan!*), for right after, David starts packing my mailbox with bulging envelopes. Logorrheic, he calls himself. Words just pour from his pen. His yards-long letters come hand-printed in weensy, meticulous mouse type, painstakingly footnoted. Soon he's pleading his troth, signing his missives Young Werther (after a tragic swain in book and opera, with a crush on an older woman).

David is the only guy rash enough ever to get my name tattooed on his bicep—in a heart with a banner. Even before we've kissed on the lips, he does this. Watching those flesh-colored Band-Aids peel off in a phalanx to show an arm scarred and bloodied, a thinking woman would've hied for the hills. My response is more pitiful. I think, *Wow, he might really like me*—a thought nobody past grade five gets to have about anything bigger than a hamster. I plant a big wet Texas mouth on his.

It's a sad testament to my virtue that an inked-up arm is all it really takes to bed me. (As one friend said later, *You gotta love a date willing to do stuff he'll regret.*) Proof of David's undying conviction, I take it as, though Lecia points out cynically that any Mary tattoo need only *Blessed Virgin* carved above it for reason to remount its throne. That and David's move to my block prove, in my moronic head, some divine power's orchestrating our future together.

For a week or so, it's bliss. Any night I don't have Dev, David and I smoke cigars in my tree fort or read Russian short stories aloud till dawn. We watch movies where stuff blows up exclusively. Within the month, he phones Mother to announce, Mrs. Karr, I plan to marry your daughter. Mother's heartless comeback: *Didn't you just get out of some place?*

Then one day, almost like a switch is thrown in us both, reality sets in, turning the whole deal inside out. I'm raking leaves, waiting to borrow David's car for after-school pickup, but he slides alongside the curb, rolls down his window, and announces he's going to the gym instead.

Can't I drop you at the gym and then get Dev? I want to know.

David prefers to pick up Dev himself, then work out.

But I'm trying to shelter Dev from David's presence in my life, which David resents. He wants to plug into the husband slot right away. Words get sharp. I throw down the rake and stalk inside. He follows.

The ensuing fight rocks the rafters—a worse tussle than Warren and I ever dragged through. And soon our every day is a rage, the whole romantic endeavor flip-flopping from cuss fight to smoochy-faced makeup—the reversals coming too fast to get down in a diary. When Dev's home, I won't let David sleep over, which pisses him off no end, as does my leaving early from a research trip he takes me on. I'm mad he doesn't fit into the slot marked *reliable.*

(Of course, his temper fits are as vivid to me now as my own are invisible. No doubt he was richly provoked, for I'm nothing if not sharp-tongued in a fight, and however young he was, neither was I in shape to partner anybody.)

If David enters the mind-set he calls *a black-eyed red-out,* he's inclined to hurl all manner of object—book and back-pack not least. And as a verbal opponent, he's a colossus, once driving me to that lowest of schoolyard attacks—personal appearance: *At least I'm not a four-eyed, broke-nosed fop* was one of many sentences I had to apologize for.

Not that anything I utter warrants his pitching my coffee table at me, my sole piece of intact furniture splintering on the wall. After, I ring a lawyer girlfriend to send him a bill for it. He fires off a check with a note arguing that since he's paid for the table, isn't it his? I shoot back that the table's still mine, but he will own its brokenness for perpetuity.

(Years later, we'll accept each other's longhand apologies for the whole debacle and resume the correspondence that held the better angels of our natures.)

Disaster, my teacher Bob explained to me once, can trans-late as *something wrong with the stars.* Our stars—David's and mine—badly misalign, yet we can't escape each other's orbits. He climbs on my balcony and bangs on the bedroom window. I slip heartfelt notes under his windshield wiper. Coming across each other at a meeting, we wind up making out in the parking lot.

By Thanksgiving, we've both changed our phone num-bers to escape each other's stalkeresque calls, and we're burnt out enough to let go, though we'll reconnect for a few sloppy goodbyes before he moves away that spring.

By December when telephone poles sparkle with red lights and green bells, I'm sunk in the grief for my marriage that I'd been running from all along. This time I vow to embrace my loneliness till some spiritual presence takes up residence in my rib cage.

But I face the holiday like my own private gallows. Dev and I shape clay elf ornaments to bake in the oven, but at night, while I'm grading papers, they take on a ghoulish, leering quality I didn't figure on. Walking to school under the gray sky, I envision my solo Christmas hunched over a hot plate boiling packaged noodles. (Forget that I don't own a hot plate.)

Patti invites me over on Christmas Day, contingent on my volunteering at the local soup kitchen—a duty I resent like hell. She says, Whatever you want emotionally, you have to start giving away. Want to find company? Open up to other people.

That's how I land behind the steam table of a homeless shelter on Christmas, hair wadded into a black net. One hand wields a long-handled spoon, the other an ice cream scoop for potatoes. Patti predicted I'd bond cheerily with my fellow volunteers. But to me, they're that most grisly of Christmas specters: a happy family. Uniformed in matching Buffalo Bills football jerseys, they nonstop grin like beauty contestants who've vaselined their teeth. The father says, *Our lives are so abundant, this is just our way of giving back.*

Maybe they don't smile at my newly divorced ass like I've got cooties, but that's what I feel, since part of my illness is a proclivity for lopping myself off from others while simultaneously blaming them for how lonely I feel.

Pretty soon I find myself staring at the blackened teeth of a crackhead, thinking, This is the bottom.

But as I hand over the tray in baby-blue plastic with its boxy compartments, a flash goes off inside. It hits me that had I kept drinking awhile, I could've ended up gumming my turkey like this woman does. And for an instant, I actually look at her. Reaching for the tray is a big-knuckled farm girl's hand shaped surprisingly like my own in the plastic glove. It's one of those head-trippy instants when my innate suspicion inverts. For a second our matching hands simultaneously hold opposing sides of the steaming item. How manufactured we both are—it briefly strikes me—things shaped and formed, as the tray is, or the long-handled spoon with its flat rivet. I guide the spoon to dive into the stuffing, thinking, I didn't grow this hand myself. It was drawn forth without my willing it into flesh.

I'd like to say I didn't have a revelation on Christmas Eve in a homeless shelter. If it seems predictable and unlikely, try it before you're snide about it. I'd ditto like to say I fell Buddha-like to the floor and began to serve mankind selflessly ever after. But the blush of compassion lasts just a millisecond, diluting soon as I start struggling to name it. Meanwhile, my thumb on the ice cream scoop mechanically pushes out a load of mashed potatoes; I ladle up cranberry.

The family in their Buffalo Bills shirts don't seem like such chowderheads for an instant, and how alive I suddenly am. Even the ache in my feet is a measure of that.

Here comes the next guy in the line, who's made a yellow turban from police crime-scene tape.

Like your hat, I say.

I did it my own self.

I can see that.

You can make yourself one. There's a whole bunch of this ribbon up on Crouse.

He gestures with the sweeping open palm of an emperor.

There's an unbidden clap of gratitude in my rib cage again. This must be what the people in meetings have been gushing about. (I once thought saying you were grateful was a nice lie, like saying *Glad to see you*.) He's passed me by and is now stuffing dinner rolls down the front of his grease-streaked parka.

After cleanup, I stand at the pay phone regaling Patti with my trite everyone-is-everyone-else revelation. She says, Oh, that, as if she expected nothing else.

But my memory for joy is still uncultivated. Right before New Year's, my head's badgering voice announces what a loser I am without a New Year's date. But Dev comes home early from Warren's, and the next day we invite over anybody with nowhere to go—foreign students, a few neighbors, a sober ex-con—for red beans and rice with greens and corn bread.

Not long after, James Laughlin sends me an acceptance letter for the book of poems, along with a check for a whopping seven hundred and fifty bucks—about a third of my credit card debt and maybe the most I've earned aggregate on poetry in the previous fifteen years.

And that's how hard that was.

38

Lord of the Flies

All men would be tyrants if they could.
—DANIEL DEFOE

One winter afternoon, waiting for Dev to come home through the snow, I hear a thrash of banging against the storm door. Running out from the kitchen, I see him fumbling with the outside handle as snowballs splatter around him. I yank open the door, and the kids scatter like mice.

Dev's cheeks are sopping and crimson, which only makes his black-lashed blue eyes brighter. They're fixed in outrage, staring past me. When I ask how many kids there are and he tells me five, I have to stop myself from busting out the door to chase the little bastards down.

Over cups of cocoa, we sit in the tiny kitchen, and he says, *Why is this happening to me?* in a voice so wholly exhausted, he might have been sixty. With his spoon, he's fishing the sodden marshmallow off his cocoa.

Because, I say, children are childish. You're new to school, relatively. They've all grown up together. You're the obvious choice.

He stuffs the marshmallow in his mouth and ponders this before asking, Why would God let this happen?

The question—the same I'd dwelled on in the past— maybe shows the effects of our nightly prayers.

Because, I say, when you grow up, you're gonna be so smart and good-looking that if something bad didn't happen to you now, you'd be a jerk then—one of those snotty kids who thinks he's all that.

Like Dan.

I'm thinking specifically of Dan, I say (I barely know who Dan is).

Dev picks at the foam atop his cocoa, saying, Dan knows karate. He only invited the cool kids to his birthday.

He studies the cocoa as if it were tea leaves foretelling the soggiest future. I get up and place a skillet on the stove for an- other supper of scrambled eggs. After a while he says, There are so many of them. I mean, the snowballs just kept coming.

Isn't there a teacher or grown-up you can appeal to at school?

They act like they're my friends in school. Then they start chasing me.

I offer to start picking him up again, and he pins me with a tired look.

I'm not a baby, he says. All the other kids walk home.

I know, I know. Okay.

We sit there listening to the wind make the windowpanes shudder. You know, I say, some people think when somebody slaps you, you should turn the other cheek.

He says, face still chapped scarlet, I only have two cheeks.

That night, tucking him in, I tell him how I'd been the

littlest kid in my neighborhood, and because I skipped a grade and had a propensity to mouth off, they beat me up all the time. I say, You know your grandpa Pete always told me to bite them.

This strikes Dev as hilarious. He says, He wanted you to bite them?

Yeah, if he wasn't around to help and they were bigger. He'd say, *Lay the ivory to 'em, Pokey.*

That's funny, Dev says.

I kiss his shampooed head, and later, standing in the doorway as I click off the light, I briefly pray for a car that I might track down and smash the little bastards like the toads they are. I tell him I'm gonna call some of the kids' parents, the ones I know.

Don't get them in trouble, he says. That'll just make it worse.

Downstairs, I call around but get no answers, and when finally I reach one mom I barely know, she harumphs into the phone, saying, Why do you think they're picking on him? You think he's innocent, I guess.

My face gets hot. I say, I have no doubt that Dev is as savage as any grade school boy, but this is five against one. This is Lord of the Flies.

Well, he must be doing something, she says.

Out of the blue, I say, I'm from the state of Texas.

What's that supposed to mean?

I know my son is gonna survive these ass-whippings no matter how many of them there are. But when it's five against one and there's not a grown-up to intervene, I'm gonna instruct Dev to pick up a rock or a stick and leave a mark on somebody. Let's hope it's not your kid.

My uncle's a lawyer, she says.

My daddy's Pete Karr, I say, and hang up.

Over breakfast the next day, I tell Dev the strategy's this: if he's away from school, and there are that many of them, he should turn and fight. Throw down his book bag and just accept the fact that he's gonna take an ass-whipping.

Slipping his backpack on, he looks completely defeated.

One ass-whipping hurts once, I says. Running home afraid every day hurts every day.

Why would they ever stop? he says.

Because you're gonna pick out one of them—the closest one you can get to—and you're gonna leave a mark. Bite the dog dookey out of him. *Lay the ivory to 'em.*

He tries to grin, but a cloud passes over his face as he pulls his royal blue watchman's cap on.

What? I say. What's the matter?

Dan does know karate, Dev says.

Do you know, I say, what would happen to Dan if you hit him full-on?

What? Dev says.

He'd topple like a pine. He's a pipsqueak of a thing. You've got a leg as big as Dan.

Dev grins all over his face. He says, Really?

Absolutely. Karate or no karate. You're twice his size.

He's out the door when he turns and hollers back, You swear I won't get in trouble?

If you hit first, you've lost TV for a month.

That afternoon he comes in shucking off his backpack. He'd run for about a block before turning to face the pack. Dan had said he was gonna karate Dev's block off, and Dev had said, You go ahead and hit me first, adding, When I hit you, you're gonna topple like a pine.

End of discussion.

Come March, after I've been praying for a solution to our transportation woes, a professor I've met once or twice through mutual friends approaches me in the quad. She's going to Italy and heard I needed a car. Maybe I could keep hers through the summer; she'd consider it a favor.

And that's how hard that was. Such unearned gifts feed the growing faith that some mystery is carrying me.

The snow's just melting when I take out the fourth credit card I can't pay—one with a five-hundred-dollar limit and a fat percentage interest rate. That same week the university flies the creative writing profs to New York for a program fund-raiser.

Once the dinner's over, the writers cross the street to the Pierre Hotel to hang out. With its checkerboard floor and ornate armchairs, it's like entering a Fred Astaire movie. That night Toby and his pals sing in loud harmony the old seventies hit "Helpless," swaying side to side like a grade-school choir.

I'm just finishing my Coke when who should come kneel at my seat but Toby's agent from almost a year back. Where, she says with both charm and entitlement, is my damn memoir?

I'm shocked she remembered me and even more shocked when I hear myself tell her the truth: I'm in the middle of a divorce and haven't done that much—less than ten pages.

She says, Send me a proposal. Maybe we can get you an advance.

Here's where grace comes in. Had I been drinking, I would've pretended to know what a proposal was, then lived in crouched fear, maybe trying to find out or not—being too afraid in my drinking form to fail at a proposal. Instead, I hear my mouth spill another truth: I don't know the first thing about writing a proposal.

She waves her hand like it's the easiest thing in the world, saying, Maybe a hundred pages. Three or four chapters.

In a poet's mind, a hundred pages sounds like two thousand. I haven't published a hundred pages in twenty years.

How long do you think, she asks, before I can get those chapters?

My head's scrambling. I figure when Dev goes to stay with his dad mid-June, I'll have a month to work, so I say, Mid-July.

Great, she says. Then just add a letter saying what else you might put in the book.

I must have a stunned look on my face.

I'll call you Monday, she says, and walk you through it.

To write the stuff down is no cakewalk, since memories from that time can ravage me. But after I get home, I start getting up mornings at four or five, praying to set down words before Dev comes down. When Dev's with Warren, I unplug the phone and apply my ass to a desk chair. Some days, I actually hear my daddy telling me stories, almost like he's risen up to ride through the pages with Mother and our whole wacky herd.

Come June, I send the agent pages on a Thursday, and she signs me the following Saturday, has an auction that week, and a few days later—while I'm chopping basil for supper—I hear the overnight envelope with payment hit my porch.

In the steamy kitchen, I draw the check out and sit studying it before I even throw pasta in the bubbly water. It's in no way a massive check, but it's the biggest I've ever seen, and it's fallen from the sky just in time to get us through the summer, plus making a down payment on a used Toyota.

Saying thanks to the invisible forces that brought it, I sit looking at the check. On the table before me, there's a giant pickle jar Dev's filled with torn grass and crickets. The bent-legged bugs are whirring to fill the room, one or two trying to climb up the curved glass. Dev bursts in, saying, Mom, let's set the crickets free tonight. And I tell him that's just what I was thinking.

39

God Shopping

Lord, You may not recognize me
speaking for someone else.
I have a son. He is
so little, so ignorant.
He likes to stand
at the screen door, calling
oggie, oggie, entering
language, and sometimes
a dog will stop and come up
the walk, perhaps
accidentally. May he believe
this is not an accident?
At the screen,
welcoming each beast
in love's name, Your emissary.

—LOUISE GLÜCK, "THE GIFT"

If you'd told me even a year before I start taking Dev to church regular that I'd wind up whispering my sins in the confessional or on my knees saying the rosary, I would've laughed myself cock-eyed. More likely pastime? Pole dancer. International spy. Drug mule. Assassin.

One Sunday I'm eating a bagel with a smear and reading the paper when Dev, age eight, intensely blue-eyed in his Power Ranger pajamas, announces he wants to go to church.

I barely look up. Despite my prayer life, organized religion still strikes me as bogus. Though Mother had pored over sacred texts of every kind, she was—as I've said before—no more able to commit to a faith than to a husband. She quoted Marx calling religion the opiate of the masses. So I'm suspect of the hierarchies.

Idly asking Dev why he wants to go to church, I'm confident that no sentence he utters will rouse me from my Sunday loll. But he says: *to see if God's there.*

The phrase straightens my slouchy spine. Some native faith lets him stare out the window at the aluminum sky and see a scrim before heaven.

Okay, I say, and I ring up a sober Episcopalian (an oxymoron, he alleges in the car), the only guy I know who goes to church. If I'd had a pal attending a mosque or temple or zendo, we'd have gone there.

So disinterested am I, so devoid of curiosity, that I climb into my friend's car toting a paperback, like the one I carry to soccer fields stiff with frost, to pass time.

It's a capital-C Church, with gray stones right out of some horror-movie castle. It sits amid red maples between the university on one side and housing projects on the other. Soon as the engine dies, Dev bolts for the huge oak doors, his loafers slapping up the leaf-strewn walk. He has on a hand-me-down sport coat. With his green clip-on bow tie, he looks like some refugee from a 1950s wedding. Going in makes me a little watery.

In the foyer, I expect to find some *Ozzie and Harriet* episode in progress, the women in pillbox hats and white gloves and ear bobs, the men in lizard-green jackets and wing tips, everybody in that old fluorescent light the color of cucumber that makes white people look so seedy. But this parish is half black, with people wearing jeans and khakis. Even the ancient blue-haired ladies have pants on.

Organ music starts in the sanctuary, and we drift into a barnlike structure with tall stained glass windows where saints I don't know are doing saintly things I can't figure out. We stand and sit and pray for over an hour. People take turns talking at the granite altar. Dev belts out hymns in his brassy alto while I flip pages. Afterward, people eat pastries in the foyer. Kids streak around. A few parents from Dev's school say hey. Somebody brings me coffee like I like.

This uninvited niceness seems like a trap. I keep waiting for them to ask me for money. In the car, I ask Dev whether God was there, expecting him to be as cynical as I am. Instead, he cocks his head and squints, as if saying, Where were *you*?

We stop going to the Episcopal church after a few weeks because I find it too cold—not emotionally but physically. To heat that vaulted space would cost a fortune, I guess. Still, the scalding baths I take to get blood back into my feet after service feel like penance.

Dev nudges me to take him to various places of worship. It's still a social exercise for me, another maternal duty I hadn't foreseen. Most places get just one visit. The Hebrew that mesmerizes me at the conservative temple frustrates Dev, who likes the Reform service, though it sometimes sounds to me—with its talk of Middle East strife—more political than spiritual. While I adore the hand-clapping gospel music of the Baptists, the anti-gay diatribe is tough to swallow, ditto the long service.

By summer, I figure my half-baked sense of a higher power might resonate with the super-liberal Protestant parishes that shun dogma, but they actually put me off. Church X has the sterile feel of an operating theater. Since the well-off parishioners send their kids to fancy camps, it's almost totally child-free. The sermon—on justice to one's fellows—has so squeezed out any mention of God or Jesus, maybe to sound modern, there's no sense of history. The pastor asks for peace and gives thanks for plenty, but the homily might come from *Reader's Digest*.

Looking for something to say to the pastor, I ask him how he deals with the problem of evil, and he says, *We don't believe in it*—a phrase so obviously untrue, I wonder how they sell it. It's like a Rotary Club meeting where everybody's agreed on the agenda in advance and is only waiting for the danish to come out.

Lots of professors go to Church Y, so again, I think maybe they'll rook me in. But where Church X avoids God altogether, Church Y sees gods everywhere, each more or less interchangeable. These gods sound no more potent than the rabbit's foot Dev carries into the batter's box on a belt loop.

The zendo wants people to sit in silence then chant for five minutes, which Dev could never do. You could be saying jump-rope rhymes, the monk informs me before the service. The breathing of the chants is supposed to relax you into a posture I couldn't hold for the appointed time if you oil-canned my knees like Oz's Tin Man.

It's a year before we follow Toby and his wife, Catherine, to their Catholic parish, maybe because I associate their church with the shame of my lapsed pals or the Inquisition's torture devices.

The whole surface of the room is sloppy with kids—toddlers zigzag down the aisles, babies squeak and yell. On the altar, Father Kane is a blue-eyed Irishman who takes us through Mass in the most unvarnished way, with none of the maudlin piety I've seen at some other churches and temples.

At the outset, he seems humble without seeming bent or cowed. As a kid, I'd been dragged to a Mass by neighbors, where the priest downshifted in prayer into this slow, syrupy—extra-holy—way of talking, as the congregation no doubt prayed to get home in time for kickoff. When Father Kane breaks up the bread, the movements are simple, stripped of any show—with the solemn dignity of an enlightened master mechanic adjusting a carburetor—nothing pro forma about it. The process somehow erases him so he's a clear conduit, and the keen quality of his attention draws me in.

Toward the end of Mass, Dev whispers, Is that a yarmulke on his head?

Since Dev goes to a Jewish after-school—the best in town—he's covetous enough of a yarmulke that he once lopped the ears off his Mickey Mouse hat to make his own.

I shush him, but Toby says under his breath, What *is* that? The priest has taped to the top of his scalp a round piece of wire mesh. From my vantage, I'd thought it was some holy hat, but now it looks like nothing so much as a small inverted sink-drain catcher.

Father Kane tips the microphone and says sheepishly, I normally wouldn't mention this, but I had a growth taken off my head. He pauses, almost blushing as he adds, I didn't want you to think I'd joined the Hair Club for Men.

Which draws hoots. Walking to the parking lot, I realize I forgot my paperback. For the first time since God-shopping, I haven't cracked it open.

Maybe I'm getting softheaded, I think, driving home. Or the burden of single-motherhood is making me a crackpot. Since Warren's moved to New Haven for love and work, a church community seems like necessary parenting ballast, though twice a month, he drives in all weather to see Dev, even staying at our house, both alone and with his sweetheart.

Still, if Dev loses the bow to his school-owned bass the night before a concert or needs his basketball hoop set to regulation height the night before his birthday party, it falls to me. And I won't say the venal thought doesn't flit through me that church folk look like they might have wrenches and lawn mowers to loan.

On Halloween, Dev joins the line of Sunday school kids costumed as various saints and taking turns telling brief, sanitized stories of martyrdom. The tiny St. George—visor askew, plastic breastplate listing—comes last, announcing, *You can be a saint, too!* like a used-car salesman, which brings down the house.

Not long after, Dev jumps the communion line—his first show of appetite for baptism. While I'm thumbing my missal, his pal Osiris crooks a finger and Dev shoots out of the pew. I lean forward to grab his sleeve, but he jerks away. The line edges up. I hiss at him to sit down, and he ignores me. Once the line curves, I lose sight of him till both boys pop up at the altar.

Before the priest, Dev stands slim and solemn. I think how ancestors on both sides of his family sought this sacrament, which is painfully carnal if you think of it. The body of the god is absorbed by the human body to nourish the spirit. Dev's mouth pops open wide as a baby bird's.

Afterward, the boys plop down beside me whispering, their hands busy. What obscene gestures, I wonder, are they practicing? But I crane over to catch them in the middle of that old hand game: *Here's the church. Here's the steeple. Open the door and see all the people.* The game's been passed down for decades, one kid teaching another how to bear long, adult-prescribed intervals of inertia—a lineage I belong to.

While the priest speaks and the responses come out, I feel myself as an animal herded among similar animals—an echo of the homeless shelter. I think how horses in the Colorado of my youth huddled together in the cold.

At one point parishioners call out their intentions, people they want prayers said for. *For my daughter whose tumor has metastasized. For the refugees from Bosnia and Rwanda. In gratitude for the safe return of my mother from Ireland . . .*

Catholics aren't who I thought they'd be, not even close. It isn't the ritual of the high Mass that impresses me, but the people—their collective surrender. If I can't do reverence to that, how dead are my innards?

Within a week or two, it's turning out that I forget to bring a paperback to Mass, so obviously, I'm not just coming for Dev anymore. It's historical interest, I tell myself, when I start reading all manner of theology.

When a married couple—he a former Jesuit, she once a nun—invite me to the Peace and Social Justice Committee, I stumble onto the lay tradition of working with the poor and against political tyranny. (I know, historically, plenty of Catholics worked *for* tyranny.) They protest nuclear arms and host refugees from Haiti and El Salvador. Every Sunday they have some batch of parolees who need jobs, or welfare moms looking for baby clothes.

Plus they argue like mad. Say what you will about Catholic dogma, like it or lump it, it sure gets people yakking it up.

I confess to this couple that Jesus Himself seems sappy—a chump or fool. For all my pretense of practicing surrender, I can't grasp signing up for crucifixion.

The wife says, Long time ago, I started focusing my faith on the Holy Spirit. She's the female pronoun in the Greek Bible.

C'mon, the husband says. It's not called Holy Spirit-anity; it's called Christianity.

After Mass one day, I challenge Father Kane on certain aspects of the liturgy that bother me. Missal in hand, I bargain like an insurance salesman to convince him how crappy Jesus is. I say something like, He's so snotty to the lady at the well. I mean, He's putting her down for sleeping around. (Worried, I must've been, about how He'd have judged any future premarital hilarity of my own.)

You think He's angry? the priest says. I always thought He was joking or teasing her. And she was just shocked He knew that stuff about her life.

It's true. Looking at the text, I've overlaid a judgmental tone on the story.

Father Kane says, You know the best part, though—or a couple things. She was Samaritan. She could only go to the well in the hottest part of the day. This was like a colored water fountain before the civil rights movement. And Jesus drinks after her—that's the radical part. The disciples are saying, Why'd you even talk to her? But Jesus didn't flinch.

Father Kane knows that Dev is studying for baptism and first communion, and he asks if I've considered doing the same.

I unload one of my key deal breakers: I don't believe the pope is the ultimate religious authority.

Father Kane says right back, Maybe someday you will. (Little did I know how outmatched I was with the modest

Father Kane, who'd clearly had this kind of talk before.) Grinning, he adds, God's after you. Struggle all you want.

I'm actually a little shocked that he cares whether I convert. Still, I sign up for instruction, claiming it's for conversations with Dev. But when the lady in charge of classes kicks me out because I have to miss a few for work travel, I run tattle to Father Kane, who sits me in a pew. He claims I've already read what they'll cover in class instruction. He wants to know my impression of Jesus.

I say, He was a peasant from a pigsty town who made all the civil and religious authorities so mad they killed Him. But for me, the Resurrection is only a metaphor for renewal.

If you can believe He made all this happen—Father Kane waves his hand around the room—right here in our little church, forget Rome and Lourdes and all that. That's a miracle, right? Somebody born into his station.

Maybe I don't belong here, I say.

But you are here, he says. What's keeping you from joining us? You come to Mass, but you're denying yourself the Sacraments. Those are the consolations of the Church.

In Mass the next week, I enter and get on my knees like everybody else, saying the prayers I usually say at home. Opening my eyes, I actually tear up. There's something different about praying in company—I can't deny it—once you get over feeling like a poser.

About a week later, Father Kane tells me he's found a way for me to miss classes and still be baptized with Dev if I want to. I can meet with Toby and talk about the gospels one-on-one. Father Kane will personally fill in any gaps.

Which is how one of my literary heroes winds up my godfather.

40

Dysfunctional Family Sweepstakes

They are passing, posthaste, posthaste, the gliding years—to use a soul-rending Horatian inflection. The years are passing, my dear, and presently nobody will know what you and I know.
—VLADIMIR NABOKOV, *SPEAK, MEMORY*

For over two years, Mother hounds me to let her read pages I'm scribbling about the worst patch of our family history, but I'm still x-ing out, deleting, starting over. She swears public opinion frets her not one whit. In fact, she and Lecia both signed off on a summary of the story before I set out.

If I gave a big rat's ass what anybody thought about me, Mother says, I'd have been baking cookies and going to PTA. Which I didn't do.

But I know reading it could hurt them, since writing it

often wrings me out like a string mop. Some afternoons after I close my notebook—I'm working longhand—I just conk out on the floor of my study like a cross-country trucker. I see a shrink who says the naps don't mean I'm repressing stuff. Don't you know, he says, feeling all that stuff again is exhausting? So the prospect of dragging Mother and Lecia through it too feels like abuse.

Mother's sole focus is money. Whatever wounds I parade through the marketplace, she's mostly just skippy I have a car, however far it is from paid off. In fact, she's sure I've misunderstood the contract somehow.

That's your money though?

That's right, Mother. My money.

What if they don't like the book?

Oh well.

What if it doesn't sell?

What poet would plan for anything different?

The next call she approaches head-on: There's no way you'll have to give the money back?

No ma'am.

No way, no how.

Right.

But do they know you've spent it already?

Once she tries to finagle a peek at the book by threatening to die: saying, What if my heart fails before you finish it?

I'll just have to regret it the rest of my life.

I remind her that as a portrait painter, she never turned the canvas around for view till it was dried, never signed it till she knew what she was endorsing.

The summer it's done, I fly her up to Syracuse. Right off, she drops her purse in the hall and falls on the manuscript like a harpie. No, she doesn't want to come to the park with

Dev and me. She waves us on. I'm not going anywhere, she says.

She takes up a lounge chair in the backyard with pages in her lap while I obsessively assemble cold soups and dips and marinades for the grill nearby, trying not to vulch over her. What am I waiting for?

Given that she takes in books the way a junkie shoots dope, I want it to mesmerize her, which—since she's its subject—is pretty much a slam dunk. I'm also hoping she'll confirm in detail what she's agreed in broad stroke is true.

But there's something more ineffable at stake, winding like thin smoke through me, unnamed. It's as if—through the writing—I've assembled some miniature replica of myself as a girl, and she's now being lowered onto Mother's lap to be verified somehow.

For all the schisms in my upbringing, the most savage scars didn't come from pain. Pain has belief in it. Pain is required, Patti likes to say; suffering is optional. What used to hurt was the vast and wondering doubt that could spread inside me like a desert, the niggling suspicion that none of the hard parts even happened. So the characters that so vividly inhabited me were phantasms, any residual hurt my own warped concoction.

I wanted Mother to see the girl I was—the girls Lecia and I were, really—to take us into her body as we've taken her so indelibly into ours. Is that love or need?

As Mother reads, I grind beans to brew her coffee. I cut her sandwich into quarters. I keep wiping her ashtray clean. I dissolve sugar into tea and shave ice into a frosted glass.

Occasionally, she hollers out, How'd you ever remember all this crazy crap? She laughs a lot. Once she says, This is your daddy to a T. I can smell him.

But her strongest emotion seems to be for an alligator belt of hers I wrote about, which she mists up over, saying, I wonder where that went to? She absorbs the material—maybe as she did being our mother—as if it were a novel she'd already seen the film of, though like any mother, she's inclined to heap on undiluted praise. No more convincing cheerleader ever shook a pom-pom.

She's almost to the end when she claims her eyes are tired.

From downstairs that night, I hear small noises from the bathroom—stifled, intermittent squeaks like a mouse might make. I tap on the door, which opens to her red-rimmed eyes.

You are so busted, I say.

She has on a black T-shirt and yoga pants. You caught me, she says, wiping her nose.

I didn't mean to hurt you, Mother, I say.

She looks surprised: I'm not the least bit hurt, she says.

You're not festive.

Living through it hurt me, she says. Reading about it's a blip on the radar.

Not a lot of mothers would make this so easy.

Can I smoke up in my attic, or are you gonna make me go on the porch?

We creak up the stairs to where she's spread pages across her mother's old wedding quilt, stitched together from men's flannel-suit samples—all manner of gray and chalk stripe with a cherry-red underside.

I hold a blue teardrop flame to her cigarillo while she takes a long draw, then blows smoke up to the rafters. She raises her arms to flatten both hands on the slanted ceiling, saying, This is like an artist's garret up here.

You could come live with us, I say. I could put in a skylight, and you could paint again.

These old bones wouldn't make it through a winter.

We sit in a silence it's hard not to scribble in with chat. Her long ash falls on the quilt, and she rubs it in, saying, It blends.

Is there anything in there you didn't know, that we hadn't talked about?

She says, I never knew you felt that way.

What way?

She shrugs and shakes her head, then asks, Didn't we have some fun?

Sure, later on some. We have fun now. But like you said, living through it . . .

I mean in Colorado. Remember we went to that department store in Denver and I got y'all those little coats with fur on the hood?

My head kecks to one side. I say, I got lost that day.

But we found you. And y'all had your horses, and the house was so fancy. There was shuffleboard at the bar y'all liked to play. You loved the jukebox.

"Ring of Fire," my favorite song. But we were afraid you were gonna go to jail.

Whatever for?

Shooting Hector.

Aw—she waves her hand in a *pshaw* motion—you knew I'd never shoot anybody.

Dev comes to the doorway, one knuckle making a screwing motion in his eye socket, saying, Are y'all crying again? Then: Why does everybody from Texas cry and smoke?

The next morning I come down about dawn, and she's on the back porch in the saggy yellow seat of an old director's chair, the final pages flipped over to the back. She's staring at her bare feet.

She glances up to say, I can't believe I was such an asshole.

You suffered the torments of the damned.

But you saw that, didn't you? All that time I thought I was so alone. I wasn't alone at all, not with you and your sister. I must've done something right. You both turned out so magnificently.

We're a lot of fun to be with, I say. The shoulders I put my arms around are small as a schoolgirl's. You did a lot of things right, I add.

When Lecia's turn comes, she meets me in Denver, renting a vast sofa of a car that I wheel through mountain passes while she turns pages. The child-abuse tour, she jokes it is, for my agenda is to double-check my words against the old landscape or school records or anybody we can drag up. But to say she's skimmed over events I couldn't forget is an understatement. She knows what happened enough to verify scenes, but it's all been packed away. She didn't have to go into therapy, she's always claimed, because I told her the insights that my own therapy had routed out. Keeping the volume down made her the brave one, the unflinching one.

In the mountains while Lecia reads, we revisit the town that held the summer cabin neither of us can find. We stand alongside the falling-down ring where our horses ran a gymkhana. We find the house where Mother left us with the stable owner's family when she ran off to marry the bartender. There's the phone booth alongside a trout pond where we once called Daddy sobbing because we'd forgotten Father's Day.

Each time we recognize a spot, it's like some book's clear overlay page falls across the old landscape, the green scene rising up articulately around us—a 3-D pop-up. We get littler at those times, standing closer like we used to as kids, and the hoots and hollers we've been making to stay brave—those dwindle down. We dwindle down, two women almost gone into girls again.

In the car, Lecia slides on her sunglasses, saying, I almost thought I'd dreamed this place up. But you've gotten down every jot and tittle.

She cheers the manuscript with all the big-sister praise she brought to my first step off the high board, and that pat on the head matters more than any review I'll get. I'd only really wanted her and Mother not to be pissed off.

Midafternoon, I steer the car across the Rockies to the town where Mother's bar was and where we went to school. That place left the most shadowy specters in Lecia, since it's no doubt where she gave up being little once and for all. The day she called Daddy collect and announced to him that he had to buy us plane tickets to get us out of there, some light in her clicked off. Doing that meant bailing out on the mother she'd spent her whole young life courting and placating. We flew from there wondering if we'd see Mother again—alive or dead. There was no visitation plan, no schedule of phone calls set up. Just my ten years' sister with the round-eyed, glassy gaze of an opium addict, as she set the big black phone in its cradle before telling me we had to pack.

We get closer to the town, and Lecia starts rifling her purse for hand unguents and lip gloss and chewing gum. She wants a Coke. She wants to stop and check in with her office by pay phone. I'd expected all this. The motel we booked—a Norman Bates–type Econo-lodge—has the only vacancy this last minute. At the check-in counter, the pinwheel mints have melted into their wrappers, their inner whirls gone smudgy pink. The TV doesn't get cable, and the bathroom sink has a tiny cup of the type dentists give you for antiseptic. In the dusty windowsills lie papery gray moths.

Sliding off her shades, Lecia peels back the flowered spread and stares down at a rough blanket the color of mustard. I was going to take a nap, she says, but there must be all species of bed louse here.

So when I head off to find our grade school, she shoulders her massive purse like a duffel bag, saying, Let's march.

We're not heading into battle.

War'd be easier for me, she says, and she follows me into the blinding sunshine.

It's strange. She's always been our navigator. You could lower her into a jungle with nary a compass, and she could machete her way out. Yet here, I have an uncanny sense where things lie. There's no map in my head either, just my torso leaning one direction or another. I follow a path straight as a spear to the pale brick schoolhouse, which now houses town offices. The heavy door closes behind us, and we're sealed in with the odor of floor wax.

As we look up the short stairway leading to a wall of coat hooks, it so exactly matches my recall that I feel a shock. *It happened.* Lecia seems enervated all of a sudden. She wants to go back to the motel, see if we can find something halfway decent to eat.

I knew this would be hard for you, I say.

She stares at me with cool brown eyes, saying, Then why the fuck did you bring me here?

Back on the main drag, tourists are gleefully buying fool's gold and Indian arrowheads and turquoise earrings. The house we lived in burnt to the ground, we find out. A neighbor lady doesn't recall us, but she names the principal who lived across the road. Maneuvering back to the hotel, I walk us smack against the bar Mother once owned—a gift shop now. Or I claim it's the same bar. Lecia says it isn't. Hell no.

(I remember one day at the bar: A horse had thrown

Lecia, and she showed up with a broken collarbone, the sharp edge poking the thin flesh. Her blond hair was tugged back in a smooth ponytail, and her round eyes were dry of tears. Mother told her, *Go stand under the wall dryer till it feels better. Does anybody have an aspirin?* Nobody did, so I stood alongside her, the hand dryer blowing its hot wind on her clavicle.)

On Lecia's big black sunglasses, the bar's doorway floats as if projected across a blindfold. She says, This isn't it. Let's go. She's rooted before the door as if a force field holds her back.

I point to the pink stucco hotel where we first stayed before Mother bought the house. We walked there with snow on our hooded fur coats.

Back and forth we quibble. Still she refuses to go in. She'll wait on the curb while I check with the shop owner. Yes, it used to be a bar, the lady says from her rice-powdered face with crinkles around her smiling eyes. Her capped teeth are big as chiclets.

I step inside, thinking, How much smaller the large places are once we're grown up, when we have car keys and credit cards. This was a harmless little gin mill once.

The clerk confirms the layout in my head, that the bathroom is over there, and I push into the small gumball-blue room. There's the spot where a wall dryer once hung. The raw hardware of its back plate faces across from a modern paper-towel holder.

In some ways, I'd relived the history of that place in the pages, and while I'm not dead to the psychic damage done here—there's a twinge of sadness for us all—the place can't overwhelm me anymore.

On my way out, I glance up at a hammered tin ceiling.

Soon as I see it, the pattern fits in a similarly jigsawed space in my memory. I could've drawn it by heart—the filigreed squares and sprouted vines. I reel back, and for an eyeblink's time, the small structure looms as large as it once did when our young mother sat sipping vodka by the window. I can see her slim in her gray pencil skirt and white crepe blouse, legs crossed, one pump near-dangling from a toe. The old grief has been mostly drained off in me for a long time now, and I'm awestruck by her grace. You're so damn pretty, I'd tell her if she'd turn around.

I step back out into the sunshine, saying to Lecia, Check out the tin ceiling.

She holds out her hand like a blind girl, and I take it. C'mon, I say, and though it's rare for her to follow, she lets me tug her in. On this expedition only, I'm point woman. One hesitant step she takes, as if afraid to get too close to a cliff edge, then another, till she's a few feet inside. She cants her wondering face up at the ceiling, then gasps, a hand covering her mouth. It's not a small breath but the lung-deep, sucked-in huff you'd take, say, finding a rat running the baseboards of your kitchen.

Outside in the sunlight, I keep holding her hand. Though her eyes are devoid of feeling, fat tears stream down, and she curses me for dragging her to this godforsaken place—me with my fucking therapy and passion for the old crap. I didn't know it'd be this hard, I tell her. Inside, I'm pissed at myself for buying her don't-give-a-damn act when I knew better. I tell her it's good we can face this place together, good that she got us out of here when she did.

Within the hour, I'm shepherding that vast chaise longue of a vehicle back toward the far side of the mountains, where she's secured a thousand-dollar-per-night hotel room for us because there are no other rooms at any inns, and the sun can't set on her in that town.

She grabs my hand in the car, palm to palm and tight, like we're fixing to bound off the pool's edge together.

Yes, she finally admits in the car, that was the place.

I recount to her how Mother told me she was surprised we didn't have fun in the mountains. Lecia shakes her head.

The next day at the airport, she kisses my hair and holds my hand and says she loves the book and what a bang-up job I did, but she's not in her eyes anymore. When I look at her, I see her at age eleven. Months from now, once she gets the bound galley, she'll read it and marvel that the opening works better with the scene of Mother at the fire, which is the exact same chapter she'd read in Colorado. The publisher set type from it, but she hadn't remembered a damn thing from that first draft. Was I sure that was written in the version she saw? I was.

41

It Makes a Body Wonder

I am only a man; I need visible signs . . .
—CZESLAW MILOSZ, "COME, HOLY SPIRIT"

Toby faces my mental block about not believing stuff from the Bible by pointing out that with my current spiritual construct, only stuff that happens to me firsthand counts as divine intervention. With total faith, I cling to the notion that God sent me—little Mary Karr, sinner deluxe—checks in the mail and healed my severely depressed head, got me car loans and a grant. I use the G-word now—God. I feel Him holding me when I'm scared—the invisible hands I mocked years before. But this same power couldn't turn water into wine or—here's the biggie—raise the dead, could it?

It's kind of like, Toby says to me at his glossy dining room table one afternoon, not believing in Bob Dylan because you've only heard the CDs and never saw him in concert. (Again: *What is your source of information?*)

Based on my experience, I say, I am the center of the universe.

Lord help us, Toby says, pulling the corner of his mustache.

The magic stuff is what runs me off, I say. Sometimes I think of Jesus as some carnival trickster. Maybe the whole Resurrection was a scam. Like some televangelists saying, *Send me a dollar and put your hand on the TV screen and I'll heal you.*

Toby tells me how being Christian during the Roman occupation was (as scams go) not so lucrative. The followers weren't rich guys but riffraff—tax collectors and whores.

So let's say Jesus was sincere. Maybe it's the Church. Maybe Paul's the big fakir.

You think Paul's conversion made him some rich cult leader? That's a laugh. He essentially resigned a CPA job to ride with the Hells Angels.

Early Christians, he tells me, partly won converts by going to death singing. I mean, a lion is eating your face and you're singing. Or you're crucified upside down and you're singing. It's undeniable that some experience changed them from the normal consciousness. Maybe they were hypnotized, brainwashed. Aren't suicide bombers gleeful?

Hell, maybe I've gone nuts already, I tell him, though no small number of people—including mental health professionals—can attest that I'm saner and happier than before I went Navy SEAL on the spiritual front.

However much I balk at Christian miracles, I think friends manufacturing secular miracles—me included sometimes—is loonier. Like Deb thinks her wind chimes tinkling are messages from her dead ex-husband. You mean to tell me, I say to her on the phone, you don't believe in the Resurrection but you think Richard controls the wind?

If Jesus isn't (a) crazy, (b) a false prophet or con man or (c) his disciples weren't, I have to at least consider the fourth possibility: that (d) some of those miracles had some foundation in fact. Somebody saw something remarkable.

Once you allow even that sliver of possibility, that crack of light, it's not long before the stone rolls away from the tomb.

Right before Easter, as our church gears up to baptize and confirm newcomers, I'm still—metaphorically speaking—staring down from the airplane door, wondering whether my parachute will open if I step out.

At one point Toby asks me, Why haven't you taken communion at any of the churches you've visited when you travel? Those priests don't know if you're Catholic or not.

The idea shocks me, and I say so.

Why not? He has a mischievous grin on his face.

That would defile the Sacrament, insult the belief of all those people in church who're committed to the faith.

So, he says, that is sacred to you?

It was, is.

In the end, no white light shines out from the wounds of Christ to bathe me in His glory. Faith is a choice like any other. If you're picking a career or a husband—or deciding whether to have a baby—there are feelings and reasons pro and con out the wazoo. But thinking it through is—at the final hour—horse dookey. You can only try it out. Not choosing baptism would make me feel half-assed somehow, like a dilettante—scared to commit to praising a force I do feel is divine—a reluctance grown from pride or because the mysteries are too unfathomable.

In the back of a dark church on Holy Saturday, I sit between Dev and Toby. In the pews, everybody holds an unlit candle, and the priest comes in with the altar's mega-candle.

Stopping at the back row, he touches its taper to the charred filament on either side of the aisle. The flame's passed one to another until we're all holding fire in our hands.

Not long after, Walt calls after a longish silence. He'd been nursing Shirley through her long battle with cancer. And other than seeing them at their son's wedding, I'd been in scant touch till her death. On the phone, I tell him how—in conference with an obstreperous student—I was about to snap at the kid when it dawned on me that he was Huck Finn. See, I say on the phone, how I'm still channeling you?

How is finding Huck Finn in your office channeling me?

Don't you remember telling me that unless you knew what was in my head, you couldn't get Ernst Cassirer in there? Knowing the kid was Huck Finn let him be who he was with me.

I remember reading Cassirer with you.

And that little rat you took care of after she'd had her babies?

There were so many of them, he says.

I tell him how my students keep shape-shifting into characters from novels. A shy, disheveled farm kid was the young stable boy Wart about to pull a sword from a stone and become a king. A flushed sorority girl who hung a ball gown in a dry cleaner's bag from my doorjamb while she spoke transformed into flushed young Kitty hoping to dance the mazurka in *Anna Karenina*.

You're one of the big reasons I believe in God.

You see the irony, he says, for his father had been a minister, and he was a rationalist to his core.

You may be a godless fuck, I say, but—what was it your colleague said—*You give secular humanism a good name*?

You give Christianity a good name, he says.

Walt's strangely pleasant about my being a Catholic, though I get a snippy postcard from a novelist I know who says, *Not you on the pope's team. Say it ain't so.*

Only Jesus keeps eluding me. I can't help noticing that all the Catholics I look up to seem very Christos-centered. But the crucifixion has started to rankle me.

At first, I'd liked the cross. You could never bring suffering there and look up and say, *Well, he didn't have it bad as me....* But after baptism, it starts to creep me out. My Episcopalian mother brags on the phone that she reveres the resurrected Christ. She likens my church to a butcher shop.

At least there's a body on the cross, I say. There's carnality there. Protestants have this Platonic—I don't know—*idea* of a body. Too subtle for me.

One Sunday after church, the kids are playing in the basement corner, and I'm studying the mangled body of Jesus on a small icon when I say to Dev—now age nine—Why the crucifixion?

He's fiddling with the knot in his shoe. What? he says. His interest in what I say is fast diminishing.

Why does redemption have to come through the crucifixion? I mean, why couldn't you play hopscotch or win at solitaire?

He rolls his eyes and picks at the knot.

I'm thinking of my pal Nick Flynn, I say. He has a poem about somebody giving him Mass cards of Jesus with His heart on fire. It ends, *My version of hell / is someone ripping open his / shirt & saying, / look what I did for you.*

That's funny, Dev says. He puts his shoe up so I can get the knot loose. I'm picking at it when he says, Who'd pay attention to hopscotch?

Whaddya mean? I say.

He says, I mean, the crucifixion is like *Pulp Fiction* (the film Mother illicitly showed him years before). Nobody would pay any attention to some goofy song that got sung. Or if God just went *poof* over you. People get baptized all the time. It's a big miracle to wash a person's sins away. Nobody pays any attention at all to it.

That's it! I say. It's marketing. God reaches people by giving them the only kind of gory crap they'll pay attention to.

But Dev has slipped off his other dress shoe and run in stocking feet to join his noisy pals in their game. The bull's-eye he hits is original sin. We are a hard-to-sell people—so venal and nuts that we'll crowd into the Coliseum, jubilant to see people hacked to death or devoured by beasts. Or we'll sit drooling before comparably horrific TV images. Only a crucifixion is awful enough to compel public imagination.

Sitting there, I remember what Dev said to me after baptism: *We belong to a great big family.* However saccharine that sounds, it's starting to seem true to me—on good days—not just in church, either. The way stick figures show our essential skeletons, so too each skeleton is a cross buried inside. Over time, it'll come out to show who we're actually kin to.

42

On the Road

. . . God I want to thank
especially, if He exists, which I believe
He does. He may not. Probably not.
But I would like to thank him. Thanks.
—BROOKS HAXTON, "IF I MAY"
(ON BEING GIVEN A POETRY PRIZE)

Dev joins the last leg of my book tour down in Texas partly because Mother's throttled the hometown librarian into hosting a book signing, which prospect niggles me. While I never set out to badmouth Leechfield or anybody in it, I sure didn't sugarcoat its charms—an opinion locals were inured to. It's not like they swanned past the oil refineries swatting mosquitoes and thinking, *Isn't this place pretty as Paris?* Hell, they know why real estate goes so cheap. They live there.

That said, it does occur to both Lecia and me that some

backwoods xenophobe might adjudge me a turncoat or car-
petbagger and fancy drawing a bead on me.

We're packing for Mother's house when Lecia says, If I see
the red laser light click on your forehead, I'll throw my body
in front of the bullet.

Neither of us can figure why Mother's so gung ho about
the whole public event, ceremony not being her forte, nor
any form of pageant. Birthday cakes were sporadic. *Let's skip
Christmas this year* was a standard executive edict starting
when we were teenagers. (The only holiday where Mother really kicked ass was Easter. Something about ham and marshmallow peeps, the conscripted basket size, and the lower
expectations inspired her—shiny geegaws in plastic eggs,
macramé belts, a skateboard. . . .)

You'd also think Mother might shy from regaling the
public with her psychotic break. But she's proud as an Eagle
Scout. When she announced to me by phone that her bridge
club wanted to host a private potluck for all of us after the big
event, I said, What have you done with my mother?

Oh, Mary, I was always like this.

She wasn't, and that's what Lecia and I bat about as we
drive—our boys lolling in back—the three hours from her
house on the Gulf to Leechfield.

All our lives down there, she was the turd in the punch
bowl, Lecia gripes. Now she wants to prop us up in front of
the bridge club like we're pigs at the state fair.

What's scariest, I say, is how excited I am that she's excited.

By the time the book hit, Mother fit the Leechfield landscape. Neighbors who once kept their kids from playing in
our yard now swap stories about her tantrums like baseball
cards. There was the time she upended the oranges in the supermarket display, the fit she threw about parmesan cheese.

She flipped off a motorcycle cop. A Baptist deacon who dared to scold her for wearing shorts in the yard heard that he could see evil in the crotch of a tree. Now church ladies holler *hey* in the afternoon. Mornings, old men jostle to buy Mother coffee at the grocery store.

Almost as worrisome is Lecia's grim focus on a brisket Mother promised to fix. Whenever we drive home, Mother tempts Lecia with some childhood dish—chicken and dumplings, fudge, red beans and rice—but never, not once, follows through.

Lecia's ongoing capacity to hope for these dishes just stumps me. On the road before her, there's a shimmering mirage of meat shredded in lush gravy with a side of buttery potato hunks. Does she bounce up and down a little in anticipation like a kid on a carousel? I believe she does, though the next instant, her face clouds. It won't be there, will it? she says, shooting me a look.

There's a newspaper cartoon of a bucket-headed boy repeatedly talked into running at the football held by a wicked pigtailed girl who yanks it away so the boy falls on his ass every time.

How many times, Lecia says, am I going to run at that football?

Many, it turns out. With scads of costly professional help, I gave up pining for maternal behavior long ago. But Lecia had once hired Mother to pick up her son Case at kindergarten until—a few weeks in—Mother forgot the boy in the parking lot. Given fat sums to answer Lecia's insurance office phones, Mother tended to snipe into the receiver *What?* The way Stalin trusted Hitler not to invade Russia, Lecia trusts Mother. In a way, I admire the simple persistence of both parties—Lecia's overfunctioning, Mother's under.

On any given holiday, Mother sits on her spreading white ass on either porch glider or couch. Which idleness—in some perverse way—I also envy. It takes fortitude to station yourself immobile before the classic-movie channel for days at a pop while hordes of individuals bake and whip, sauté and sear; serve and clear; and eventually scrub cheese crusts off casseroles and pan drippings from a blackened oven.

For weeks I've hounded Mother daily about brisket, and she's sworn to ante up. But yesterday her corns hurt, and as late as dawn this morning, the meat hadn't been bought. She was having palpitations, but I swore if the stove was cold when we walked in, I'd head back to the airport.

It could kill me to go to the store with my heart fluttering this way, she said.

If you drop dead making this brisket, I said, you'll go straight up to live with Baby Jesus.

I'm thinking of going back to being a Buddhist, she said.

Then you'll escape the wheel of rebirth, I said.

Minutes after we pull in, my sister's face floats cherublike above an electric skillet holding a mess of peppery brisket. She uses her hand to wave toward her nose the white ribbons of steam swiveling up. Mother breathes frost on her big square glasses, then wipes them. She looks stunned we're making such a big deal.

Oh, she says with a distracted look, I forgot to get the blow-up mattress. (Lecia and I sent her—separately, it turns out—cash to buy an extra mattress.)

My sister's deaf to this. She's forking up saucy meat with a beatific expression. Such a token might not exactly undo past hurts, but they might reshape our mouths to savor what's now being served up.

That night, at opposite ends of the bulbous sofa, Lecia and

I have lain our respective heads like characters in a storybook rowboat under tinfoil stars, with a faded blue quilt covering our middles. In the saggy double bed we used to share, our boys have sacked out—Dev blond like her, Case dark like me.

At the schoolyard basketball court today, we'd watched Dev drag in Case's wake as I had Lecia's. Just thirteen, Case can just barely palm the ball for a second or two, his hand like a giant spider holding it aloft as Dev gapes. Ready? Case said, and he bounce-passed it to the smaller boy.

Dev two-stepped through a layup, the orange ball slipping through the white net, which prompted Case to shout out *swish*. Leaping for the rebound, Case stepped back and started to lecture, detailing proper form for a shot with the rigor of a ballet master. Bend your knees. Hold it here. Finish with the tips of your fingers right over the front rim.

That night on Mother's sofa, Lecia asks, Who does Case remind you of?

In terms of the need to expound? You and Daddy, I say.

Frightening, she says.

About then Mother stumps in, hair every which way, a piece of cheese disappearing into her maw. She says, What're y'all talking about so late?

Our deep and abiding love for you, Lecia says.

Mother slumps down on the facing chair, staring at the grassy shag carpet. When she lifts her head, there are tears in her eyes. I wish your daddy was here for this, she says, us all together this way.

Look at both those boys, Lecia says, Pete Karr times two.

He's the only person who ever really loved me.

What are we? I say.

Mother shrugs. The only man, I mean. I miss him like crazy.

He did adore you, I say.

He felt sorry for me, she says, but he stood by, thick or thin.

She runs a hand over her spiky hair, asking, Does this haircut look like feathers?

In the library the next day, Mother's bridge club marches in—a troop of ladies bearing into the small room trays of baked goods big as coffee tables.

The day unfolds like that old TV show *This Is Your Life*, where producers conspire to drag before you the past's every character. In aging form, they parade. There's the doctor who examined me the night Mother went to the hospital; my first-grade teacher; the principal who told me I'd be no more than a common prostitute. John Cleary, the first boy I ever kissed, is there with his daughters. My friend Clarice from grade school, Meredith from high school (in lawyer's garb and big as a linebacker), Doonie with his whole tribe. There's the judge Mother charmed into freeing me from jail—nearly a hundred, he is, his liver-spotted hand still clutching Mother's, and he still gazes at her like she's a jam-stuffed biscuit. The druggist, the guy who ran the lumberyard, girls who snubbed me at the skating rink, girls who didn't.

I feel every school photo I ever took pass over my face to melt into the forty-year-old I am now. Seen by so many pairs of old eyes, I become my every self.

Then above the crowd, a disembodied head comes gliding as if carried on a pole. From the corner of my eye, I catch the silhouette, and my head whips to track it. The profile vanishes behind a pillar. The room around me clicks off as the face eases back into view—black-haired with snow at the temples. I stand so fast, the chair I'm in tips over. The crowd parts, and the eras collapse into each other. All the notches on the time line are stripped off like thorns. It's Daddy approaching me like a smiling phantom.

Though it's not Daddy, of course, but my cousin Thomas, unseen since our grandpa's funeral in sixth grade, wearing the exact face Daddy had at fifty, and Lecia must think so, too, since she's rushed to his side, hand over her mouth.

Maybe that day's bounty bumped my sales up, plus Lecia's inflicting copies on virtually everybody she knew—clients, friends, cleaning people. Out of the trunk of her car, she hawks them like a hot dog vendor (I swear), and being as she could sell snow to an Eskimo, she reorders often. In any bookstore, she remerchandises so that my book's in front.

So the book was a sleeper hit, which floored me. Before it came out, I'd actually warned the publisher not to print so many, since the thought of them growing cobwebs in warehouses flooded me with dread. Having spent my fifteen-year career reading to a few loyal pals, I was shocked to find that now bookstore crowds wrapped around the block as I signed till my hand cramped. Mail flooded in. Magazines would pay me astonishing sums to write a few thousand words. Lecia and Mother were wild with glee, my sister joking that I'd never have to call collect again.

But in another way, nothing much changed. A single mom can't hit the road and stay gone. Mostly I lived like before. I taught. I stood around a Little League field with a clipboard and a whistle around my neck. Maybe once a week, some mom might say she'd seen me in *People* magazine. Then once or twice a month I'd make a surreal overnight trip where I felt—as writer Ian McEwan once said—like an employee of my former self.

The big win? Money. My bills were paid. I could hire a student to help with Dev, grocery shop, fold laundry. Other than that and some journalism jobs—and the monthly photo session or far flung reading or lecture—I was a single mom in a small town.

Which is how I wind up in a sweltering theme park come August—by selling books. Before I went on the road, I promised Dev if we made it on one big best-seller list, I'd take him to Disney World. For a week: my idea of an electric chair with no off switch.

Still, being there turned out to be a thrill, but for one hair-raising ride called the Tower of Terror, where they dropped us in an elevator a dozen floors. In the group photo, everyone's hands are up in the air as they grin. I'm hunkered down as if for a bomb blast. (I have too many frames per second for Tower of Terror.)

After five days of more palatable rides, Dev and I abandon the blistering park, so I can rent a speedboat we can't afford. With his new blue captain's hat on, he steers us bouncing over the waves.

At night, while he soaks in the bathtub, I talk to Walt for way longer than I promised his kids I would. He's suffering some asbestos-related disease caught in a car factory as a teenager. Now it's devouring the lungs in his barrel chest, and every breath costs him.

In St. Paul the year before, I'd visited him. His daughter Pam had moved home, and he'd needed an oxygen bottle.

From Florida that night, I ask what can they do.

Not much, he says, panting. Morphine. It's progressive.

You're telling me you're gonna die?

That's right.

You can't die, I say. That's just unacceptable to me.

Well, I'm not a big fan of the idea, either. He wheezes for a minute before saying, I can't talk. Tell me your adventures.

So I tell him about the long drop in the tower; and the

wonton soup at Epcot; and Tinker Bell sliding down on her cable through fireworks; and a baby bird we found under a park bench, fallen from a nest, how it looked like a purplish dragon, how we sat with it till a guy with a broom swept it into his dustpan.

Great job, he gasps. You've done.

The line between us is crackling, and I know I'm keeping him on the line for myself. His breath comes in like a tide and goes out farther every time.

Tell me some noble deaths, he says.

I remind him that when Socrates had drunk the hemlock—in the *Phaedo* we read together—the cold was creeping up his legs, how his students bent over him, saying, *Don't you have anything more to tell us.* . . . And in the Chekhov biography I just finished, he was coughing into his napkin bright red arterial blood, and once the doctor announced it was hopeless, champagne was called for.

Dev comes out wrapped in an oversize bathrobe, and he's got that crease in his forehead that comes when he sees me cry. He knows Walt's fading, and his hand settles on my shoulder.

Remember back when I was in school, I finally say into the putty-colored receiver, how you bought all those lunches and theater tickets for me, when I asked how I'd ever pay you back? Remember what you said?

He's too breathless to respond.

You said, *It's not that linear. You're gonna go on to help somebody else.* Well, I got a chance to help my assistant out of a pinch. And she asked how she'd pay me back, and I told her the story. I'd never have done that without you.

He's struggling to say something, barely audible his voice is, a plume of air, the smoke trail a voice leaves behind. He says, Tell her to thank me.

43

The Spiritual Exercises of St. Ignatius

Late have I loved you, O Beauty, so ancient and so new, late have I loved you. For behold you were within me, and I outside; and I sought you outside and in my unloveliness fell upon those lovely things which you have made. You were with me, and I was not with you. I was kept from you by those things, yet had they not been in you, they would not have been at all. You called and cried to me to break open my deafness and you sent forth your beams and you shone upon me and chased away my blindness. You breathed fragrance upon me, and I drew in my breath and now do pant for you . . .

—ST. AUGUSTINE, *CITY OF GOD*

After ten months praying in a cave in Manresa, St. Ignatius received a vision that permitted him *to see God in all things—*

the stated goal of his Spiritual Exercises, which are part of each Jesuit's novitiate.

This doesn't innately appeal to me. Despite my conversion, I don't much care to see God in all things. I prefer to find God in circumstances I think up in advance, at home in my spare time—circumstances God will fulfill for me like a gumball machine when I put the penny of my prayer into it.

It's not virtue that leads me to the Exercises but pain. Only a flamethrower on my ass ever drives me to knock-knock-knock on heaven's door. Pain, in my case, is the sole stimulus for righteous action.

After six years in Syracuse—Dev's eleven—I lost a love; or more accurately, I drove one away with a stick. It seems unfair to drag him in kicking and screaming for the purposes of this narrative, so here's the short version. On tour in London, I'd taken up with a tall Cambridge-educated Brit met through work. (Let's say his job was in TV.) Our months-long transatlantic affair had a glittery aspect. He owned more tuxedos than a maître d', and I jetted over for his black-tie soirees. He spent a summer month in green Syracuse with Dev and me. But the distance was a misery. He ran a company in London, and I could never move Dev from his dad. Still, the Brit and I wound up engaged—as in to be married. He'd leave London for Syracuse and consulting.

For a few months I deluded myself that my old dream of family was assembling. I splurged on fancy barrister bookcases for his five thousand, first-edition books, which arrived in duct-taped bubble wrap. I cooked steamship roasts.

But Syracuse was drearier than London, with exactly zero tuxedo-specific events beyond the occasional prom. Plus an underemployed thirty-something bachelor with time on his hands wasn't exactly a couture fit for a forty-something workaholic with a six-foot son who giggled while chucking a basketball at said bachelor's crotch. (You make him stop, I said, staring into my computer.)

The burden of the move quite literally broke the Brit's back—a slipped disk flattened him. After months of hauling his dinner to him on a tray, I wanted to bubble-wrap him and stick stamps on his forehead. (So much for *in sickness and in health*.) We scheduled back surgery in London, Dev and I letting a summer place while he healed. But by then I was already wondering if we could get the deposit back on the reception hall, envisioning the dress I'd bought boxed up with mothballs. (If I'd been thinking like an adult instead of a grade-schooler with a Cinderella costume, I'd never have permitted anybody to give up a fancy job and house in Notting Hill.) I broke things off, but his departure tore open an old wound.

Once he's gone, I begin to sense—as I shove my cart through the supermarket amid the Republican families on Sunday—a giant S on my chest for Spinster. Dev's preoccupied with friends and rap records. Despite Patti and friends, the old lack of close family makes me fumingly mad at God, who, it may seem nutty to say, is real to me after years of prayer, not like the Easter Bunny or anything. All pain still makes me mad at God.

Running into Big John, who steers me into overhauling how I pray, strikes me as grace. We make best pals playing racquetball at my health club—a joke, given he's six-five and a former Olympic contender for the water polo team. With our handicapping, I only have to score a single point to win.

As a young man, John had been torn between a career as an athlete and the Jesuit seminary, but he'd drunk his way out of both businesses. On getting sober, he'd started a swim club to pursue his dream of coaching Olympic-caliber competitors. A lumbering guy with curly brown hair and eyes the color of pool chlorine, he pursues that Olympic vision waking and sleeping.

When we meet, he's sober longer than I am, and—due to his own heartbreak—he's reconsidering whether he's called to be a Jesuit. To discern the answer, he undertakes a lay version of the Exercises, emerging nine months later like a creature dipped in fine metal, heartbreak cured. Right after, his coaching career takes off like gangbusters. His swimmers start taking national prizes, and four are pulling down Olympic-level times. One gold-medals in Sydney. In short, following Ignatius jacked up both his mood and his productivity, and—competitive bitch that I am—this spiked my interest.

Still, I waffle when a nun outlines the time commitment—classes, spiritual direction, hours of prayer, journals. Also, while I wasn't—for longer than I care to admit—boinking anybody, I didn't want to scare off any future prospects. Imagine saying to your date that you can't give up any nay-nay till your Franciscan spiritual advisor gives the thumbs up.

Then coming back from New York on the train one day, I slip into a familiar gap. It's right before Christmas in a packed coach car, the overhead shelves crammed with suitcases and spilling bags and packages. I settle into a window seat with the backrest tilted far back. It's the only place left. Behind me, a young woman—maybe nineteen—asks me to move my seat up. After fiddling with it for a second, I tell her it's stuck in a deep recline. Then I lie back while passengers clot the aisles and jam in their overhead bags. She leans forward and says, very close to my ear, *I bet if I yanked your hair, you could move that seat.*

And from my sagging state of half-sleep, I snap awake and shoot back, You picked the wrong bitch to fuck with on this train.

Around us, the entire car stops. People hold gestures mid-air. She starts to kick the back of my seat—hard and rhythmically, which I don't respond to at first. If I were thinking like anything but an animal, I would've apologized to her by now. But I sit there fuming instead, telling myself stuff like, *She's just doing this because I'm a woman of a certain age.* I'm determined not to respond to the kicks that keep coming, but eventually, she says with force, You better not get off in Albany, bitch, 'cause I'll slap your face.

With blood pounding in my temples and all the venom that a woman disappointed in love can bring to an instant, I press my face into the slot between the seat and the window and hiss, If you touch me, I'll cut your fucking hand off.

I don't even know where this sentence comes from. Not to mention that—in terms of cutting off a hand—I lack even a pair of cuticle scissors. All human activity within sound of me ceases. The entire car is throbbing with hatred for us both. The girl withdraws like a slug doused with salt, and the train lurches west.

About twenty minutes out of the station, while I sit infused with acid at the outburst, I try to write the girl a note, but I wind up crouching by her seat to apologize. She shrugs coolly.

Once home, I call my sobriety coach, Patti, who says, What d'you expect, Mare? Run around without a meeting, and eventually, you'll start acting like a drunk again.

I wasn't that bad back then.

Silence from Patti, who knows better.

Okay, sometimes I was.

She suggests I doctor bathwater with lavender salts, set votive candles all over, kill the lights, then step into my own baptismal fount. Maybe there I can rethink events on the train. Follow that, she says, with a list of how your life has changed since you quit drinking.

Lying back in the fragrant water, I let a washcloth obliterate my features, rewinding to the days and hours before I got on the train.

It's the old story. Underslept and underfed, I'd been running with my shoulder bag thumping against my butt, doing quarterback dodges and rolls on crowded holiday streets, while behind me, pedestrians dove for cover. I was behind in every conceivable way. So the old attack dog started howling through my head as I'd loped. Take the subway, the sane voice had said. Take the subway, you can buy a sandwich. Then counterattack claimed I needed cardio for the blubber on my ass. A sandwich isn't the solution. You need to refinance. You need five hundred dollars this week or Dev's Christmas is Tiny Tim's.

You might as well call it the voice of the Adversary, for once I tune in to it, I've lost my real self—the God-made one, akin to others. The Adversary's voice can suck me into the maelstrom of my tornado-force will, which'll chew up anybody in its path, me included.

The washcloth steams my features soft, and once the water's cold, I oil myself up like a bodybuilder, slip on sweats, then towel-wrap my hair like a Turkish pasha.

Heating up meatballs for Dev and his pals loudly playing air hockey in the basement, I do Patti's list of what's changed in ten years. The boys clattering downstairs are a nightly antidote to the shipwrecked household I grew up in, and we no longer have to roll coins from the sofa cushions in order to afford meatballs. Last month at Mother's surprise birthday, I floated in the pool alongside her and Lecia while brother-in-law Tom worked the grill and Dev and his cousin did cannonballs.

The night after the train debacle, I drive under a sky black as graphite to meet my new spiritual director for the Exercises—a bulky Franciscan nun named Sister Margaret, patiently going blind behind fish-tank glasses that magnify her eyes like goggles.

Asked my concept of God, I mouth all the fashionable stuff—all-loving, all-powerful, etc. But as we talk, it bobs up that in periods of uncertainty or pain—forlorn childhood, this failed relationship—I often feel intentionally punished or abandoned.

How's that possible, I say, if I have no childhood experience of a punishing God?

Margaret says, We often strap on to God the mask of whoever hurt us as children. If you've been neglected, God seems cold; if you've been bullied, He's a tyrant. If you're filled with self-hatred, then God is a monster making inventor. How do you feel sitting here with me now?

I don't know, like some slutty Catholic schoolgirl.

She laughs at this and says, I see you—she peers through those lenses—what I can see of you, as my sister, God's beloved child. The hairs on your head are numbered, and we've been brought together, you and me, to shine on each other a while.

So you don't judge me? I want to know.

For what? she said. I don't even know you.

Well, I say, I'm not married, and I aspire to be sexually active again some day.

She says, I'm not naive. But Jesus might ask: Should you be vulnerable to a man without some spiritual commitment? Is that God's dream for you?

God has a dream for me? I say. I love that idea. It sounds like a Disney movie.

I know, Margaret says. Her pale round face opens up. Everybody uses the phrase *God's will* or *plan*. That has a neo-Nazi ring to it.

I like the Disney version.

I feel you, she says, and I sit for a minute silently disbelieving she's a nun. She adjusts her heavy glasses, and her eyes once again magnify.

Let's eat a cookie and pray for each other's disordered attachments, she says. Mine involves pride and cookies.

Mine, I say, involves pride and good-looking men.

Together we bow our heads.

44

The Bog Queen

Where did they bury the dog after she hung herself,
and into the roots of what tree are those bones entangled?
I come blessed like a river of black rock, like a long secret,
and the kind of kindness that is like a door closed
but not locked. Yesterday I was nothing but a road
heading in four directions. When I threatened to run away
my mother said she'd take me wherever I wanted to go.
—TERRANCE HAYES, "THE BLUE TERRANCE"

The house I grew up in sat in a bog, and in the middle of the house sat my mother, well into her dotage. All my life, she'd blamed the place—*anus of the universe,* in her parlance—for robbing her of every artistic inclination. Daily, she willed it to slide back into the Gulf it sat on the edge of.

In my thirties, it actually started to sink: plots of land once three feet below sea level got to four. Houses sagged and listed on their brick stilts, and one end of a church parking lot disappeared into a sinkhole. The refineries that pumped toxins into the sky were showing around their rivets starbursts of rust, and fewer and fewer pickups lined up for parking slots every year. Young people started to move away after high school.

Among those left behind in tract houses and trailer parks, the occasional meth lab set off a spectacular explosion. Due to the acid-green poisons poured into bayous and backwaters, the cancer rate shot through the roof. Every family had its fair share of tumor scars and chemo stories. For others, the guns their fathers once pointed at squirrels and possums were increasingly turned on each other or taken between the teeth.

You'd think the destruction of the town would've left Mother, who'd cursed it for decades, doing some celebratory chicken dance on Main Street. But in a wry twist, Mother has come to love the house in the bog. She's had it painted eggyolk yellow. With the red roof and green lawn, it looks like a child's crayon piece, with my mother inside it dwindling into a line drawing.

But the swamp is eating Mother's house, too. Wet rot gobbles at the window fittings, and purple wisteria vines edge in, followed by various species of lizard and beetle. She finds, sleeping in the clothes hamper, a chicken snake big around as her wrist. A neighbor has to come with a hoe and a garbage bag to haul it off while Mother stands aside with a small snub-nosed revolver. All the house's screens are imploding, their frames no longer square, and the back doorjamb is edged with encroaching honeysuckle.

Mother sits in the house reading the Bible along with histories of lost civilizations and books of gnostic mystery ordered from far away. Plus *The New Yorker* and *Artforum*. Her hair's grown out from spiky to thick cumulus cloud, and the curves of her body have started to burn off. Though she's shrinking down toward the underlying bone, her mind is unquenchable fire.

She's grown saner with age, but she still has the lackadaisical whims of a kid. Even after a quadruple bypass has reamed the four chambers of her heart, she smokes nonstop and exists on a diet—I once heard her announce to her careworn cardiologist—of provolone cheese and summer sausage, fruit, and the occasional Ho Ho. Two suitors come to see her at regular intervals, but their romantic beseechings have become as matter-of-fact as her refusals. Afternoons, she plays dominoes with them at the kitchen table, speculating at length on which of them will die first.

And she says, I don't know why I'm still here.

She lights one long cigarette after another and despite all this, fails to seem—exactly—unhappy.

She still has some arrows in her quiver. For instance, when she feels hungry for Mexican food or merely wants company, she'll call my sister more than two hours away with killer traffic.

Lecia's family of six (her son and four stepkids plus executive husband) keep her busy. She runs an insurance business that's paid for a house, inside which are a waterfall and a pond with plump orange koi trained by regular feedings to recognize my sister's shadow and swim to her with their mouths blowing her kisses from the pond's surface. On the edge of that, a golf course where tall Husband Tom—nickname: Big, both for his height and after the romantic lead in a TV show—putts with an accuracy almost surgical. There's even a metal-lined room to hide in if the revolution comes and bandits or insurgents show up. The Scar-face House, I dub it.

But to run all this, my sister gets up at four or five most mornings, following a regimen fit for a five-star general executing a military coup. At night Big entertains executives by cooking vast carcasses on that grill the size of a station wagon. They take a lot of trips—some involving golf, which Lecia hates—and the rest of which she mostly doesn't think up. In short, she's as much slave as empress to her realm.

Yet when Mother calls to report a heart attack coming on, my sister grabs her bag and dashes out of the house, floor-boarding her Batmobile down to the sagging corner of earth sliding toward the Gulf, only to find Mother affably awaiting her, palpitations miraculously improved. No, they needn't visit the doctor, but that place on the corner has the best en-chiladas and virgin margaritas.

Even after I urge my sister to ask Mother point-blank if she's lying about her ailments to yank Lecia's chain, and even after my Mother baldly confesses that she makes up about 95 percent of her maladies, my sister can't stop herself from galloping toward the town of our birth, since forty years of training can't be shaken off, and codependence is a terrible thing.

While we sisters agree it's time to sell the sagging house and move Mother closer to one of us, each time we sound serious about this, Mother gets weepy and suffers shortness of breath and unprecedented rises in blood pressure that twist my sister's innards.

A few times I fly Mother to New York City, the mecca of her youth, and roll her through museums in a wheelchair until she says, I feel like a fool; why don't I push you awhile? We horrify many citizens of that great city as she limps behind me and I recline, swigging water. At night, though she swears to stay out of the minibar, she forces me nearly to bankruptcy by devouring as many fifteen-dollar Cokes and twenty-dollar PayDay bars as she can in her brief stay. At one breakfast, I find her hands smeared with chocolate.

But I'm the prodigal, the long-gone daughter, and I can't send home enough checks to pay down that guilt. And when one night she tells me her mother hasn't come back with the car, and I have to remind her that her mother is forty years dead, I can hear the hoofbeats of the apocalypse galloping unwilled toward her.

So I fly home, crossing the patio whose bricks are being split by grass. I walk in, drop my bulging bag, holler, *Honey, I'm home,* and I find the dining room ceiling caved half in, the central air conditioner dangling down through plaster on a slanted slab of plywood, hanging in midair as if by magician's wires.

Mother, I say, rushing into the room and feeling under my sandals the squish of water in the green shag carpet, which exudes moldy odors of a color I don't want to picture. I say, Mother, what happened here?

I stare up into the hole while standing off to the side, fearing the rest of the ceiling is on the verge of collapse. Finally, I ask, Why didn't you call somebody?

I didn't know who to call, she says. She's distractedly studying a crossword in one hand, her brass glasses on the tip of her narrow nose till she says, What's an eleven-letter word for coinage of Alexander the Great?

I squish my feet, saying, The rug's ruined. Can't you smell that?

No worse than outside, she says.

This didn't happen just today?

She looks up saying, Of course not. This week. Maybe last week.

I still don't understand why you didn't call somebody before the whole floor soaked through.

She perches on the side of an easy chair and studies her puzzle. She says, I'm bad on coinage. Can you call your sister?

I flip open my cell phone and punch redial. Lecia answers as she does when busy, like one of those cartoon tycoons—or the mother of five children, which she is. She says, Do you need something?

Coin of Alexander the Great.

How many letters?

Eleven.

Tetradrachm, she says, then spells it. Is that it? she adds, I'm covered up with work here.

We trade love before I snap the phone shut.

Got it, Mother says, and moves to the next clue while saying, I figured you or your sister would come along and fix it.

The eleven-letter word?

The ceiling, she says.

I track down and cajole into action air-conditioner repairmen and electricians and plaster workers to glue back together Mother's crayoned house.

That's it, I say when the bills are presented. We're selling this cracker box.

We chip in to buy Mother a condo in the same small town as Lecia's office. We know Mother will rail about the change, but to prop up the rotting house would cost twice what it's worth. I can envision driving up someday to find the walls caved in, Mother sitting amid mossy ruins with book in hand and birds nesting in her hair.

You tell her it's a fait accompli, Lecia says. She'll raise holy hell. You make her take the hit. Tom and I'll move her.

If y'all do that, I'll clean out the house.

Once again Mother promises to be packed and ready, and once again Lecia finds her staring, coffee cup in midair, at three empty supermarket boxes, not a single plate news-papered.

I need y'all to start me up, Mother says.

Over a period of two days, Lecia and her husband pack and manhandle Mother's possessions into a truck with the energy of newlyweds. They ferry it all two hours away, near Houston, into the corner unit we bought, staying till every picture is hung.

Making up Mother's new bed with plush linens, Lecia finds a Polaroid of the egg-yolk crayon house under Mother's pillow.

The old house is cleared of big pieces when I fly in to clean it out, which involves sorting through letters and paint-ings and stuff we may want to tenderly tuck away in tissue, though in truth, we partly long to bulldoze the place.

I'm not without help. My high school friend Doonie, now the fence king of San Diego County, flies home to help. So does John Cleary—boy next door, first kiss. They show up on the steps as if dismounted from white chargers to shovel out the pigsty of a house.

By dusk, it's down to the baseboards, and I'm alone. John and Doonie head off to drive a final truckload to the dump. My legs are streaked with dirt, and it's as if some key on my back has unwound, for I've dropped in my tracks in Mother's once magical closet. I've folded up where I'd so often played hide-and-seek inside the silks of her bespangled wardrobe, inhaling like so much hash smoke her minty Salem smoke and Shalimar.

Other people kept marriage and divorce decrees, birth announcements, scrapbooks. Mother kept clothes—but she'd trashed all the good stuff. Gone the Dior couture and pearl-snap rodeo shirts, the shirred beaver coat the color of clotted cream whose ecru lining had chocolate lace at the hem.

Today I pulled off hangers the oddball crap she wore when she got old—a red sweatshirt with Santa Claus on it, a pink one whose cat appliqué had jeweled eyes. (What do you like about that, Mother? And she said, Sparkly.) I strip from the hangers big-shoulder jackets from the eighties and splashy tropical shirtwaists. The slanted high heels my once small feet had disappeared into got upended into the charity box. When the last white polyester blouse slipped free, the coat hangers rang against each other with a high-pitched keening.

Seeing that closet so bare brought back when Daddy first hammered it together, for he'd built their whole bedroom out of our garage. We had made this house and grown into and—finally—out of it.

When Doonie and John come back from the dump, they find me in that musty closet under a bare bulb and a rod holding dozens of crow-black hangers. I'm thumbing ancient *Playboys*. I don't know who these belong to, I say.

Get out of there, Mary Marlene, John says.

Right before we leave, one of Mother's old friends shows up with her station wagon. We load in the massive easels on which Mother will never again tilt a gessoed canvas. She'd quit painting, quit buying pretty clothes. Petal by petal, she's been shedding herself. We box up the rusted coffee cans from which brushes of fine Russian sable protrude like so many furred blossoms.

Then John and Doonie drive me in a chilly rental car to a seafood joint with sawdust on the floor. There we all drink sweet iced tea, and from giant ovals of crockery we draw the hard shells of barbecued crabs and break them open with our greasy hands. Napkins tied around our necks, mouths shining with oil, we tear at and suck from the intricate chambers and corridors of those stone shells before they're dropped on the sawdust floor.

45

My Sinfulness in All Its Ugliness

Which way I flie is Hell; my self am Hell.
—JOHN MILTON, *PARADISE LOST*

That night I'm driving back to Mother's condo not having prayed, which seems no accident from this juncture. Cleaning out the childhood home that day had been heavy duty. Plus, it's a dark time in terms of the Exercises—the season of Lent, atonement—when you daily pray to be shown your own sinfulness in all its ugliness. Over bayous my rental car goes low-flying like a steel-coated bat. Since I didn't quite believe that spiritual forces for good and evil tug us to and fro, I fancied that failing to pray was understandable, an accident, for I'd risen at four to catch a plane down to Houston.

In the rental car, I fly over foggy blacktop alone, with the sciatic kink in my lower back keeping me edged toward the phosphorescent dash. But swelling in my chest is—what unknown sense—pride? I've been able to help Mother for once with more than a check in the mail. My sister hasn't borne the burden alone. And the company of my Leechfield brothers has left me feeling all shiny inside.

Sister Margaret had warned me that praying to know your own sins may prompt an arid season, with no consolations. Which makes you—in her scary parlance—a juicy morsel for the Adversary. Okay, I said, if a guy in a red suit with horns and a long scaly tail appears, I'll shake a crucifix at him. Margaret told me, He might appear as future pleasure, or he'll appeal to your intellectual vanity. Asked what I should do to prevent these dark assaults, she said, During Lent, don't miss a single minute of prayer, no matter what comes up. Err on the side of overkill, even if you feel yourself only going through the motions.

That night driving from the homestead, the black sky sliding off my windows, I don't consider sending up any hosanna of thanks, nor do Margaret's warnings echo through me. I feel exhausted, sure, but contrarily swell about myself, like the best daughter. Sin? What sin? The hours spent cleaning out the house have left me in weary ease—proud of the good works I've done. The fog holds me in the car's hull, and I drive suspended in time.

Reaching Mother's condo about eleven, I climb the stairs swinging a light garment bag, expecting to find her asleep. But she's ensconced in her mushroom-colored recliner, a giant magnifying lamp burning like a halo alongside her. An old movie with the sound muted unrolls across the screen. I ready myself for the praise and approbation she'll heap on me for squiring her into this luxury.

She says, Did you have fun?

I see from the set of her jaw she's fired up and ask her what's wrong.

Nothing's wrong. How could anything be wrong? I'm here in the little white hole you and your sister have buried me in. You've stripped me of all my possessions, robbed me of anything I held dear.

Mother, what are you talking about?

I've been sitting here wondering whether it would make you happy to come in and find me with my brains blown out. That's what would really make your day.

It's an ambush I never saw coming, and where I'd been sizzling with tired satisfaction before, I've suddenly got a kink between my shoulder blades. I say, I'm exhausted, Mother. Don't start this shit now.

(Maybe normal people don't have to beseech God at such junctures to stay level, but I do. But it's as if I've never prayed. No space exists in me for any perspective.)

In a flash, the fishy crab taste sours my breath, and I bend to rummage my bag for a toothbrush. Instead, I get a glowing vision of my toiletries bag, forgotten in the old house. I ask Mother if she has a fresh toothbrush or some mouthwash.

I have nothing, she says. She's sobbing. I have nothing.

To escape the image of her pitched forward, her back heaving, I shut the bathroom door. I wash the grit off my face and neck. Spying a frayed toothbrush upside down in a glass, I squeeze paste on it and start to scrub my mouth out when I taste bleach—and do I detect the odor of shit on its bristles? It's been used to scrub the toilet. I spit and rinse my mouth and spit, holding back the urge to vomit.

And, in that instant, my mouth scalded with bleach and shit, I feel the entire fabric of the world began to undergo a profound shift. I cease to be myself, or rather, my adult self. Time arcs back, carrying me in it.

On the ends of my arms, I feel the length of my fingers dwindle. Though standing upright, I sense the floor escalating closer as my legs get shorter. My arms shrink in their sockets. My eyes no longer sit flush to the front of my face; they've retreated far back into my head, as if my true self is crouched in terror in the back of my skull, staring out at Mother from far off.

And, into each strand of my mother's white hair, fiery color floods back. Her shoulders square, and she's tall and slim again, facing me with the enraged pout of her former drunker self. In an eyeblink, our old forms devour us.

When you've been hurt enough as a kid (maybe at any age), it's like you have a trick knee. Most of your life, you can function like an adult, but add in the right portions of sleeplessness and stress and grief, and the hurt, defeated self can bloom into place.

Standing before Mother that night, I hear her spewing the kind of bile I listened to for most of the worst evenings of my life, and God no longer exists, nor any road for me other than to let land whatever barbs Mother might pitch. She's God then, or my fear is God. Her face warps into the old mask as she shrieks, You raped me, you and your sister raped me.

I inhale her fury as I might fumes from glue tubes squeezed into a paper bag. The adrenaline that flushes through me inflates me again into a fire-breathing rage. What I shout is more messy and furious than these lines, but the general gist goes:

You could talk to me like that when I was little and I didn't have any way out.

But I spent all day throwing out all the canvases you never had the balls to paint on. Every shit-sucking day of my whole life, you blamed me and Daddy and Lecia for you not painting. The truth is: You never had the balls to paint, Mother. You were too fucking scared to reveal your ugly self to the world. So you stayed home, and you vomited all that pent-up poison on all of us. And having made not a single plan for your old age, you sit in the house we paid for, trying to screech me back into submission.

I don't fucking think so, Mother. You don't like it here? Get in your fucking car and go. And Lecia and I will sell this place and enjoy the first vacation either of us has had in years, you selfish fucking bitch.

I think is what I said.

When I stop speaking, I see my terrified eighty-year-old Mother, small and white-haired. She's collapsed on a recliner, using a magnifying glass to read the labels of pill bottles, sobbing. She's looking for her nitroglycerin tablets.

Which I retrieve for her.

And that's how I find my sinfulness in all its ugliness— not in prayer but in its absence. Without God, any discomfort makes me capable of attacking with piety the defenseless— including a frail, confused old lady who's lost her home of fifty years. And it's for this type of realization that God—in His infinite wisdom—created mirrors. I put Mother to bed and catch a glimpse of us as I pull the covers up to her chin. I'm saying I'm so sorry, and she's claiming to understand.

In the next room at the side of the unfamiliar bed, I get on my knees and try to pray, but my pinballing consciousness slams side to side against my curved rib cage, blasts up to the top of my skull and down against my pelvic cavity, and keeps slamming around that way in vectors I can't follow. I kneel there for fifteen minutes or so, then climb into bed and implode into sleep as if smashed up inside with a ballpeen hammer.

Fitful, this rest is. At one point I dream I'm picking up a child's stuffed animal—a Beanie Baby of the type Dev collected as a kid. In my dream hand, I look down, and the stuffed toy has morphed into a pit viper. With its triangular head, it lunges at my face. I scream myself awake and sit up and see—with eyes wide, a night terror—snakes lunging from the bed's tufted headboard.

Sweaty, heart rattling against my ribs, I look at the digital clock—just after three in the morning I'd gone to bed about two. I pull on running shorts, then tie on a pair of sneakers, thinking that a few miles of road will bang the ugly out of me.

Instead, I lie facedown on the carpet, repeating the prayer about God taking my will. Speaking it, I feel the words sucked from my mouth into a vacuum where God is not. My head's a hurricane, and to pray at all is like screaming into a gale.

Lying there, I remember the Scriptures I've forgotten for days. Margaret specifically gave me two passages, saying, While I was praying this week, these pieces came to me. I'm very strongly guided to give them to you. How touched I'd been when she handed them over, but I hadn't picked them up.

I find in Mother's still-boxed books a Bible, floppy and old, its binding cracked and peeling like a batwing. Opening it, I see Mother's name carefully inscribed: *For Charlie Marie Moore, from her loving Mother Mary, Christmas 1927.*

I flip through the onionskin pages to my first assignment, verses seven through twelve of Psalm fifty-one. What I see makes the skin of my scalp prickle, for the lines are marked in pale blue chalk. A child's hand has drawn a wavy line in the margin—not across the whole psalm, only alongside the lines I've been steered to—verses seven to twelve, which very deliberately traverse two sections of verse from the middle of one to the other. Kneeling, I sit back on my feet and feel the flesh on my scalp creep. I read the words. (Later, I'll learn this is *the hanging psalm* read to English prisoners as they approached the gallows.)

7   True I was born guilty, a sinner even as my
        mother conceived me.
8   Still, you insist on sincerity of heart; in my
        inmost being teach me wisdom.
9   Cleanse me with hyssop, that I may be pure;
        wash me, make me whiter than snow.
10   Let me hear sounds of joy and gladness; let the
        bones you have crushed rejoice.
II
11   Turn away your face from my sins; blot out all
        my guilt.
12   A clean heart create for me, God; renew in me a
        steadfast spirit.

How odd, I think, for I never thought of Mother as particularly devout in childhood—she wasn't. But it seems vaguely significant still.

Only when I flip to my second assignment—the Epistle of James—does my breath catch, for as I turn page after page after page, there are no other blue marks in the Bible, not one, until I reach the New Testament, where Margaret has assigned a passage about temptation, James one through thirteen. Mother's childhood hand has marked one through twelve, using the same blue chalk as the other passage.

Blessed is the man who perseveres in temptation, for when
he has been proved he will receive the crown of life that
he promised to those who love him. No one experiencing
temptation should say, "I am being tempted by God"; for
God is not subject to temptation to evil, and He Himself
tempts no one. Rather each person is tempted when he is
lured and enticed by his own desire. Then desire conceives
and brings forth sin, and when sin reaches maturity, it
gives birth to death.

This is not the parting of the Red Sea. This is not a dead
friend arisen from his gauze windings and peering out of the
stone tomb or stilling the waves about to upend my boat.
This is not the healing of a leper, nor a bullet hole entering the
front of my helmet and exiting out the rear without touching
the head that wore it.

As miracles go, it may not even seem like one. But it feels
as if God once guided my mother's small hand, circa 1920-
something, to make two notes I'd very much need to find seventy years later—a message that I could be made new, that I
am—have always been—loved.

I see the small blonde my mother had been, on the cusp
of running like a shithouse rat into her own torments. And I
know how specifically designed we are for each other. I feel in
a bone-deep way the degree to which I'm watched over—how
everyone is. And how my stone heart is moment by moment
softening as I embrace that.

Maybe all any of us wants is to feel singled out for some
long, sweet, quenching draft of love, some open-throated guzzling of it—like what a baby gets at the breast. The mystery of
the Bible passages, marked just for me, does that.

I stay on my knees a long time, and sometime near dawn,

my cell phone trills, and I ask my sister the math genius what are the odds—in terms of probability—that those two passages would've been marked of all the verses possible. And she says, Very slender.

Seeing the marked Bible, Mother's not in the least flabbergasted, saying, I knew we were born to be together a long time ago. Maybe you do now, too.

Mock that experience as random chance if you like, but from then on, I start to arrive in the instant as never before, standing up in it as if pushed from behind like a wave, for it feels as if I was made—from all the possible shapes a human might take—not to prove myself worthy but to refine the worth I'm formed from, acknowledge it, own it, spend it on others.

Easter, I visit Father Kane, recently ensconced in the home for retired priests, to make my confession. I sit weeping across from him, fully aware of the ingratitude I've occasionally nurtured and fertilized like a garden of black vines. Which posture rankles him. Oh, get up, Mary, he said, you know damn well God loves you.

And I do. I (mostly) always do.

I'd like to say I never waver from that place, but on a crowded subway, I still pine for a firearm some days.

Though by the time Mother died, any of the old anger had been siphoned out of me like poison from a snakebite. Major organ system failure, the young doctors said. Old age, said the older ones.

I'm sick of this shit, she said. She'd set her jaw to die fast, I think. To lodge one last cry of outrage against Daddy's lingering five years' death, she let go in as many days.

I hate that you're leaving, I said to her. I just got used to you.

Well, I'm not doing it on purpose, she said with vigor.

How old was she? She'd lied so much, nobody knew—eightyish, we're guessing.

Your husband's outside, Miz Karr, the nurse said when one of her suitors showed up, hat in hand.

He must look like hell. He's been dead two decades.

If Daddy lived his final years in a haze, Mother's hazel eyes—when they were open those last days—stared at you sharp as a pair of ice picks.

Who's the president? the doctor said, to determine if she was cogent enough to say no to life support.

Bill Clinton, she said.

Who was the president before Clinton?

That asshole George Bush, she said, and before him, that asshole Ronald Reagan.

She opened her eyes once to find Lecia powdering her nose while I caked on another load of mascara. What are y'all getting fixed up for? she said.

The handsome cardio dude's coming to examine you, I said.

Oh my God, she said, pooching her lips out—Put my lipstick on.

Ten years, she's dead, and I still find myself some mornings reaching for the phone to call her. She could no more be gone than gravity or the moon.

Sometimes when I walk the New York streets, I find in the occasional pedestrian's face my long-dead parents. An Indian garment worker in overalls ferries a bin of Chinese silk—the bright rolls at different heights like pipes in some candy-colored organ. Beneath his baseball cap, his eyes glance off mine, and it's Daddy for an instant. Or gliding off a shopwindow, I see Mother's winged cheekbones and marble complexion that halt me in my tracks. But it's only my face impersonating hers, and if ever I miss her broad, sharecropper's hands, I have only to look at my own, growing from the ends of my own arms, which are replicas of hers. Good days, I see myself in others, and I know—in my bone marrow—nothing we truly love is ever lost, no matter what form it assumes. There are days when through fear and egoism I shake my fist at the sky, afterward feeling silly and worn out as a toddler post–temper tantrum.

Every now and then we enter the presence of the numinous and deduce for an instant how we're formed, in what detail the force that infuses every petal might specifically run through us, wishing only to lure us into our full potential. Usually, the closest we get is when we love, or when some beloved beams back, which can galvanize you like steel and make resilient what had heretofore only been soft flesh. (Dev, you gave me that.) It can start you singing as the lion pads over to you, its jaws hinging open, its hot breath on you. Even unto death.

Mary Karr 2009 Pax Christi

Acknowledgments

From conception to forward, Courtney Hodell practiced her extraordinary midwifery, birthing this book from my obstreperous psyche. Without her and Jennifer Barth of Harper-Collins and my agent, Amanda Urban, I'd no doubt still be writhing on the delivery table.

Readers vetting pages to keep me honest include my ever-patient family plus Joan Alway, Mark Costello, Doonie, Deborah Greenwald, John Holohan, Deb Larson, Thomas Lux, Patti Macmillan, and Tobias Wolff. Special thanks to Elizabeth Auchincloss and Patricia Allen. Spiritual guidance came from most of the above as well as Uwen Akpan, S.J.; Father Joseph Kane; Sister Marisse May; and Matthew Roche, S.J.

Writers granting the right to excerpt their lit'rary works gratis include Don DeLillo, Nick Flynn, Louise Glück, Robert Hass, Brooks Haxton, Terrance Hayes, Sebastian Matthews, Heather McHugh, George Saunders, Charles Simic, Chris Smither, Franz Wright, and Dean Young. Katherine Beitner of Harper kicked publicity ass. Poetry permissions were valiantly rustled up by Chris Robinson and Jason Sack.

My sister, Lecia Scaglione, and her husband, Tom, helped me through innumerable hard stretches; so did Rodney Crowell, Don DeLillo, Dan Halpern, Robert Hass, Brooks Haxton, Terrance Hayes, Brenda Hillman, Ed Hirsch, Patti Macmillan, Mark and Lili Reinisch, George Saunders, Case Scaglione, J. W. Shenk, Mark Scher, Kent Scott, and Donna Zeiser.

My rabbi and champion was Michael Meyer.

About the Author

Mary Karr is the author of three award-winning bestselling memoirs: *The Liars' Club, Cherry,* and *Lit.* A Guggenheim Fellow in poetry, Karr has won Pushcart Prizes for both verse and essays. Other grants include the Whiting Writer's Award, PEN's Martha Albrand Award, and Radcliffe's Bunting Fellowship. She is the Jesse Truesdell Peck Professor of Literature at Syracuse University.

COOL PAPERBACKS, COOL PRICE

Tales of the City	Beautiful Ruins	Alas, Babylon	The Bridge of San Luis Rey
Armistead Maupin	Jess Walter	Pat Frank	Thornton Wilder

OLIVE EDITIONS for $10 EACH

Available for a Limited Time Only

Black Boy	Lit	The Dispossessed	Crazy Heart
Richard Wright	Mary Karr	Ursula K. Le Guin	Thomas Cobb